Student Workbook

Contents

Preface

To the Student

This *Workbook* has been designed to help you excel in the study of abnormal psychology. While abnormal psychology is a fascinating course that should become one of the most memorable classes of your college experience, it is also one that is filled with detailed topics and numerous terms and concepts—so much so that you may find it a little intimidating at times. A key purpose of this workbook is to help you organize your study in this course so that you will have the time and the knowledge to delve more deeply into the disorders and the ideas presented.

The utility of the *Workbook* goes beyond simply being a concise way to organize the raw topic coverage of the textbook. A great deal of effort was put into designing review exercises that call upon you to apply rote information in a way that gets you thinking about the underlying meaning of the ideas. In addition to fill-in-the-blank and short-answer questions, many exercises present a hypothetical set of facts relating to a patient or a psychological disorder. Applying your knowledge to hypothetical situations helps to bring the information to life. We have tried to "mix up" exercise types wherever possible, in order to keep things more engaging for you.

Ways to Use the Workbook

There are at least a couple of ways that you can use this *Workbook*. We recommend that students first read the textbook a section at a time, and then attempt the corresponding section of review exercises in the *Workbook*. Exercises explicitly follow the textbook's order of coverage, and each section and subsection is clearly delineated in the *Workbook*. The topic headings within the chapter review exercises provide the page numbers of the coverage in the textbook. Many of the exercises call for a detailed knowledge of the material in the textbook—perhaps in far more detail than may be required on your exams. This is intentional, as one of our goals is to prepare you for anything you might see on an exam. If you take a week, or even a day, between reading the textbook and attempting the review exercises, you may be surprised at how difficult it can be to recall all the details.

There is an additional benefit to completing the exercises in the manner we have suggested. It provides you with an excellent set of study notes that can be used in conjunction with your lecture notes.

An alternative way to use the *Workbook* is to try to complete the review exercises after you have read the book and attended your instructor's lectures. This is a way to identify areas where you need to concentrate your remaining study time before a test. The risk is that you may discover that you don't understand the material as well as you believed, and that you haven't left yourself enough time to learn it.

We hope that your studies with the *Workbook* will be a rewarding experience that truly helps you to understand, appreciate, and profit from the study of abnormal psychology.

To the Instructor

During a class term, time is a valuable commodity—especially with a topic-filled course like abnormal psychology. As an instructor, you already know that there never seems to be sufficient time to cover everything you would like in a term. Just imparting the strictly factual information can take so much time that you are left with little time to go into greater depth. If your students are using this *Workbook,* it can mean that you will have more time to devote to the conceptual and applied aspects of the factual material of abnormal psychology.

The *Workbook* is structured to enable you to assign it to your students in sections that correspond to the topic headings in the textbook. Each *Workbook* chapter begins with an outline of the chapter presentation, which facilitates assigning parts to students, and also helps your students keep their studies better organized.

Our experience has been that the students who apply themselves to the kinds of review exercises you will find in this *Workbook* are usually the ones who are the most prepared and the most engaged. They are also the ones who tend to perform better on exams.

We have recommended ideas, but please use the *Workbook* in the manner that will serve you best. It could easily be used for homework to check that your students have completed and understood their reading assignments, especially in smaller classes. Also, if you have the opportunity for class involvement in your lectures, the *Workbook* can help your students come to class better prepared to discuss specific issues.

Acknowledgments

We are deeply indebted to Carmen R. Wilson VanVoorhis and Katherine M. Nicolai, who authored previous editions of this *Workbook*. We would also like to thank Christine Ondreicka, Sharon Prevost, and Jenny Chiu of Worth Publishers for their editorial input, as well as Stacey Alexander for her production expertise.

Ron Comer
Greg Comer

Student Workbook

CHAPTER

1 Abnormal Psychology: Past and Present

CHAPTER OUTLINE

I. What Is Psychological Abnormality?

A. Deviance
B. Distress
C. Dysfunction
D. Danger
E. The Elusive Nature of Abnormality

II. What Is Treatment?

III. How Was Abnormality Viewed and Treated in the Past?

A. Ancient Views and Treatments
B. Greek and Roman Views and Treatments
C. Europe in the Middle Ages: Demonology Returns
D. The Renaissance and the Rise of Asylums
E. The Nineteenth Century: Reform and Moral Treatment
F. The Early Twentieth Century: The Somatogenic and Psychogenic Perspectives

IV. Current Trends

A. How Are People with Severe Disturbances Cared For?
B. How Are People with Less Severe Disturbances Treated?
C. A Growing Emphasis on Preventing Disorders and Promoting Mental Health
D. Multicultural Psychology
E. The Growing Influence of Insurance Coverage
F. What Are Today's Leading Theories and Professions?

V. Putting It Together: A Work in Progress

Multiple Choice

REVIEW EXERCISES

I. and II. What Is Psychological Abnormality? What Is Treatment?, 2–6

Although no single definition of abnormal mental functioning is universally accepted, most definitions share four common features: the notions of deviance, distress, dysfunction, and danger. You can think of these as the "four D's" of defining abnormal functioning. All four are covered in this part of the workbook.

1. Complete this table by first identifying the feature (or the "D") associated with each definition listed, then giving a hypothetical example of a behavior that illustrates the defining feature.

Feature	Definition	Example
a. danger	Patterns of behavior, thoughts, and emotions that pose a risk to one's well-being and safety are considered abnormal.	A young woman abuses cocaine and alcohol on a daily basis, drives recklessly when high, endangering herself and others.
b.	For patterns of behaviors, thoughts, and emotions to be labeled abnormal, the individual must experience them as unpleasant and adverse.	
c.	Behaviors, thoughts, and emotions that violate cultural norms are considered abnormal.	
d.	Patterns of behavior, thoughts, and emotions that interfere with an individual's ability to maintain important aspects of life are considered abnormal.	

2. The major difficulty in defining abnormality is that the concept of "abnormality" is relative. Write a paragraph explaining what this means.

____

____

____

____

3. **Treatment** or therapy is defined as a procedure to help change _______________ behavior into more _______________ behavior.

4. Jerome Frank, a clinical theorist, has written that all forms of therapy have three essential features or ingredients. Complete the following list of these key features.

   a. A _______________ seeks help or relief from

   b. a trained, socially sanctioned _______________, in

   c. a structured series of contacts between the two that is designed to produce changes in the help-seeker's _______________ state, attitudes, and _______________ .

5. Clinicians differ on whether to use the term "patient" or "client" to describe those who seek help through counseling or psychotherapy. Identify which term *you* would prefer if you were to seek therapy services, and briefly describe why.

____

____

____

III. How Was Abnormality Viewed and Treated in the Past?, 6–16

1. Given that as many as 30 percent of adults in the United States display psychological dysfunction serious enough to warrant treatment, some speculate that certain aspects of our modern world foster emotional maladjustment. List two recent societal developments that may contribute to psychological dysfunctioning.

   a. _______________

   b. _______________

A Closer Look: Marching to a Different Drummer: Eccentrics, 7

1. Researcher David Weeks suggested that eccentrics do not typically suffer from mental disorders, because their unusual behavior patterns are chosen ________ and provide ________.

2. David Weeks found that eccentrics that he studied had ________ emotional problems than individuals in the general population.

A. Ancient Views and Treatments, 7

1. It is believed that people in prehistoric societies viewed the human body and mind as sites of battle by ________ forces, and they viewed both normal and abnormal behavior as the outcome of battles between good and evil spirits.

2. List and briefly describe two treatments for abnormality that may have occurred in prehistoric societies.

   a. trephination; _______________

   ____

   b. ________; _______________

   ____

B. Greek and Roman Views and Treatments, 8

1. Define each of the following mental disorders that were identified by early Greek and Roman physicians.

   a. Melancholia: _______________

   b. Mania: _______________

2. Complete the following statements regarding **Hippocrates,** called the father of modern medicine.

   a. He saw abnormal behavior as a disease caused by internal medical problems; specifically, he thought that ________ pathology was the culprit.

   b. Hippocrates believed that like all forms of disease, abnormal behavior resulted from an imbalance of the four fluids, or ________, that flowed through the body.

C. Europe in the Middle Ages: Demonology Returns, 10

1. What was the primary reason for the return of demonological views of psychological abnormality in the Middle Ages?

____

____

2. Large outbreaks of ______________ ______________, in which large numbers of people shared similar delusions or hallucinations, are an example of abnormal behavior present during the Middle Ages, a time of great societal stress and unrest.

3. List and briefly describe two prevalent forms of these shared delusions.

   a. ______________; ____

   ____

   b. ______________; people thought they were possessed by wolves or other wild animals, and acted as though they were these animals.

4. If you could go back in time to the Middle Ages and witness clergymen performing exorcisms on people who behaved abnormally, what do you think you might see?

____

____

____

5. At the end of the Middle Ages, naturalistic or medical explanations of abnormal behavior had replaced demonological explanations. Give two examples of possible naturalistic explanations of a person's "madness" or "lunacy" during this period.

____

____

Psych Watch: Modern Pressures: Modern Problems, 9

1. Hundreds of therapists practice the treatment approach called ____________ to treat those who suffer from "eco-anxiety."

2. In the wake of the September 11, 2001 terrorist attacks, some individuals have been afflicted with __________ __________, or the obsessive concern that they will soon be the victim of a terrorist attack.

3. The fear of being bombarded and overloaded with information from the Internet and other mass media sources is known as __________ __________.

D. The Renaissance and the Rise of Asylums, 11

1. The German physician Johann ______________, thought to be the first medical practitioner to specialize in mental illness, rejected the demonological explanation of abnormality.

2. What was the purpose of the Gheel Shrine?

____

____

3. In the sixteenth century, the idea of asylums grew. Though usually founded with excellent intentions, such institutions as London's Bethlehem Hospital, the Lunatics' Tower in Vienna, and La Bicêtre in Paris

degenerated into sites of degrading conditions where treatments of unspeakable cruelty flourished. List some of these horrible conditions.

____

____

A Closer Look: The Moon and the Mind, 12

1. Though no research has established a conclusive link between the moon and human behavior, some scientists have advanced theories for possible explanations. Describe two of these dubious theories that have been put forth.

   a. ____

   b. ____

E. The Nineteenth Century: Reform and Moral Treatment, 13

1. What was the initial site of asylum reform (around 1793), and who was the man most responsible for the reform?

   ______________________; ______________________

2. Describe an overall theme of the reforms in the treatment of patients during this period.

   ____

   ____

3. In England, William ______________ founded a "retreat" where rest, talk, prayer, and manual work replaced mechanical restraints and unfounded medical interventions as treatments for mental patients.

4. The methods of Pinel and Tuke were called ______________ treatment.

5. Benjamin Rush was the person who is credited with bringing moral treatment to the United States. List two of his major innovations.

   ____

   ____

6. In 1841, a Boston schoolteacher named Dorothea Dix was shocked by the conditions she witnessed at asylums throughout the United States. Dix began a 40-year campaign of reform that addressed the plight of the mentally ill. Write a paragraph describing her remarkable effort.

   ____

   ____

   ____

7. Complete these statements describing how each of the following three factors contributed to the decline of moral treatment.

   a. Moral treatment had advanced so quickly that many hospitals were built in a short period of time, leading to shortages of funding and ______________ .

   b. The basic assumptions of moral treatment—that patients would begin to function normally if they were treated with ______________—proved too optimistic.

   c. Many people reacted to the trend of patients being removed to large, distant mental hospitals with a new wave of ______________ against the mentally ill.

F. The Early Twentieth Century: The Somatogenic and Psychogenic Perspectives, 14

1. In the late nineteenth century, the **somatogenic perspective**—the idea that abnormal psychological functioning has physical causes—once again gained acceptance and support. Explain how (a) the work of Emil Kraepelin and (b) the discovery that general paresis is caused by syphilis were important to the resurgence of the somatogenic perspective.

   a. ______________________________

   ____

   b. ______________________________

   ____

2. The **psychogenic perspective** has the view that the primary causes of abnormal behavior are ______________ in nature.

3. Some scientists believed that the successes of the treatment called *mesmerism* (later called *hypnotism*) in treating patients with ______________ disorders resulted from patients being induced into a trancelike state.

4. Briefly describe the disorders you identified above.

   ____

5. Two French physicians, Bernheim and Liébault, settled the debate over the cause of hysterical disorders by showing that they could be induced and then removed in otherwise normal subjects by means of ______________ ; thus, these disorders were largely ______________ in origin.

6. ______________ , a Viennese doctor who later worked with Freud, discovered that his hypnotized patients sometimes awoke free of hysterical symptoms after speaking freely about past traumas under hypnosis.

7. Freud's theory of ______________ posits that ______________ psychological processes are at the root of both normal and abnormal functioning.

8. Freud's form of therapy was designed to help people gain ______________ into their problems and was conducted usually in the therapist's office—a format now known as ______________ therapy.

IV. Current Trends, 16–22

A. How Are People with Severe Disturbances Cared For?, 17

1. The discovery and use of **psychotropic drugs** resulted in the nearly immediate discharge of many severely disturbed patients from public mental hospitals. This policy is now known as________ ______________________ .

2. ______________ care has become the primary mode of treatment for people with severe psychological disturbances as well as for those with more moderate problems.

3. Although the community mental health approach has admirable goals and has been effective in helping many people with mental disorders, it has not been entirely successful. Briefly, describe how the community mental health approach has failed in some respects.

   ____

   ____

B. How Are People with Less Severe Disturbances Treated?, 18

1. Over the last several decades, more people than ever have had access to treatment for psychological problems. Briefly describe the reasons for this trend that are associated with the key words provided.
   a. Cost: ____________________
   ____
   b. Settings: ____________________
   ____
2. Recent studies have suggested that one out of every ____________ Americans receives treatment for psychological problems each year.
3. Almost 50 percent of people in therapy suffer from ____________ or depression, and about 20 percent seek help for problems with ____________, family, job, ____________, or community relationships.

C. A Growing Emphasis on Preventing Disorders and Promoting Mental Health, 18

1. Ms. Jenkins, a school social worker, has developed an educational group on proper nutrition and exercise for sixth grade girls. She hopes to teach the girls skills to use to avoid problematic eating and exercising behaviors and ultimately eating disorders. Ms. Jenkins's approach is a form of ____________.
2. Write a short paragraph explaining how Ms. Jenkins might use **positive psychology** in her work with the sixth grade girls.
   ____
   ____
   ____
   ____

D. Multicultural Psychology, 20

1. What do multicultural psychologists study?

E. The Growing Influence of Insurance Coverage, 20

1. Most insurance programs today require clients to choose from a list of approved therapists and dictate the cost and number of sessions for which the client will be reimbursed. These types of programs are known as ____________ ____________ programs.
2. List three reasons clients and therapists dislike managed care programs.
   a. ____________________
   b. ____________________
   c. ____________________

F. What Are Today's Leading Theories and Professions?, 21

1. At present no single theoretical perspective dominates the clinical field. Many theories have influenced the current understanding and treatment of abnormal functioning. Complete the following statements about some of the perspectives.

a. Before the 1950s, the _______________ perspective, with its emphasis on _______________ conflicts as the cause of psychopathology, was dominant.

b. The somatogenic or _______________ view of abnormality grew in stature in the 1950s with the discovery of effective _______________ drugs.

c. Some of the influential perspectives that have emerged since the 1950s include the behavioral, cognitive, humanistic-existential, and sociocultural schools. They explain and treat abnormality in very different ways.

2. Complete the following statements regarding professional careers in psychology.

a. Psychotherapy was the exclusive province of _______________ before the 1950s. These people are physicians who have completed _______________ to _______________ years of training after medical school in the treatment of abnormal mental functioning.

b. Clinical psychologists are professionals who earn a doctorate by completing four years of graduate training in abnormal functioning and its treatment and also complete a one-year _______________ at a mental hospital or mental health agency.

c. Counseling psychologists, educational psychologists, psychiatric nurses, marriage therapists, family therapists, and—the largest group—_______________ _______________ _______________ fall into a category of professionals who have completed a graduate training program in their specialty area.

V. Putting It Together: A Work in Progress, 22

1. In your own words, describe some reasons why students of abnormal psychology can benefit from learning about historical perspectives on abnormal behavior and its treatment.

____

____

____

____

____

MULTIPLE CHOICE

1. Mary dresses exclusively in men's clothes (including the underwear). This is an example of the feature of the definition of abnormality called
   a. distress.
   b. deviance.
   c. dysfunction.
   d. danger to self or others.

2. Rae, who is running for public office, seems to be developing a fear of crowds. To which aspect of the definition of abnormality is this example most relevant?
   a. distress
   b. deviance
   c. dysfunction
   d. danger to self or others

3. An eccentric person is likely to display all of the following except
   a. intelligence.
   b. nonconformity.
   c. noncompetitiveness.
   d. disordered thinking.

4. Some ancient societies practiced trephination, which consisted of
   a. blood letting.
   b. removing part of a patient's skull.
   c. imposing social isolation on a sufferer.
   d. a kind of exorcism practiced by a shaman.

5. During the Middle Ages, the dominant model of explanation for abnormal behavior was
   a. scientific.
   b. humanistic.
   c. philosophical.
   d. demonological.

6. The person now believed to be the founder of the modern study of psychopathology was
   a. Hippocrates.
   b. Johann Weyer.
   c. Philippe Pinel.
   d. Sigmund Freud.

7. The real beginning of the humane treatment of people with mental disorders began in
   a. Spain.
   b. France.
   c. England.
   d. the United States.

8. Which of the following is most consistent with the somatogenic view of mental illness?
   a. hypnosis
   b. physical ailments can cause psychological disturbances
   c. the symptoms of mental illness can be described and classified
   d. hysterical symptoms such as partial paralysis can be induced with hypnosis

9. The original developer of psychoanalysis was
   a. Josef Breuer.
   b. Emil Kraepelin.
   c. Sigmund Freud.
   d. Ambroise-Auguste Liébault.

10. Since the beginning of the deinstitutionalization movement in the 1950s
    a. the prescription of psychotropic drugs has significantly decreased.
    b. the daily patient population in American mental hospitals has increased.
    c. the number of violent crimes committed by mentally ill persons has doubled.
    d. outpatient care has become the primary treatment for persons with psychological problems.

CHAPTER

2 Research in Abnormal Psychology

CHAPTER OUTLINE

I. What Do Clinical Researchers Do?

II. The Case Study
- A. How Are Case Studies Helpful?
- B. What Are the Limitations of Case Studies?

III. The Correlational Method
- A. Describing a Correlation
- B. When Can Correlations Be Trusted?
- C. What Are the Merits of the Correlational Method?
- D. Special Forms of Correlational Research

IV. The Experimental Method
- A. The Control Group
- B. Random Assignment
- C. Blind Design

V. Alternative Experimental Designs
- A. Quasi-Experimental Design
- B. Natural Experiment
- C. Analogue Experiment
- D. Single-Subject Experiment

VI. Putting It Together: The Use of Multiple Research Methods

Multiple Choice

REVIEW EXERCISES

I. What Do Clinical Researchers Do?, 28–29

The scientific method is the process of systematically acquiring and evaluating information by observation to gain an understanding of the phenomena being studied. It is a key concept of modern science. This section's exercises relate to this important basis for research.

1. Clinical research looks for a general, or a ________________ ________________ of abnormal behavior, such as truths about the nature, causes, and treatments of abnormalities, whereas clinical practitioners search for truths regarding the abnormalities in individuals, which are called idiographic truths.
2. To formulate a nomothetic explanation of abnormal psychology, scientists try to identify and explain relationships between **variables.** Any characteristic or event that can vary, whether from time to time, place to place, or person to person, is a variable. List some of the variables that are of particular interest to clinical researchers.

   ____

3. Clinical researchers seek to determine whether two or more variables change together and whether

   ____ .

4. The three primary methods of investigation—the case study, the correlational method, and the experimental method—enable clinical researchers to formulate and test **hypotheses.** Define the term *hypothesis.*

   ____

   ____

II. The Case Study, 29–32

1. What are the characteristics and goals of the case study method of research?

   ____

   ____

A. How Are Case Studies Helpful?, 31

1. Fill in the missing words in the following list of nomothetic roles case studies serve.
   a. They are a source of ideas about ________________ and can provide tentative support for a ________________.
   b. They may serve to challenge theoretical ________________ .
   c. They serve as a source of ideas for new therapeutic ________________ .
   d. They offer opportunities to study unusual problems that ____ .

B. What Are the Limitations of Case Studies?, 31

1. Case studies are reported by **biased observers.** Why does this limit the usefulness of the research method?

   ____

   ____

2. A study is said to have internal accuracy, or **internal validity,** when an investigator can show that

3. Why do case studies have limited internal validity?

4. A study is said to have **external validity** when

5. Why do case studies have limited external validity?

6. Although case studies provide rich detail about single individuals, they do not provide nomothetic insights, or information about large groups of people. Only **correlational** and **experimental** methods can accomplish this. Below, summarize the three important characteristics of correlational and experimental research methods that allow investigators to gain nomothetic insights.

   a.

   b.

   c.

III. The Correlational Method, 32–38

1. Define **correlation.**

2. Formulate a question that might be asked by a researcher using the correlational method that includes the variables "procrastination" and "test anxiety." (*Hint:* Be sure the word "cause" is not used in your question—you'll discover why later.)

3. Why must a **sample** be representative of the larger population of interest?

A. Describing a Correlation, 32

1. Imagine that you are a researcher interested in studying the relationship between marital satisfaction and number of pre-marriage sexual partners. On the following graphs, draw in the "lines of best fit" that illustrate the labeled relationships between marital satisfaction and the number of pre-marriage sexual partners.

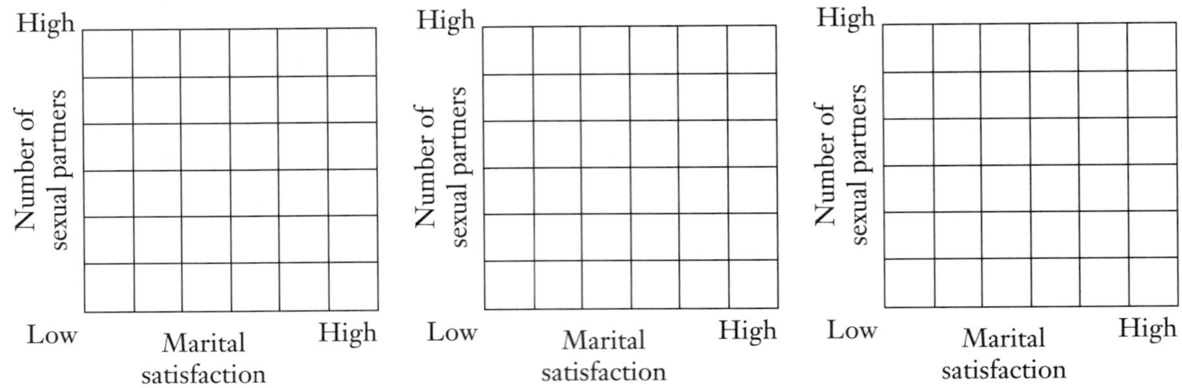

Positive Relationship *Negative Relationship* *No Relationship*

2. Other than knowing whether a correlation is positive or negative, it is important to know the magnitude, or ________________, of the relationship between variables.

3. The statistical term known as the ________________ ________________, symbolized by the letter *r*, expresses the direction and the magnitude of the relationship between two variables.

4. Put the following list of coefficients in order of their strength of correlation:

   .61 −.01 .50 −.58 −.82

   Strongest correlation _______ _______ _______ _______ _______ *Weakest correlation*

The Media Speaks: On Facebook, Scholars Link Up with Data, 33

1. Identify several drawbacks to the kind of research on Facebook users described in this section.

   ____

   ____

B. When Can Correlations Be Trusted?, 35

1. Statistical analyses of data are performed in order to discover how likely it is that a given correlation has been found by mere ________________.

2. What does the statistical notation $p < .05$ mean?

   ____

   ____

C. What Are the Merits of the Correlational Method?, 36

1. Correlational studies typically exhibit more ________________ validity than case studies because findings can be ________________ to people beyond those in the study.

2. However, correlational studies lack ________________ validity because they do not explain the ________________ between variables.

3. Let's say that in your study of marital satisfaction you also discover that couples who are satisfied with their marriages exhibit better communication skills than those who are less satisfied. (You find a correlation of .65, which is significant at the $p < .05$ level.) What are the three possible reasons for

this relationship?

a. ______________________________

b. ______________________________

c. Both marital satisfaction and good communication skills are caused by a third variable, such as a nondefensive personality style.

D. Special Forms of Correlational Research, 37

1. An **epidemiological study** determines the incidence and prevalence of disorders. Define:

   Incidence:

   ____

   Prevalence:

   ____

2. List two findings of the epidemiological studies reported in your text.

   ____

   ____

3. Longitudinal research methods provide information about the ______________ of events, so they are more likely than conventional correlation studies to shed light on which events may be ______________ and which may be consequences. However, they still do not pinpoint ______________.

IV. The Experimental Method, 38–40

1. Circle the term that best describes each variable in the experimental method.

   In the experimental method, researchers:

   a. manipulate the (independent / dependent) variable that is thought to cause some effect.

   b. observe the effect of the manipulated variable on the (independent / dependent) variable of interest.

2. Complete the following exercise by identifying the independent and the dependent variables of each fictional "study."

Hypothesis	Independent Variable	Dependent Variable
Drinking warm, as opposed to cold, milk causes people to be sleepy		sleepiness
Using shampoo X causes hair loss		
Group therapy is more effective than individual therapy in the treatment of depression	type of therapy	

3. Give a thorough definition of the term **confound.**

   ____

   ____

4. Why does the presence of confounds make it difficult to establish cause-and-effect relationships in experimental studies?

____

____

____

A–C. The Control Group, Random Assignment, and Blind Design, 38

The three features that researchers incorporate into their experiments in order to control potential confounds are (1) ***control groups,*** *(2)* ***random assignment,*** *and (3)* ***blind design.*** *After completing the following set of questions that relate to these procedures, you will be asked to critique and redesign a study that contains numerous confounds.*

1. Experimental methods require at least two groups of subjects: a control group and an experimental group. Ideally, what is the *only* difference between the control group and the experimental group?

____

Read this! Students are often confused about how the control group and the experimental group can be exactly "the same" except for the independent variable, when, after all, the two groups consist of *completely different people.* How can researchers say that the independent variable *caused* a change in the dependent variable, when perhaps the difference between the two groups on the dependent variable was simply a result of the fact that one group was different to begin with (more outgoing, happier, more aggressive, etc.)?

When researchers **randomly assign** subjects to either the control or the experimental group, they assume that *preexisting differences between the groups are reduced* (or "evened out") so that the *average* level of outgoingness, happiness, aggression, and so on, is approximately equal for both the control and the experimental group.

2. How might researchers randomly assign subjects to groups?

____

3. Subjects may bias the results of an experiment because they have attempted to please or _______________ the experimenter to get the results he or she wants; if this occurs, changes in the dependent variable could be a result of _______________ _______, rather than the independent variable.

4. How might experimenter bias, also known as the **Rosenthal effect,** occur in an experiment?

____

____

5. Provide a thorough definition for the following terms.

   a. blind design: ____

   ____

   b. double-blind design: ____

   ____

   c. triple-blind design: ____

Here is your chance to improve a study that is full of confounds. Read through the following description of a study on classical music therapy and respond to the questions that follow it.

6. There are numerous confounds present in the classical music therapy study that follows that could easily explain the results. List three of them.

   a. ______________________________

   b. ______________________________

   c. ______________________________

Case Study

Study:	Classical Music Therapy
Hypothesis:	People experience mood elevation after listening to classical music (i.e., listening to classical music causes people to feel happier).
Subjects:	Subjects were identified and recruited at a "Mozart by Moonlight" concert. Researchers told potential subjects, "We think listening to classical music will make you feel better. Will you help us?"
Method:	Subjects filled out a questionnaire designed to assess mood prior to engaging in experiment. They were then asked to sit in comfortable recliners in the research lab. Subjects were given headphones and told by an attractive, pleasant research assistant to relax and listen to 30 minutes of classical music. After listening to the music, subjects removed their headphones and filled out the same mood questionnaires in order to assess pre- and postmusic differences. Sandwiches and soft drinks were provided to the subjects as they filled out the postmusic questionnaire.
Results:	Pre- and postmusic scores were significantly different in the hypothesized direction. The experimenter concluded that classical music therapy results in people feeling happier.

7. Now, rewrite the Subjects and Method sections of this study (making sure that you address the confounds you identified in question 6) so that the experimenter's conclusion is justified.

Case Study

Study:	Classical Music Therapy
Hypothesis:	People experience mood elevation after listening to classical music (i.e., listening to classical music causes people to feel happier).
Subjects:	
Method:	
Results:	Pre- and postmusic scores were significantly different in the hypothesized direction. The experimenter concluded that classical music therapy results in people feeling happier.

V. Alternative Experimental Designs, 40–45

Workbook coverage of subsection V is divided into four parts—one for each of the variations of experimental design discussed in the textbook. They are: "Quasi-Experimental Design," "Natural Experiment," "Analogue Experiment," and "Single-Subject Experiment."

A Closer Look: Humans Have Rights, Too, 41

1. Name four types of drug studies that have been cited in recent years as having placed sufferers of severe mental disorders at risk during the 1980s and 1990s.

   a. ______________________________

   b. ______________________________

   c. ______________________________

   d. ______________________________

2. In 1999, the National Institute of Mental Health (NIMH) suspended some of its ____________-__________ studies, as the clinical community has grown more aware of the risks associated with these studies.

A. Quasi-Experimental Design, 42

1. Quasi-experimental designs make use of groups that already exist in the real world as opposed to "true" experiments in which subjects are ________________ assigned to ________________ and ________________ groups.

2. Why must researchers who study the psychological effects of rape on women use a quasi-experimental (rather than a "true" experimental) design?

   ____

   ____

   ____

3. What is the benefit of using the quasi-experimental design of **matched control subjects?**

   ____

   ____

   ____

B. Natural Experiment, 42

1. Natural experiments are those in which nature rather than the experimenter manipulates a(n) ________________ variable, and the experimenter ________________ the effects.

2. The natural experiment conducted by research teams on the psychological effects of the December 26, 2004, Indian Ocean earthquake and resulting tsunamis showed that survivors were significantly more depressed and anxious than control subjects. List some other results of the experiment.

   a. ______________________________

   b. ______________________________

   c. ______________________________

3. Limitations of the natural experimental method include the facts that natural experiments cannot be ________________, and broad ________________ drawn from a single study could be incorrect.

C. Analogue Experiment, 43

1. A major strength of analogue designs is that researchers can manipulate the ________________ variables, while avoiding some of the ________________ and practical limitations of other research designs.
2. How do analogue studies provide information about real-life abnormal behavior?

   ____

   ____

   ____

3. **Martin Seligman**'s hypothesis about the cause of human depression says that people become depressed when they believe that they no longer have any ________________ over the good and bad events that occur in their lives—that they are helpless.
4. Describe (a) the method and (b) the findings of Seligman's analogue research with humans.

   a. ____

   ____

   b. ____

   ____

5. What is the primary limitation of analogue designs?

   ____

   ____

D. Single-Subject Experiment, 44

1. Explain how experimentation is possible with only a single subject.

   ____

   ____

2. In single-subject experiments, **baseline data** are pieces of information gathered during an observation period before any ________________ or interventions, which establish a standard with which to compare later change.
3. Why is it so important to collect baseline data in single-subject designs?

   ____

   ____

4. Subjects serve as their own ________________ in ABAB, or reversal, designs.
5. When are researchers most likely to use a single-subject experiment design?

   ____

   ____

   ____

The information in the following case study will be used in exercises covering each of the two most commonly used single-subject experimental designs: the ABAB design and the multiple-baseline design.

Case Study

Nathan is an 8-year-old boy who is in a classroom for severely disturbed children. He has been diagnosed with autism, a pervasive developmental disorder whose central features are a profound unresponsiveness to others, poor or absent communication, and a range of unusual—even bizarre—responses to the environment. Recently, Nathan's teachers have grown very concerned about his safety in the classroom. He has begun to repeatedly bang his head on his desktop, resulting in bruises and abrasions on his forehead. Autistic children who demonstrate this behavior are frequently equipped with helmets to prevent serious injury. However, Nathan became extremely upset when his teachers attempted to use this form of intervention. In fact, he became almost uncontrollable when the helmet was placed on his head.

Because Nathan has responded favorably to being rewarded with fruit juice for positive behavior in the classroom, his teachers would like to find out if this method of reinforcement would be effective in reducing or eliminating his head-banging behavior. They would like you, a clinical researcher, to design a single-subject experiment to test their hypothesis.

6. Use the preceding information to complete the following chart of an ABAB design for this sample case.

Reinforcement Program (The Independent Variable)

Nathan will be rewarded with fruit juice for every 10-minute period of time that he does not bang his head on the desk.

A The frequency of Nathan's head-banging is measured before the introduction of the independent variable (in the baseline period).

(Think of each of the following steps as the test of a separate hypothesis.)

B *Step Taken:* Nathan is given a reward of juice for not banging his head

Expectation:

A *Step Taken:*

Expectation: Head-banging behavior will increase

B *Step Taken:*

Expectation:

7. If your predictions are supported in this ABAB design, what conclusion can be drawn about the reintroduction of the independent variable?

8. Like the ABAB design, the **multiple-baseline design** is also a single-subject experimental design.

Complete the following statements addressing two important differences between the ABAB design and the multiple-baseline design.

a. The multiple-baseline design does not contain the _______________ found in the ABAB design (i.e., the alternating introduction and removal of the reinforcer).

b. In the multiple-baseline design, at least _______________ distinct behaviors (the dependent variables) are identified, and the _______________ variable (the reinforcer) is manipulated to examine its effect on those behaviors.

9. By examining more than one behavioral _______________, the researcher can eliminate _______________ variables from his or her interpretation of findings.

10. What is the primary difference between single-subject experiments and case studies?

____

VI. Putting It Together: The Use of Multiple Research Methods, 45–46

1. Describe the factors that complicate or limit what we can learn about abnormal behavior and its treatment through clinical research. Try using your own words. That is, see how well you can explain these five scientific ideas without using the textbook's exact wording.

a. ____

____

b. ____

____

c. ____

____

d. ____

____

e. ____

____

MULTIPLE CHOICE

1. A psychologist doing research on anxiety studies a large and diversified group of anxious individuals in the hopes of understanding the phenomenon and developing a treatment. He is doing ________________ research.
   a. case study
   b. nomothetic
   c. idiographic
   d. experimental

2. The data that Freud used to develop psychoanalysis came from the use of
   a. correlational studies.
   b. experimental studies.
   c. the case study method.
   d. the nomothetic approach.

3. Dr. Vue gave a group of general psychology students a survey that measured their level of depression and substance use. Dr. Vue wanted to know if any relationship existed between the two. Which research method is Dr. Vue using?
   a. experiment
   b. quasi-experiment
   c. natural experiment
   d. correlation

4. If a difference is judged statistically significant, that means that the
   a. result has external validity.
   b. probability of a chance result is small.
   c. difference was experimentally determined.
   d. probability of the result being due to change is zero.

5. Which of the following is a characteristic of longitudinal studies in general?
   a. There is repeated measurement of the participants.
   b. There is manipulation of a variable by the researcher.
   c. There is the use of blind or double-blind control procedures.
   d. There is the ability of repeated observations to allow the conclusion of causality.

6. Research has demonstrated a **positive correlation** between children's behavior disorders and marital stress. Children with the worst behavior disorders tend to come from families in which the parents have the most marital problems. What can be said about this relationship?
   a. Children's behavior disorders are a result of the marital distress.
   b. Children's behavior disorders cause an increase in marital distress.
   c. Some outside factor, such as poverty, causes both the children's behavior disorders and the marital distress.
   d. Nothing can be said about the causation of behavior disorders or marital distress.

7. Dr. Ramirez required half of a group of healthy volunteers to study a passage for 1 hour. The other half of the group read the passage once (5 minutes). When both groups were finished, she administered a memory test to the participants who had studied for an hour and then to the participants who had just read the passage. She found that the participants who studied more remembered more. Which of the following was true?
   a. The results of the memory test were confounded.
   b. Study time and recall interval were confounded.
   c. She found that increased studying increased memory.
   d. The independent and dependent variables were confounded.

8. The principle behind random assignment is that
   a. placebo effects are eliminated from the study results.

b. every person in the population is equally likely to be selected.
c. it guarantees that the two groups will contain the same kinds of participants.
d. a participant is as likely to be in the control group as in the experimental group.

9. Kira conducted an experiment under two conditions in which she dropped a pile of books while another person approached her on a sidewalk. In the first, she dressed like a typical college student, wore make-up, had her hair neatly fixed, etc. In the second, she wore ragged clothing and no make-up, had messy hair, and muttered to herself. She then recorded whether the other person helped her pick up her books. The independent variable in Kira's experiment is
a. the dropped books.
b. the passerby's helping behavior.
c. Kira's appearance.
d. there was no independent variable in this study.

10. Which of the following is true of quasi-experiments?
a. They allow a clear conclusion of causality.
b. They employ random selection of subjects.
c. They employ random assignment of subjects.
d. The experimenters do not use random assignment.

11. One limitation of analogue studies is a potential lack of
a. control.
b. external validity.
c. the placebo effect.
d. the ability to rule out alternative explanations (by design).

CHAPTER

3 Models of Abnormality

CHAPTER OUTLINE

In Chapter 1, you explored various modes, or ***paradigms,*** *that were used to explain abnormal behavior from ancient times through the early twentieth century. You saw that treatment strategies (exorcism, moral treatment, hypnotism, etc.) followed directly from the assumptions of the particular model of abnormality that was popular at the time. Chapter 2 examined some of the research in abnormal psychology and the methods used by clinical researchers to discover the features of abnormal behavior.*

Contemporary researchers and clinicians adhere to one or more of several models discussed in Chapter 3. You will discover that each of the contemporary models articulates a unique set of assumptions related to how abnormal behavior develops and how it should be treated. Furthermore, each model has unique strengths and limitations. Students are often frustrated by the fact that there is no one "right" model that can explain all aspects of abnormal behavior. As you study Chapter 3, keep in mind that each model sheds light on a different aspect of human functioning, and that a solid understanding of the basic tenets of all the models will foster a greater appreciation for the complexities of human behavior—including abnormal behavior.

This chapter of the workbook parallels the structure of the textbook, covering six central models of abnormality: the ***biological model*** *(focusing on physical processes), the* ***psychodynamic model*** *(emphasizing unconscious processes), the* ***behavioral model*** *(concentrating on learning and overt behavior), the* ***cognitive model*** *(emphasizing thought processes), the* ***humanistic-existential model*** *(concentrating on issues of identity, values, meaning, and responsibility), and the* ***sociocultural model*** *(focusing on family-social and cultural influences).*

REVIEW EXERCISES

I. The Biological Model, 51–56

A. How Do Biological Theorists Explain Abnormal Behavior?, 51

1. Biological theorists believe that mental disorders are linked to problems in _______________ functioning.
2. _______________ are the nerve cells in the brain, and _______________ are the supporting brain cells.

Be sure you have studied and can identify the various regions of the brain described and illustrated on page 51 of the textbook.

3. In this exercise, give the names of the six terms relating to a typical neuron that are being described.
   a. Found at the axon's terminus: _______________
   b. Neuronal chemicals: _______________
   c. Extensions located at the end of the neuron that receive impulses: _______________
   d. Sites located on the dendrite that receive neurotransmitter: _______________
   e. A long fiber on which electrical impulses travel: _______________
   f. A tiny space separating one neuron from the next: _______________

Study the following diagram, which depicts how messages get from the nerve endings of one neuron to the dendrites of another neuron.

Electrical impulses travel down the axon to reach a neuron's ending.
The nerve ending is stimulated to release a chemical (neurotransmitter).

↓

The neurotransmitter travels across the synaptic space.

↓

The neurotransmitter reaches receptors on the dendrites of the adjacent neurons.

↓

The neurotransmitter leads the receiving neuron either to . . .

↓ ↓

. . . generate another electrical impulse OR cease firing.

4. Abnormal neurotransmitter activity has been implicated in several mental disorders. Complete the following statements regarding these activities.
   a. ________________ disorders have been linked to low GABA activity.
   b. Schizophrenia has been linked to excessive ________________ activity.
   c. ________________ has been linked to low activity of serotonin.
5. Biological researchers have also focused on abnormal activity of the ________________ system, which controls the release of ________________ that affect many important bodily functions (such as sexual activity, heart rate, and responses to stress).
6. Anxiety and mood disorders have been tied to abnormal secretions of ________________, which is released by the adrenal glands.
7. A person's genetic makeup can influence brain anatomy and neurotransmitter and endocrine abnormalities. ________________ are segments within the chromosomes of each cell that control the traits each person inherits from his or her parents.
8. Although specific genes that cause abnormal behavior have not yet been identified, genetic factors have been linked to the development of certain mental disorders. List these below.

   ____

   ____
9. Evolutionary theorists believe that human behavior and the genes that guide human behavior survive because they have helped individuals to ________________ and ________________.
10. Explain how behavior considered abnormal in current times could have been adaptive for our ancestors.

    ____

    ____
11. Research suggests that schizophrenia may be related to exposure to certain ________________ during childhood or *in utero*.
12. Recent research has linked ________________ infections to ________________, mood, and ________________ disorders.

B. Biological Treatments, 54

1. Complete the following tables of characteristics of drug therapies. *Organizing information from the textbook in this manner should help with studying.*

Antianxiety drugs	
Purpose	
Type (and trade names)	alprazolam (Xanax), diazepam (Valium)
Antidepressant drugs	
Purpose	
Type (and trade names)	
Antibipolar drugs	
Purpose	help stabilize mood of person diagnosed with bipolar disorder (manic-depression)
Type (and trade names)	
Antipsychotic drugs or neuroleptic drugs	
Purpose	
Type (and trade names)	

2. A second form of biological therapy is **electroconvulsive therapy,** or ECT. Complete the following statements related to ECT procedure and effectiveness.
   a. ECT is used to treat patients suffering from ________________ .
   b. Electrodes pass _______ to _______ volts of electrical current through the brain, causing a ________________ (or convulsion) that lasts a few minutes.
   c. ECT treatment usually consists of _______ to _______ sessions, spaced two or three days apart.
3. In a lobotomy procedure, the connections between the brain's __________________ __________________ and its lower centers are severed.
4. Although neurosurgery, or psychosurgery, is still considered an experimental procedure, it is used in the treatment of very severe disorders that have _______ _______ to years of other forms of treatment.

C. Assessing the Biological Model, 55

1. The textbook lists two major criticisms of the biological model. Complete the summary of the first criticism, then give a summary of the second and third.
   a. Although biological processes certainly do affect our behavior, thoughts, and emotions, they are just as certainly affected *by* our behavior, thoughts, and emotions. Our mental life is a(n) ________________ of biological and nonbiological factors.
   b. ____
   ____
   c. ____
   ____

II. The Psychodynamic Model, 56–62

1. One belief of psychodynamic theorists is that our behavior is determined by interacting, dynamic psychological forces outside of our awareness. Complete the following list of additional assumptions of the psychodynamic model of abnormal behavior.

   a. Abnormal behaviors are the result of _______________ between internal forces.

   b. Psychological conflicts are related to early _______________ and _______________ experiences in childhood.

   c. Psychodynamic theories rest on the _______________ assumption that no symptom or behavior is "accidental."

A. How Did Freud Explain Normal and Abnormal Functioning?, 56

Exercises covering this portion of the text are broken down in the same manner as the textbook's discussions. Coverage of the id, the ego, and the superego are followed by coverage of the Freudian developmental stages.

Freud believed that the "personality" is comprised of three unconscious forces: the id (instinctual needs), the ego (rational thinking), and the superego (moral standards). Complete the following list of characteristics that define each of these forces.

1. The Id, 56

1. The id operates according to the _______________ principle, which means that it always seeks _______________.

2. Id instincts are primarily _______________ in nature. _______________ is the term that describes the person's dynamic, intrapsychic sexual energy, which fuels the id.

2. The Ego, 57

1. The ego operates according to the **reality principle.** What does this mean?

   ____

   ____

2. The ego develops strategies designed to control unacceptable id impulses that may create anxiety if they are "allowed" into conscious awareness. After reading Table 3-1 on textbook page 58, complete the following table by matching each ego defense mechanism with the appropriate illustration from the list of examples below. Then write a brief definition for each in your own words.

Ego defense mechanism	Example	Definition
Repression	d.	primary Freudian defense mechanism: dangerous or painful thoughts aren't allowed into consciousness
Rationalization		
Denial		
Projection		

Ego defense mechanism	Example	Definition
Displacement		
Intellectualization		

Examples:

a. Eric is extremely upset when he sees his girlfriend, Donna, talking and laughing with her ex-boyfriend. Later Eric accuses Donna of being excessively jealous of any woman who happens to glance at him.

b. After Nancy's supervisor comments that her work is less than satisfactory, Nancy responds by telling the supervisor she will try harder, then goes home and yells at her children to clean up their rooms.

c. When the police arrested him on a domestic violence charge, 48-year-old Steven stated that his wife deserved the beating because she had burned dinner again.

d. At the age of 8, Anne witnessed her father severely abusing her mother, an event that Anne quickly "forgot" and still has no memory of at the age of 42.

e. Even after her third arrest for drunken driving, 30-year-old Loretta claims that she "doesn't have a problem" with alcohol.

f. When Shawna breaks up with her boyfriend, Anthony, after a two-year relationship, Anthony responds by calmly identifying the main reasons why they are, in fact, incompatible.

3. The Superego, 57

1. The superego is developed when we realize that many of our id impulses are unacceptable. This realization comes as we unconsciously adopt, or ________________, our ________________ moral values and standards.

2. Another name for the superego is the ________________.

4. Developmental Stages, 57

1. Certain demands or pressures are so threatening to a growing child that the id, ego, and superego do not mature properly and result in the child becoming ________________ (or entrapped) at a particular developmental stage.

2. Freud suggested that individuals move through five distinct stages in their development. Each stage corresponds to a particular area of the body (called the ________________ zone) that Freud believed was most important to the developing person at a given point in time. In the table to the right, list the five stages and the age range encompassed by each stage.

Stage	Age Range
Oral	–
	–
	–
	–
	–

3. Freud believed that at each stage, people face certain conflicts that must be resolved if they are to develop into psychologically healthy adults. Read through the text material on the oral stage and notice the photograph and caption related to the anal stage at the bottom of page 59 in your text. Fixation at the oral stage and at the anal stage of development can result in the emergence of certain "oral" or "anal" characteristics in adulthood. Describe these characteristics below.

   "Oral" characteristics: ____________________

   "Anal" characteristics: ____________________

B. How Do Other Psychodynamic Explanations Differ from Freud's?, 58

Exercises in this subsection of the workbook cover three of the most influential psychodynamic theories: ego theory, object relations theory, and self theory.

1. What is the basic assumption of ego theorists?

   ____

   ____

2. What is the basic assumption of self theorists?

   ____

   ____

3. What is the basic assumption of object relations theorists?

   ____

   ____

C. Psychodynamic Therapies, 59

1. List two of the primary goals of psychodynamic therapy.

   ____

   ____

2. What is the therapeutic purpose of **free association?**

   ____

   ____

3. The following terms describe some of the phenomena that psychodynamic clinicians attempt to **interpret** during the course of therapy. Define each term.

   a. **Resistance** is the unconscious block in a patient's __________ __________, or a change of subject so as to avoid a potentially painful discussion.

   b. **Transference** is when a patient acts toward the __________ much as he or she did toward important figures such as his or her parents.

4. Freud considered **dreams** to be the "royal road to the unconscious" because he believed __________ and other defense mechanisms operate less completely during sleep.

5. Psychodynamic therapists translate the __________ content of dreams into symbolic, or __________, content.

6. Define **catharsis:** ____________________

7. "__________ __________" is the process of examining the same issues over and over again in psychodynamic therapy—each time with a deeper level of clarity and insight.

8. Traditional psychodynamic therapies can take many months, even years, to complete. In more recently developed short-term dynamic therapies, patients choose a single problem, called a ________________ ________________, that they would like to work on in therapy.
9. A contemporary school of psychodynamic therapy, ________________ ________________ therapy, argues that therapists' reactions and beliefs should be included in the therapy process.

D. Assessing the Psychodynamic Model, 62

1. Strengths of Freud's psychodynamic theory include the fact that it provided an alternative to ________________ theories and treatments of abnormality and that for the first time theories and techniques were applied ________________ to treatment.
2. A reason why this model has received little research support is that processes such as id drives and ego defenses are abstract and operate at a(n) ________________ level, making it nearly impossible to determine if they are occurring.

III. The Behavioral Model, 63–66

1. What is the basic assumption of the behavioral model about abnormal behavior?

   ____

   ____

2. The behavioral model was the first perspective to be developed in ____________________. Psychologists in these laboratories conducted experiments on learning that takes place through ________________.
3. Behavioral principles established by research psychologists were applied to clinical problems in part because clinicians were becoming frustrated with ____.

A. How Do Behaviorists Explain Abnormal Functioning?, 64

1. The three types of conditioning described in your text include (a) **operant conditioning** and (b) **modeling.** Briefly describe these types of learning/conditioning.

   a. Operant conditioning: ____

   ____

   b. Modeling: ____

   ____

2. The textbook states that classical conditioning is a process of *learning by temporal association.* Briefly explain what this means.

   ____

   ____

After reviewing Pavlov's famous experiments with dogs in your text, read and respond to the following case study relating to classical conditioning.

Case Study

Thirteen-year-old Diane was riding her bicycle home one day after school while listening to her favorite Foo Fighters song on her headphones. She was thinking about what to wear to a party her friend Jackie was having that night and paid more attention to the song than to the traffic around her. She glided through a red light at a busy intersection. Her preoccupation was suddenly interrupted by the sounds of a car screeching to a halt and blaring its horn. Diane swerved around the car, narrowly avoiding a collision. As she walked her bike home, Diane's entire body trembled with fear—she thought she might vomit. Later, when Diane arrived at the party, her friend Jackie put on the CD of the same Foo Fighters song, which she knew Diane liked. Jackie was surprised to see Diane turn pale and rush to the bathroom. "I guess she doesn't like this song," thought Jackie as she went to check on her friend.

3. Complete this diagram by providing the **unconditioned stimulus** and the **conditioned stimulus** in the preceding case study.

______________	⟶	fear, nausea
Unconditioned stimulus		**Unconditioned response**
______________	⟶	fear, nausea
Conditioned stimulus		**Conditioned response**

Demonstrate your knowledge of classical conditioning by explaining the following case of a young boy named Abe.

Case Study

Five-year-old Abe developed an intense fear of the dark after experiencing horrible nightmares for a period of three months. Abe's fear of the dark was classically conditioned: nightmares (UCS) resulting in a fear response (UCR) were repeatedly paired with the darkness of his bedroom (CS). Darkness eventually evoked a fear response (CR) in Abe even when he did not have a nightmare. Abe's parents are puzzled, however, when their child starts screaming every time he sees a stuffed animal (just like those that sit on Abe's bed).

4. Briefly explain how classical conditioning principles could explain Abe's fear of stuffed animals.

____

____

B. Behavioral Therapies, 65

1. Complete the following flow chart by providing missing information relating to the steps in **systematic desensitization,** a classical conditioning technique frequently used with people who suffer from phobias.

Step 1:	Client learns ______________ over the course of several sessions.
Step 2:	Client constructs a ______________, which is a list of least to most anxiety-arousing situations.
Step 3:	Client either imagines or is physically exposed to situations on the list while maintaining a state of ______________ .
Step 4:	Client moves up the hierarchy until he or she can ______________________ .

C. Assessing the Behavioral Model, 65

1. Complete the following list of strengths and limitations of the behavioral model as described in the textbook.

   Strengths:

   a. Behavioral explanations can be tested in the laboratory and predicted effects can be observed and measured.

   b. ______________________________

   c. ______________________________

   Limitations:

   a. It is not certain that abnormalities are ordinarily acquired in the same way as clinically induced symptoms.

   b. ______________________________

   c. ______________________________

2. Some behaviorists believe that the traditional focus on overt (observable) behaviors does not adequately capture the complexities of human behavior. For example, Albert Bandura argues that one's behavior is affected by one's sense of ______________, an assessment of whether one can master and perform necessary behaviors.

3. Behaviorists who take into account covert (unobservable) behaviors such as thoughts and beliefs represent the ______________________ model.

IV. The Cognitive Model, 67–69

The cognitive model suggests that in order to understand human behavior we must investigate WHAT and HOW people think—the CONTENT and PROCESS of human thought.

A. How Do Cognitive Theorists Explain Abnormal Functioning?, 67

According to cognitive psychologists, we create representations of the world in our minds that dictate the way we perceive and understand events in our lives. "Errors" or inaccuracies in these mental representations can lead to maladaptive functioning.

1. Cognitive theorists suggest that some people hold *assumptions* and *attitudes* that are maladaptive and inaccurate. Read through the excerpt from a cognitive therapy session on pages 67 and 68 of your text. Identify at least one maladaptive assumption that the patient seems to hold in this case.

   ____

   ____

2. Cognitive theorists also focus on the **illogical thinking process**—based on maladaptive assumptions—that some people demonstrate. Look again at the cognitive therapy excerpt on pages 67 and 68. Can you identify an example of the patient's illogical thinking processes (e.g., overgeneralization)?

   ____

   ____

   ____

B. Cognitive Therapies, 67

1. Cognitive therapists help their clients develop new, more adaptive ways of thinking about themselves, others, and the world. Specifically, cognitive therapists help clients to:

   a. recognize the ______________ thoughts, biased ______________ , and logical errors that lead to dysfunction.

   b. ______________ their dysfunctional thoughts, and try out and apply new interpretations in their day-to-day lives.

C. Assessing the Cognitive Model, 68

1. Describe two strengths and two limitations of the cognitive model.

   Strengths:

   a. ______________________________

   b. ______________________________

   Limitations:

   a. ______________________________

   b. ______________________________

2. One example of the new wave of cognitive therapies that have emerged in recent years is the ____________ and ____________ therapy (ACT).

3. ACT and other new wave cognitive therapies often employ ____________-____________ techniques to help clients achieve ____________ of their troublesome thoughts without judgment, in the hopes that the thoughts will eventually trouble the clients less.

Psych Watch: Surfing for Help, 72

1. What are the possible advantages of Internet support groups in coping with depression, substance abuse, anxiety, eating disorders, and other psychological disorders?

   ____

   ____

   ____

   ____

2. What are possible drawbacks to "chat group therapy"?

   ____

   ____

   ____

3. What are some things advocates point to which indicate computer software programs may help those suffering from emotional distress?

   a. ______________________________

   b. ______________________________

   c. ______________________________

   d. ______________________________

4. Describe audio-visual e-therapy, which is on the rise. Identify key advantages and disadvantages to this type of therapy.

____

____

____

V. The Humanistic-Existential Model, 69–75

1. Humanistic and existential perspectives of behavior focus on broader dimensions of human existence such as: ____

____

2. Humanistic models assert that human beings are born with a natural drive to fulfill their innate potential for goodness and growth. This is known as the drive to ____________________ .

3. Which perspective (humanistic or existential) is considered to be more pessimistic, and why?

____

____

4. Carl Rogers called this humanistic approach ____________________ therapy.

5. The existential perspective is based on the ideas of existential philosophers who believed that people attempt to derive the meaning of their existence through their ______________ .

A. Rogers's Humanistic Theory and Therapy, 70

1. Describe the humanistic theory according to Carl Rogers.

   a. The road to ______________ begins in infancy.

   b. All of us have a basic need to receive positive ______________ from the significant people in our lives (primarily our parents).

   c. Those who receive unconditional ______________ ______________ early in life are likely to develop unconditional ______________ .

   d. Children who do not, acquire **conditions of worth** as a result.

2. Rogers's client-centered therapy requires clinicians to demonstrate three important characteristics when they are working with clients. Describe each characteristic below:

   a. Unconditional positive regard: ____

   ____

   b. Accurate empathy: ____

   ____

   c. Genuineness: ____

   ____

   ____

3. Although the effectiveness of Rogers's therapy has received mixed research support, his approach did open up the practice of psychotherapy to new ______________ and to psychologists (before, psychotherapy was the "exclusive territory" of ______________).

B. Gestalt Theory and Therapy, 71

1. Gestalt theory and therapy were developed by Frederick (Fritz) ________________ in the 1950s and are part of the humanistic approach.
2. Both client-centered and gestalt therapists help their clients move toward self-recognition and self-________________, but gestalt therapists achieve this goal by ________________ and challenging clients.
3. Gestalt therapists urge clients to become increasingly self-aware through several techniques. Complete the table below by briefly describing each gestalt technique and the specific goal of each technique.

Technique	Description	Goal
Skillful frustration		
Role-playing		
Rules		

C. Spiritual Views and Interventions, 73

1. Clinicians only recently began to view spirituality as a positive factor in mental health. What were the reasons for the belief that religion could be potentially damaging?

____

____

____

2. Recent research suggests people who view God as warm and caring are less ________________, pessimistic, ________________, or ________________ than those who view God as cold and unresponsive.

D. Existential Theories and Therapy, 73

1. Complete the following flow chart that illustrates the existential explanation of psychological distress and abnormal behavior.

A person hides from personal responsibility and choice when he or she becomes engulfed in constant change, confusion, and the emotional strain of present-day society, as well as the particular stress of his or her immediate environment.

BECAUSE OF THIS,

he or she overlooks his or her personal ________________ and won't take ________________ for his or her own life. This abdication can be a form of refuge, but can

LEAD TO

the person being left with an empty, "inauthentic" life and experiencing

- anxiety
- ________________
- ________________
- ________________
- ________________

2. What are the goals of existential therapy?

____

____

E. Assessing the Humanistic-Existential Model, 75

1. Among the strengths of the humanistic-existential model of abnormal behavior is that it emphasizes issues with which people struggle (e.g., existence, meaning, values, and choices) that are important to effective (or ineffective) psychological functioning. List two other strengths of this model.

   a. ____

   b. ____

2. What is a primary limitation of the humanistic-existential model?

____

VI. The Sociocultural Model: The Family-Social and Multicultural Perspectives, 75–84

1. Sociocultural theorists are particularly interested in answering questions about a person's social and cultural environment in order to understand his or her abnormal behavior. Complete the following list of questions that are posed by the sociocultural model.

   a. What are the _______________ of the person's society?

   b. What _______________ does the person play in the social environment?

   c. What kind of _______________ background or _______________ structure is the person exposed to?

   d. How do other people _______________ and react to the person?

A. How Do Family-Social Theorists Explain Abnormal Functioning?, 75

Sociocultural explanations of abnormal behavior focus on three areas: social labels and roles, social networks and supports, and family structure and communication. The following exercises parallel the textbook's coverage of these areas.

1. Social Labels and Roles, 76

1. Complete the following diagram that depicts the "vicious cycle" that contributes to the development of mental illness according to sociocultural theorists.

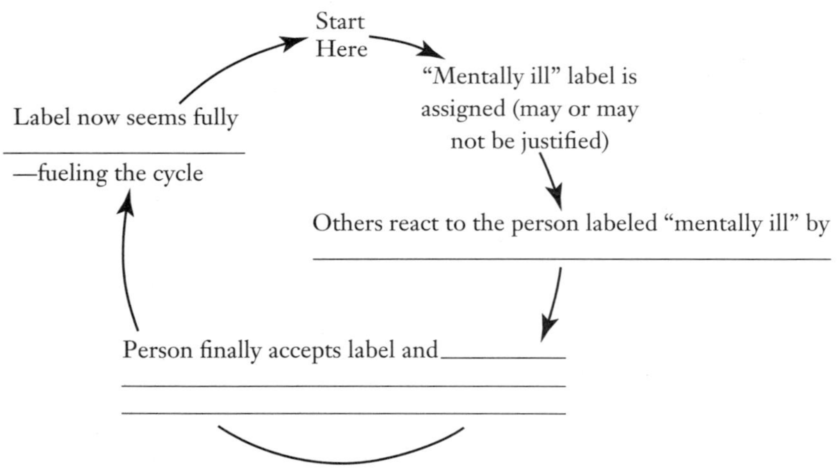

2. Complete the following statements related to the method and findings of David Rosenhan's study of the effects of diagnostic labeling on psychiatric "pseudopatients."

Rosenhan's "Pseudopatient Study"

Method:

*Eight normal people ("pseudopatients") went to several psychiatric hospitals and complained of the following symptom:

____

____

*All the pseudopatients were admitted to the hospitals with diagnoses of ________________ .

*Once they were admitted, the pseudopatients behaved normally (i.e., did not exhibit any "symptoms").

Findings:

*The pseudopatients' hospitalization ranged from _______ to _______ days, despite the fact that they showed no symptoms of mental disorder while in the hospital.

*The diagnostic label seemed to influence the way that the _______________ viewed and dealt with the pseudopatients.

*The pseudopatients reported the following feelings during their hospital stay:

____

2. Social Networks and Supports, 76

1. Sociocultural theorists believe that the quality of a person's social and professional relationships is sometimes linked to abnormal behaviors. Researchers have identified certain qualities that characterize the social relationships of people who become depressed under stressful conditions. Describe these qualities below.

____

____

3. Family Structure and Communication, 76

1. How, according to family systems theorists, do some families force individual members to behave in ways that society at large would deem abnormal?

____

____

____

2. Families whose members are grossly overinvolved in each other's lives have a(n) ________________ structure, whereas families with overly rigid boundaries between members are said to display a structure of ________________ .

3. Even if only one member of the family is identified as "sick," family therapists treat the family system as a whole. Based on your knowledge of family systems theory, why do you think this is the case?

____

____

____

B. Family-Social Treatments, 77

The following exercises follow the textbook's structure of coverage of four special sociocultural strategies: group, family, couple, and community treatment therapies.

1. Group Therapy, 77

1. List some of the important benefits experienced by clients in group therapy.

____

____

____

2. Research findings indicate that group therapy is often just as effective as _______________ therapy for people with a range of psychological problems and educational needs.

3. In the self-help group format, people who share similar problems meet without the leadership of a professional _______________ .

4. In the United States today there are between ______ and ______ self-help groups attended by ______ to ______ percent of the population.

2. Family Therapy, 79

1. Regardless of their theoretical orientation, family therapists adhere to the principles of family system theory. Describe the principles of this theory.

____

____

____

2. **Structural family therapists** focus on the family _______________ structure, the role each family member plays, and the _______________ between family members.

3. Therapists pay special attention to family communication patterns in the _______________ family therapy approach.

3. Couple Therapy, 80

1. Describe the goals of the following two forms of couple therapy.

   a. Behavioral couple therapy:

   ____

   ____

   ____

   b. Integrative couple therapy:

   ____

   ____

   ____

2. Although couples who receive therapy show more improvement in their relationship than couples who do not receive therapy, less than _____ of treated couples report they are "happily married" at the end of therapy.

3. Couple therapy seems to be most effective for couples who are _______________ , well-adjusted,

and less rigid in their ________________ ________________ .

4. Community Treatment, 80

1. In 1963, President John F. Kennedy called for a "bold new approach" to the treatment of mental illness, and the Community Mental Health Act was passed by Congress soon after. Describe how the **community mental health movement** changed the way that people with severe psychological problems received treatment services.

____

____

2. Complete the following statements relating to the three types of prevention practiced in community treatments. Then, give an example of each.

   a. ________________ *prevention* consists of efforts to improve community attitudes and policies with the goal of preventing mental disorders altogether.

   Example: ____

   b. The goal of *secondary prevention* is to ________________ and ________________ mental disorders at their earliest stages.

   Example: ____

   c. In *tertiary prevention,* treatment providers try to prevent severe disorders (that already exist) from becoming ________________ problems.

   Example: ____

3. Community programs have often failed to provide tertiary services needed by severely disturbed persons. Why?

____

____

C. How Do Multicultural Theorists Explain Abnormal Functioning?, 81

1. *Culture* is the set of ________________, attitudes, ________________, ________________ and behaviors shared by a group of people.

2. Eating disorders are more prevalent in Western cultures than in non-Western cultures. How does this evidence support a multicultural explanation of the development of eating disorders?

____

____

3. The ________________ perspective suggests that an individual's behavior, whether normal or abnormal, is best understood in the context of his or her unique cultural context.

4. Poorer people are more likely to suffer from severe psychological problems than wealthier people. What are some of the unique pressures that exist for the former group that could be related to higher levels of stress and a greater potential for psychological dysfunction?

____

____

____

____

5. *"Racial and sexual prejudice contribute to abnormal functioning."* For each of the following groups of people, list a piece of evidence that supports this statement.

Group	Evidence
Women	Women in Western societies are diagnosed with anxiety and depressive disorders at least twice as often as men.
African Americans	
Hispanic persons	
Native Americans	

6. Name eight of the typical elements of culture-sensitive therapy approaches.

a. ____________________

b. ____________________

c. ____________________

d. ____________________

e. ____________________

f. ____________________

g. ____________________

h. ____________________

D. Multicultural Treatments, 82

1. Research has illuminated several differences in how people from ethnic and racial minority groups respond to and utilize therapy. What are these?

   a. People from ethnic and racial minority groups seem to make fewer improvements in clinical treatment than people from majority groups.

   b. Members of ethnic and racial minority groups use mental health services _______ _______ than members of majority groups.

   c. ____________________

   ____________________.

2. Approaches geared toward the unique issues and special pressures of being a person of color or a woman in Western society are called ________________ and ________________ therapies, respectively.

E. Assessing the Sociocultural Model, 83

1. The sociocultural model has influenced clinicians to take into account family and societal issues and has highlighted the impact of diagnostic labels. However, two important limitations of this model are:

   a. ____________________

   ____

b. ____

____

V. Putting It Together: Integration of the Models, 84–85

1. Contemporary models of abnormality take into account the biological, psychological, and sociocultural aspects of abnormal behavior; likewise, contemporary clinicians are increasingly utilizing ______________ theories as they conceptualize and treat their clients'/patients' problems.
2. Many contemporary theorists and clinicians adhere to a **diathesis-stress model** of abnormal functioning. Complete the diagram on the next page, which depicts this model.

A person has a diathesis—a biological, ______________________,
or sociological ____________________ to develop a disorder.

↓

The person then experiences episodes of extreme ________________.

↓

Onset of the psychological disorder is "triggered."

Other theorists and clinicians favor the idea that **reciprocal effects** *of biological, psychological, and sociocultural factors can best explain abnormal behavior.*

Case Study

Since early childhood, Jenna has been a very anxious and tense person. Even as an infant she was "nervous and high-strung," according to her parents (who happen to be somewhat tense and anxious themselves). Jenna is also very intelligent and driven, and has maintained a 4.0 grade point average throughout her years at college. Unfortunately, Jenna's unrelenting, intense anxiety has contributed to physical problems (e.g., headaches and frequent gastrointestinal distress), as well as unpredictable, and very frightening, panic attacks. Because of these problems, Jenna cannot bring herself to take the GRE (the exam most graduate schools require for admittance), despite the fact that she desperately wants to go to graduate school. Jenna is unable to sleep at night, worrying that her "life won't go anywhere" and that she is "a huge failure." In addition, Jenna has virtually no network of friends or social supports; she avoids social activities because of her fatigue, feelings of worthlessness, and fear of having a panic attack. Jenna decides to seek professional counseling because her anxiety and depression are worsening, and she feels as though her "mind is spinning out of control."

3. Go through this case, and discuss the **reciprocal effects** of Jenna's biology, psychology, and environment on her current problems. *(Be sure you understand how this model differs from the diathesis-stress model described earlier.)*

____

____

____

____

MULTIPLE CHOICE

1. A paradigm is
   a. a specific law of behavior.
   b. another name for a theory.
   c. a set of the basic assumptions that organize one's approach to an area under study.
   d. a research study that determines the fundamental causes of a specific mental disorder.

2. A part of the brain that is involved in memory is the
   a. amygdala.
   b. basal ganglia.
   c. hippocampus.
   d. corpus callosum.

3. Neural information gets from one neuron to another via
   a. a chemical messenger.
   b. an electrical nerve impulse.
   c. the movement of receptors across the synapse.
   d. direct contact between an axon and a dendrite.

4. Which of the following is an antipsychotic drug?
   a. Xanax
   b. Prozac
   c. diazepam
   d. haloperidol

5. The originator of psychoanalysis was
   a. Jung.
   b. Freud.
   c. Breuer.
   d. Charcot.

6. Which of the following terms is used to describe a person's instinctual needs, drives, and impulses?
   a. id
   b. ego
   c. superego
   d. conscience

7. Focusing on past traumatic events, particularly from childhood, as causes of one's abnormal behavior is a major part of treatment in
   a. psychoanalysis.
   b. cognitive therapy.
   c. behavioral therapy.
   d. biological treatment.

8. Short-term psychodynamic therapies usually
   a. work well with alcoholics.
   b. are best for severely disturbed patients.
   c. require the therapist to be more confrontational.
   d. demonstrate better outcome than longer traditional therapy.

9. If you close your eyes and imagine biting into a big juicy sour lemon, you are likely to salivate. The image of the lemon is the
   a. conditioned stimulus.
   b. conditioned response.
   c. unconditioned stimulus.
   d. unconditioned response.

10. Which of the following is a cognitive concept?
    a. behavior
    b. self-efficacy
    c. reinforcement
    d. unconditional positive regard

11. Carl Rogers is considered the pioneer of the
    a. behavioral model.
    b. cognitive model.
    c. existential theory.
    d. humanistic theory.

12. What is the type of therapy in which a psychologist treats several unrelated clients together?
    a. psychodrama
    b. group therapy
    c. couple therapy
    d. a self-help group

13. The divorce rate in the United States and Canada is about
    a. 10%.
    b. 25%.
    c. 50%.
    d. 75%.

14. Which of the following would be an example of tertiary prevention of mental health problems?
    a. establishing a suicide hot line
    b. building a sheltered workshop where psychiatric outpatients can work
    c. advocating for establishing a day-care center for neighborhood children
    d. consulting with teachers to identify children who may benefit from services

CHAPTER

4 Clinical Assessment, Diagnosis, and Treatment

CHAPTER OUTLINE

REVIEW EXERCISES

I. Clinical Assessment: How and Why Does the Client Behave Abnormally?, 89–105

1. Complete the following list of the uses of clinical assessment techniques.

   a. to determine how and why someone behaves abnormally.

b. ______________________________

c. ______________________________

2. A clinician's ______________ orientation will influence his or her decision about what type of assessment technique to use.

A. Characteristics of Assessment Tools, 90

1. How would you **standardize** the scores of an alertness test for airline pilots?

____

____

____

2. Each of the following exercises relates to one of four kinds of clinical test **reliability** described in the textbook.

   a. The reliability of a test refers to the ______________ of assessment measures and test results.

   b. How would you go about demonstrating that the "Glass Is Half-Empty Test," a measure of pessimism, has adequate test–retest reliability?

   ____

   ____

   c. Interrater, or interjudge, reliability is demonstrated when several evaluators (or "judges") independently ______________ on how a test should be ______________________ .

3. An assessment tool's **validity** is the ______________ with which it measures what it is intended to measure.

4. Each of the following exercises relates to one of five kinds of validity described in the textbook.

   a. ______________ validity means that the items on a test "look like" they are measuring what they are supposed to measure; this kind of validity, however, does not necessarily establish that the test is ______________ .

   b. Imagine that the "Glass Is Half-Empty Test," which is designed to measure pessimism, is being considered as a tool to identify people who are at risk for developing a clinical depression later in life. What kind of validity would the test need to demonstrate in order for it to be used for this purpose?

   ____

   c. Concurrent validity is the degree to which test scores agree with:

   ____

B. Clinical Interviews, 91

1. What pieces of information are typically gained through clinical interviewing?

____

____

2. The textbook describes how clinicians give special attention to topics that are important to their particular theoretical orientation. Complete the following table by providing the name of the orientation that fits each description of topics.

Interview Topics	Orientation
Try to discover assumptions and interpretations that influence the way a person acts and feels	
Pinpoint signs of any biochemical or neurological dysfunction	
Relevant information about the stimuli that trigger the abnormal functioning, the precise nature of the abnormal responses, and the consequences of the responses	
The person's needs and fantasies, relevant memories about past events and relationships	
The person's self-concept and unique perceptions	
The person's family, living arrangements, and work relationships	

3. Unstructured interviews are comprised of open-ended questions (questions that cannot be answered with a simple "yes" or "no"). The textbook gives the example "Would you tell me about yourself?" Try to think of two more open-ended questions that might be asked in an clinical interview.

   a. ____

   b. ____

4. Clinicians who use ________________ interview strategies sometimes rely on published interview ________________ that provide a standard set of questions.

5. List some of the areas of functioning assessed on a mental status exam.

   ____

   ____

   ____

6. Complete the description of four of the limitations of clinical interviews.

   a. Information gathered at the interview is—to some extent—preselected by the client and may be self-serving and less than accurate.

   b. Some clients are simply unable to provide ________________ information in an interview.

   c. ____

   ____

   d. Clients respond differently to different interviewers. List some characteristics of clinicians that clients may respond to in one way or another.

   ____

C. Clinical Tests, 93

Coverage in this important subsection is broken into six parts, devoted to each of the six most prominent kinds of clinical tests.

Be sure you understand the coverage of reliability and validity, as they serve as a basis for "testing" the usefulness of each type of test.

I. Projective Tests, 94

1. The primary assumption of projective tests is that clients will "project" aspects of their own ________________ into the ________________, which is to interpret ambiguous stimuli.

2. Look at the **Rorschach inkblot** depicted in Figure 4–1 on page 94. This is similar to the 10 inkblots that Hermann Rorschach selected for use in the assessment of personality. Below, write a response to the question "What might this be?"

____

____

____

____

3. Rorschach believed that the images seen in the inkblots corresponded to a person's ________________ condition. *(After reading over your own response in #2 above, do you agree?)*

4. Most clinicians who use the Rorschach method today pay primary attention to the "style" of patients' responses to inkblots, such as whether they respond to the whole blot or specific details of it. Give two examples of the kinds of "styles" that different people demonstrate in their responses.

   a. ____

   b. ____

5. Complete the following flow chart relating to the questions a clinician using the **Thematic Apperception Test** would ask.

People who take the TAT are shown one picture at a time and asked to make up a dramatic story about it stating . . .

↓

1. What is happening?	3. What are the characters ________________ and ________________
2. ________________	4. ________________

↓

Clinicians then interpret the stories as an expression of the person's own circumstances, needs, emotions, etc.

6. Other projective tests include the ________________-completion test and the Draw-a-________________ Test, which is the most prevalent drawing test.

7. List three of the reliability and validity problems of the projective tests.

   a. ____

   ____

   b. Studies that "test" how well clinicians can describe personalities based on the results of projective tests have repeatedly shown inaccuracies.

   c. ____

   ____

Table 4-1: Multicultural Hot Spots in Assessment and Diagnosis, 97

Reread Table 4-1 on page 97 in your textbook. Incorporating some of the multicultural "hot spots" described in the table, create a case study in which a dominant-culture assessor attempts to assess, diagnose, and treat an ethnic-minority client.

____

____

____

____

____

____

____

____

____

____

2. Personality Inventories, 96

1. Currently there are two versions—original and revised—of the MMPI, or the Minnesota ____________ ____________ ____________ .

2. Complete the following table by matching the MMPI clinical scales with the letter corresponding to the content description from the list following the scales.

Number	Scale	Content Description
1 or HS	Hypochondriasis	
2 or D	Depression	
3 or Hy	Conversion Hysteria	
4 or PD	Psychopathic deviate	
5 or Mf	Masculinity-femininity	
6 or Pa	Paranoia	
7 or Pt	Psychasthenia	
8 or Sc	Schizophrenia	
9 or Ma	Hypomania	
0 or Si	Social introversion	

Content descriptions:

a. Obsessions, compulsions, fears, and guilt

b. Suspicion, delusions of grandeur, persecutory delusions

c. Excessive concern with bodily functions

d. Shyness, insecurity, little interest in people

e. Conventional masculine and feminine styles
f. Emotional shallowness, disregard for social norms
g. Pessimism, hopelessness, lethargy
h. Bizarre thoughts and behavior, hallucinations
i. Use of symptoms to avoid conflicts and responsibilities
j. Excitement, overactivity, racing thoughts

3. People can score from 0 to _______ on each MMPI scale, with scores of _______ or above indicating clinical significance or deviance.
4. List three problems that the MMPI-2 assesses that were not included in the original MMPI.
   a. ____________________
   b. ____________________
   c. ____________________
5. Complete the following list of advantages of structured personality inventories over projective tests
   a. short administration time
   b. ____________________
   c. ____________________
   d. ____________________
   e. greater validity (although it is still limited)
6. In addition to limited validity, a criticism of personality inventories is that they often fail to consider ______________ differences in people's responses.

3. Response Inventories, 98

1. Complete the following table by describing the purposes of the listed response inventories.

Inventory	Purpose
Affective inventories	
Social skill inventories	
Cognitive inventories	

4. Psychophysiological Tests, 99

1. Psychophysiological tests have become important assessment tools since the discovery that certain ______________ responses—such as changes in heart rate or blood pressure—often indicate ______________ problems—such as anxiety disorders.
2. Describe how **polygraphs** are used.

____

____

3. One limitation of psychophysiological assessment methods is that the equipment is expensive and must be expertly maintained. List two more limitations.

   a. ______________________________

   b. ______________________________

A Closer Look: The Truth, the Whole Truth, and Nothing but the Truth, 100

Although movies and television shows portray polygraphs (lie detectors) as being very accurate, actually they do not work as well as we would like. Research shows that _______ out of 100 truths, on average, are labeled lies by polygraph testing.

5. Neurological and Neuropsychological Tests, 100

1. List several causes of neurological damage in the brain that can result in psychological or behavioral problems.

   ____

   ____

   ____

2. In recent years, technological advances have allowed clinicians and researchers to get a closer, more detailed look at the brain in order to pinpoint potential sites of brain dysfunction. Describe each of the following neurological tests:

   a. Electroencephalogram (or EEG): ______________________________

   ____

   b. Computerized axial tomogram (or ______________ scan): ______________________________

   ____

   c. Positron emission tomogram (or ______________ scan): ______________________________

   ____

   d. Magnetic resonance imaging (or ______________): ______________________________

   ____

3. **Neuropsychological tests** can identify subtle brain abnormalities by measuring skills such as visual ______________ , recent ______________ , and visual-motor ______________ .

4. Describe the procedure used to detect neurological impairment by the **Bender Visual-Motor Gestalt Test.**

   ____

   ____

5. Because no single neuropsychological test can distinguish between specific kinds of impairment, clinicians often use a ______________ of tests to measure multiple skill areas.

6. Intelligence Tests, 102

1. Why is it impossible to measure intelligence directly?

   ____

   ____

2. The overall score on an intelligence test is called the ______________ ______________ or ______________ .

3. List the three most widely used measures of intelligence.

4. Intelligence tests generally demonstrate high validity and reliability, but they do have several shortcomings. Describe two of these important limitations.

   a.

   b.

D. Clinical Observations, 103

1. Describe how clinicians use the following strategies to observe behavior.
   a. Naturalistic observations:
   b. Analog observations:

2. Describe how the following factors can limit the validity of clinical observations.
   a. Observer drift:
   b. Observer bias:
   c. Subject reactivity:

3. Why may clinical observations lack cross-situational validity?

4. Imagine that you are a clinician and a 26-year-old man suffering from obesity comes into your clinic for help. You would like him to begin **self-monitoring** immediately. What are some of the things that you would like him to record?

The Media Speaks: Tests, eBay, and the Public Good, 104

1. To date, eBay has denied all requests to restrict the sale of Wechsler intelligence tests through its Web site. Identify several ways in which these tests might be misused if their sale is not limited to clinical psychologists and trained professionals.

II. Diagnosis: Does the Client's Syndrome Match a Known Disorder?, 105–112

A. Classification Systems, 106

1. A clinician makes a **diagnosis** when he or she determines that a person's pattern of symptoms (or ______________) constitutes a particular ______________ .

2. What are the (a) ICD and (b) DSM-IV-TR?

   a. ____

   ____

   b. ____

   ____

Eye on Culture: Culture-Bound Abnormality, 106

1. Briefly describe the system used by DSM IV-TR to handle culture-bound forms of abnormality, such as those described in the textbook on pages 106 and 107. Identify the major arguments that have been made to support and to criticize this system.

   ____

   ____

   ____

B. DSM-IV-TR, 108

1. The DSM-IV-TR includes descriptions of about _______ mental disorders.

2. Each entry in the DSM-IV-TR contains numerous pieces of information. What are they?

   ____

   ____

   ____

3. The following table relates to the five axes (branches of information) of DSM-IV-TR. Match each of the first four axes with the appropriate examples (there are none for Axis V) from the list of entries following the table, then give a short description for each axis. The numbers in parentheses under "Examples" are the number of examples you should choose for that particular axis.

Axis	Examples	Description
Axis I	(6) m, c, h	an extensive list of clinical syndromes that typically cause significant impairment
Axis II	(3) d	
Axis III	(3) n	
Axis IV	(3) o	
Axis V	(none)	

Examples:

a. Major depression
b. Recent death of a spouse
c. Schizophrenia
d. Antisocial personality disorder
e. Leukemia
f. Obsessive-compulsive disorder
g. Mental retardation
h. Autism
i. Ongoing sexual abuse
j. Bipolar disorder
k. Dependent personality disorder
l. AIDS
m. Anorexia nervosa
n. Epilepsy
o. Chronic unemployment

C. Is DSM-IV-TR an Effective Classification System?, 109

1. What does "reliability" mean in the context of a diagnostic classification system?

____

____

____

2. Describe the two steps taken by the DSM-IV-TR task force to maximize the reliability of the DSM-IV-TR system.

   a. ____

   ____

   b. ____

   ____

3. A diagnostic classification system that is most useful to clinicians is one that demonstrates ________________ validity in that it helps predict future symptoms.
4. A growing number of theorists believe the two fundamental problems that weaken the DSM-IV-TR are:

   a. Its basic assumption that clinical disorders are ________________ different from normal behavior rather than different in degree only.

   b. Its use of ________________ diagnostic categories, with each category of pathology considered to be separate from all the others.

D. Can Diagnosis and Labeling Cause Harm?, 111

1. List some examples of how clinicians, in interpreting assessment data, may be "flawed information processors."

____

____

____

2. Some theorists believe that diagnostic labels may be self-fulfilling prophecies. Explain the reasoning behind this belief.

____

____

____

III. Treatment: How Might the Client Be Helped?, 113–117

A. Treatment Decisions, 113

1. What factors influence or contribute to clinicians' treatment decisions? Complete the list of factors below.
   a. Information about the _______________ and _______________ of a client's problems that is gained through the assessment process.
   b. _______________ information that includes which techniques have been helpful for the particular type of problem.
   c. The clinician's theoretical _______________ .
   d. Other sources of information, such as _______________ results, colleagues, workshops, and books.

B. The Effectiveness of Treatment, 114

1. One of the problems with answering the question, "Is treatment 'X' successful?" is that researchers and clinicians could define "successful" in many different ways. What is one other problem with answering this question?

____

____

2. According to reviews of hundreds of studies on the effectiveness of therapy, the average person who receives therapy is better off than _________ percent of those who do not receive treatment.
3. The _______________ _______________ describes the false belief that all therapies are the same despite differences in therapists' theoretical orientation, personality, etc.
4. List some of the "common therapeutic strategies" that seem to characterize all effective therapies.

____

____

5. Complete the following table by identifying the most effective treatment approach(es) for the listed psychological problems/disorders.

Disorder	Effective Treatment Approach(es)
Schizophrenia	
Phobic disorders	

Psych Watch: Dark Sites, 115

1. It has been reported that there are currently more than __________ pro-anorexia Internet sites.
2. Identify an argument that has been made in favor of allowing pro-suicide Web sites to exist unimpeded.

____

____

____

IV. Putting It Together: Renewed Respect Collides with Economic Pressure, 117–118

1. During the 1960s and 1970s, many therapists lost confidence in the degree to which assessment and diagnosis could benefit clinical practice. More recently, however, assessment and diagnosis are again viewed by therapists as being an integral part of their clinical work. List three reasons for this shift.

   a. ____

   b. ____

   c. ____

MULTIPLE CHOICE

1. In order to understand a client's problems, a clinician uses a process that includes
   a. behavioral analysis and functional analysis.
   b. projective testing and interviewing.
   c. structured observation and classification.
   d. assessment and diagnosis.

2. Jillian is a participant in a study to evaluate a new measure of depression. She takes the depression test once, waits one month, then takes the test again. Her scores were almost identical. If other participants also have near identical scores, the test likely has good
   a. test-retest reliability.
   b. interrater reliability.
   c. predictive validity.
   d. concurrent validity.

3. If a test accurately measures what it claims to measure, that test is said to have
   a. concurrence.
   b. reliability.
   c. validity.
   d. standardization.

4. A clinician who looks for information concerning assumptions, interpretations, and coping skills during an interview probably takes the ________________ approach.
   a. biological
   b. behavioral
   c. cognitive
   d. humanistic

5. Current users of the Rorschach now pay attention mostly to the
   a. style of the response.
   b. affect of the responder.
   c. thematic content of the response.
   d. symbolic meaning of the response.

6. Simone is afraid of people and not at all assertive. Which MMPI-2 scale would she most likely score high on?
   a. schizophrenia
   b. psychasthenia
   c. social introversion
   d. psychopathic deviate

7. The PET scan makes a picture of the brain
   a. using X-rays that are projected at several different angles.
   b. that reflects the degree of activity of the various areas scanned.
   c. that reflects the magnetic properties of the atoms in the cells scanned.
   d. using a recording of the electrical impulses produced by the neurons in the brain.

8. One of the drawbacks of clinical observation is that the very presence of an observer might influence the behavior of the subject being observed. This is called
   a. reactivity.
   b. observer bias.
   c. observer drift.
   d. external validity.

9. Who developed the first influential classification system for abnormal behavior?
   a. Sigmund Freud
   b. Emil Kraepelin
   c. the American Psychiatric Association
   d. the American Psychological Association

10. What does Axis V include?
    a. a global assessment of functioning
    b. any relevant general medical condition
    c. any relevant psychosocial or environmental problem
    d. vivid clinical syndromes that typically cause significant impairment

CHAPTER

5 Anxiety Disorders

CHAPTER OUTLINE

I. Generalized Anxiety Disorder
- A. The Sociocultural Perspective: Societal and Multicultural Factors
- B. The Psychodynamic Perspective
- C. The Humanistic Perspective
- D. The Cognitive Perspective
- E. The Biological Perspective

II. Phobias
- A. Specific Phobias
- B. Social Phobias
- C. What Causes Phobias?
- D. How Are Phobias Treated?

III. Panic Disorder
- A. The Biological Perspective
- B. The Cognitive Perspective

IV. Obsessive-Compulsive Disorder
- A. What Are the Features of Obsessions and Compulsions?
- B. The Psychodynamic Perspective
- C. The Behavioral Perspective
- D. The Cognitive Perspective
- E. The Biological Perspective

V. Putting It Together: Diathesis-Stress in Action

Multiple Choice

REVIEW EXERCISES

I. Generalized Anxiety Disorder, 122–133

1. People with generalized anxiety disorders are often described as having ______________ anxiety because they experience worries about so many things in their lives.
2. In order to qualify for a diagnosis of generalized anxiety disorder, individuals must experience anxiety about numerous activities, situations, or events, and they must have symptoms that are present for at least how long?

   ____

3. List four of the symptoms of generalized anxiety disorder.

   a. ____

   b. ____

   c. ____

   d. ____

4. Generalized anxiety disorder usually emerges in ______________ or ______________, and ______ times as many women as men are diagnosed with this disorder.

A. The Sociocultural Perspective: Societal and Multicultural Factors, 123

1. Sociocultural theorists suggest that people who are confronted with societal situations that are truly ______________ are more likely to develop generalized anxiety disorder.
2. Several important studies suggest generalized anxiety disorder is more prevalent among individuals who live in poverty or face other societal pressures. Sociocultural factors, however, do not completely explain GAD. Why not?

   ____

   ____

3. Hispanics in both the United States and Latin America suffer from __________, a culture-bound disorder that bears great similarity to generalized anxiety disorder.

Table 5-2: Eye on Culture: Anxiety Disorders, 123

1. Compared to the general population, people who earn low incomes suffer a __________ rate of generalized anxiety disorders, specific phobias, social phobias, obsessive-compulsive disorders, and panic disorders.
2. Compared to the rate in the total population, women suffer the disorders listed in question 1 at a higher rate, with the exception of __________, which they suffer at the same rate as the total population.
3. Hispanic Americans suffer all of the disorders listed in question 1 at the same rate as the total population, with the exception of __________, which they suffer at a higher rate.

B. The Psychodynamic Perspective, 124

1. Define the three kinds of anxiety delineated by Freud.

   a. Realistic anxiety: ____

   ____

b. Neurotic anxiety: ____

c. Moral anxiety: ____

2. Freud suggested that people can develop generalized anxiety disorder when their defense mechanisms break down. The textbook lists two ways that this breakdown can occur and result in generalized anxiety disorder; describe them.

3. The textbook cites two lines of research that appear to support the psychodynamic explanation of generalized anxiety disorder. Briefly state the findings of studies on each of them.

   a. Excessive use of defense mechanisms: ____________________________

   b. Extreme punishment for id impulses: ____________________________

4. List two major criticisms of research on psychodynamic explanations of generalized anxiety disorder.

   a. ____

   b. ____

5. Describe the goals of the following two types of psychodynamic therapists in the treatment of generalized anxiety disorder.

   a. Freudian therapists: ____

   b. Object relations therapists: __________________________________

C. The Humanistic Perspective, 125

1. According to Carl Rogers, people can develop generalized anxiety disorder when, as children:

2. Rogers's treatment approach is called ________________-________________ therapy.

3. Humanistic therapists believe that if they provide an atmosphere of genuine acceptance and caring, clients will experience relief from their anxiety or other symptoms of psychological distress. How would providing this type of atmosphere result in client change?

D. The Cognitive Perspective, 126

1. Initially, cognitive theorists believed that generalized anxiety disorders are caused by ____________ ____________.

2. The letters a–e represent a jumbled set of steps in the process of how a person could develop generalized anxiety disorder according to the work of cognitive theorist **Albert Ellis.** Demonstrate that you understand this process by numbering the steps 1–5 in the order that fits Ellis's explanation.

   _____ a. Maladaptive assumptions are applied to more and more life situations.

   _____ b. A stressful event such as an exam or a date occurs.

   _____ c. A person holds a maladaptive assumption, such as "It is catastrophic when things are not the way one would very much like them to be."

   _____ d. The person develops generalized anxiety disorder.

   _____ e. The event is interpreted as highly dangerous and threatening, leading a person to overreact and experience fear.

3. According to cognitive theorists, people whose lives have been filled with ________________, ________________ events are likely to have exaggerated expectations of danger.

4. Identify and briefly describe the three "new wave cognitive explanations" of generalized anxiety disorder.

   a. ____

   ____

   ____

   b. ____

   ____

   ____

   c. ____

   ____

   ____

5. Albert Ellis's **rational-emotive therapy** consists of three important components. Complete the list.

   a. The therapist points out the client's irrational assumptions.

   b. ____

   c. ____

6. In __________-__________ cognitive therapy, therapists help clients to become aware of their troubling thoughts as they occur and to accept them as mere events of the mind.

E. The Biological Perspective, 130

1. Biological theorists believe that **family pedigree studies** will shed light on the question of whether a biological predisposition toward generalized anxiety disorder (GAD) might be inherited. In this exercise, (a) describe this research method and (b) describe a research finding that supports the notion that GAD might be heritable.

   a. ____

   ____

   ____

b. ____

____

____

2. Researchers have focused on the role of **gamma-aminobutyric acid** (GABA) and GABA receptors in fear reactions. Study the following "scenario" relating to normal fear reactions. (This diagram for study only).

Fear Reaction		Feedback System
Threatening stimulus perceived ↓ Key neurons throughout the brain fire rapidly creating . . . ↓ . . . a state of hyperexcitement in the brain and body ↓ Person experiences fear and anxiety	→	Feedback system is triggered ↓ GABA-producing neurons throughout the brain release GABA ↓ GABA binds to GABA receptors on receiving neurons and induces those neurons to stop firing ↓ Excitement is thereby reduced and fear and anxiety subside

3. Researchers believe that people with generalized anxiety disorders may have a problem in their anxiety feedback system. List three possible problems that researchers have speculated may be causing this problem.

   a. ____

   b. ____

   c. ____

4. Several discoveries have complicated the possibly overly simplistic explanation that GABA plays the central role in generalized anxiety disorders. Complete the following list of these complicating factors.

   a. GABA is one of several chemicals that can bind to ________________ receptors.

   b. Most of the biological research has been done on laboratory animals, so researchers can only assume that subjects are experiencing something that approximates ________________ ________________.

   c. No ________________ relationship has been established. In other words, it is possible that chronic anxiety eventually leads to poor ________________ ________________, rather than the other way around.

5. Until the 1950s, ________________ drugs were the primary drug treatment for anxiety disorders. What were some of the problems associated with these drugs?

____

____

6. Benzodiazepines are effective on anxiety disorders because the receptor sites that receive them also receive ________________, a neurotransmitter that ________________ neuron firing. What happens when benzodiazepines bind to these receptor sites?

____

7. Complete the following statements that address the potential risk of benzodiazepine use.
   a. When anxious people stopped taking the drugs, the anxiety returned.
   b. People who take them in large doses over a long period of time can become ______________ on them, and can experience many undesired side effects, such as drowsiness, memory loss, and depression.
   c. Although they are not toxic by themselves, they seem to ______________, or multiply, the effects of other substances, such as alcohol.
8. If, as is now suspected, low serotonin plays a key role in generalized anxiety disorder, why would benzodiazepine drugs, which reduce serotonin, be helpful in treating the disorder?

   ____

   ____

   ____

9. The basic premise of **relaxation training** is that ______________ relaxation will eventually lead to ______________ relaxation, especially after continued practice.
10. In biofeedback training, the ______________ (EMG) device provides visual and/or auditory feedback that informs the client when his or her ______________ are more or less tense.
11. The goal of biofeedback training is for people to become skilled at voluntarily ______________ muscle tension through a process of trial and error.
12. **Biofeedback** techniques seem to be more helpful in the treatment of ______________ problems than psychological problems.

II. Phobias, 134–143

1. A **phobia** is defined as a persistent and ______________ fear of a particular ______________, ______________, or ______________.
2. What were the most important findings of the Burlington, Vermont, study of relationship between fears and stage of life?

   ____

   ____

   ____

3. Complete the following statements. They relate to the characteristics that, according to the DSM-IV-TR, differentiate normal fears from phobic fears.
   a. Fear experienced in a phobic disorder is more intense and ______________.
   b. The phobic person's desire to ______________ the object or situation is more compelling.
   c. People with phobias experience such distress that their fears often interfere dramatically with their personal, social, or occupational functioning.

A and B. Specific Phobias and Social Phobias, 134

1. The three categories of phobias distinguished by the DSM-IV-TR are agoraphobia, social phobias, and specific phobias. Complete the table below by describing characteristics of each of these disorders.

Phobias	Characteristics
Agoraphobia	
Social phobia	
Specific phobia	

3. In several studies, African and Asian American participants have scored ____________ on surveys of social anxiety and other social concerns.

C. What Causes Phobias?, 137

1. Behavioral Explanations: How Are Fears Learned?, 137

1. One behavioral explanation of phobias is that fear is acquired through ________________ conditioning.

Read the following case study and answer the questions pertaining to it.

Case Study

It was 1:00 AM and Malcolm was driving home to North Dakota for his sister's wedding. It was snowing heavily, and the roads were icy; he was driving as fast as he safely could, but the trip had already taken two hours longer than it normally would. As Malcolm was fiddling with the radio dial, he looked up to see a huge semitrailer swerving dangerously in front of him. Malcolm pumped his brakes, but his car began to spin toward the truck, which was now facing him head-on. Malcolm leaned on the steering wheel and swerved into the ditch. His small car crashed into a fence by the ditch, but fortunately he suffered no physical injuries. Malcolm's heart was pounding, and he had never been so frightened in his life. Since his near-fatal accident, Malcolm cannot travel in a car. Simply contemplating a short drive fills him with panic and dread. In short, Malcolm has developed a phobia.

2. Using the case study and adhering to the behavioral explanation, complete this diagram.

Unconditioned stimulus (US)	→	fear response **Unconditioned response (UR)**
Conditioned stimulus (CS)	→	**Conditioned response (CR)**

3. Why would one fear-provoking experience (such as Malcolm's accident) develop into a long-term phobia?

4. Behaviorists posit that phobias could develop into a generalized anxiety disorder through __________ __________ .

5. Describe how Malcolm's phobia specifically could develop into a generalized anxiety disorder.

2. How Have Behavioral Explanations Fared in Research?, 139

1. Describe the findings of the "Little Albert" experiment.

2. Experiments have also produced evidence that fear can be acquired through **modeling.** Describe the (a) method and (b) findings of the research in this area by Bandura and Rosenthal in 1966.

   a.

   b.

3. Findings from several studies (particularly studies that have attempted to replicate previous findings) have failed to support the behavioral view of anxiety disorders. What is the conclusion that the textbook draws in light of this failure?

3. A Behavioral-Evolutionary Explanation, 139

1. "__________" is the idea that human beings, as a species, are predisposed to develop some fears (e.g., of snakes, lightning, heights) rather than others (e.g., of trees, rabbits, candy).

2. Refer to the study conducted by Ohman and his colleagues on conditioned fears in humans, then summarize (a) its method and (b) its findings.

a. ____

____

____

b. ____

____

____

3. The textbook describes two possible explanations of why humans might be predisposed to certain fears. Briefly, describe the underlying arguments of each.

   a. Evolutionary predisposition: ____

   ____

   b. Environmental predisposition: ____

   ____

D. How Are Phobias Treated?, 140

1. Treatments for Specific Phobias, 140

1. ______________ therapy appears to be the most effective form of treatment for phobic disorders.
2. **Systematic desensitization, flooding** and **modeling** are known collectively as ______________ treatments because clients are ______________ to the object or situation they dread.
3. Provide a description of each of the three phases of **systematic desensitization**

   a. Relaxation training: ____

   ____

   b. Construction of fear hierarchy: ____

   ____

   c. Graded pairings: ____

   ____

4. Behavioral therapists who use **flooding** techniques believe that when phobic clients are repeatedly ______________ to feared stimuli, they will see that the stimuli are quite ______________ .
5. Unlike desensitization strategies, flooding procedures do not use ______________ training or a ______________ approach to confronting a feared object or situation.
6. In **modeling** procedures, the ______________ confronts the feared object or situation while the ______________ watches.
7. Actual exposure to the feared object or event (also known as ______________ exposure) is more effective than imaginal or observational exposure (also known as ______________ exposure).

2. Treatments for Social Phobias, 141

1. People with social phobias have incapacitating social fears. What is the second distinct component of the social phobias?

   ____

2. Unlike specific phobias, social fears and phobias appear to respond to ______________ medications.

3. Gradual _______________ therapy, often coupled with homework assignments, helps people with social phobias learn to face the situations they dread most.
4. What makes group therapy an ideal setting for exposure-based treatment of social phobias?

____

____

5. Cognitive approaches such as Ellis's _______________ _______________ therapy help clients challenge and confront underlying assumptions and beliefs that can lead to social anxiety.
6. Complete the following flow chart that depicts basic elements of social skills training.

Therapists		Clients		Therapists provide
_______________	→	_______________	→	_______________
appropriate social behavior		social behaviors with the therapist or other clients		to clients regarding their "performance"

III. Panic Disorder, 143–149

1. Panic attacks usually reach a peak within _____ minutes.
2. List some symptoms of panic attacks.

____

____

3. People diagnosed with a panic disorder experience panic attacks without apparent _______________, recurrently, and _______________.
4. The DSM-IV-TR states that a diagnosis of panic disorder is warranted if, after having at least one unexpected panic attack, the person spends one month or more:
   a. worrying persistently about _______________________________,
   b. worrying about the _______________________________,
   c. and/or planning his or her _______________________________.
5. How are panic disorder and **agoraphobia** linked together?

____

____

____

Psych Watch: Panic: Everyone Is Vulnerable, 145

1. After reading the news account in this section, reflect on a time in your life when you might have experienced a sensation of panic. Describe how you felt and how you reacted.

____

____

A. The Biological Perspective, 146

1. Unexpectedly, it was found that people with panic disorders seem to respond most favorably to antidepressant drugs, rather than to _______________ drugs.

2. There are a large number of neurons that utilize **norepinephrine** in the area of the brain known as the ________________ ________________. When this area is electrically stimulated in monkeys, the monkey displays a paniclike reaction.

3. Name four brain areas included in the brain circuit that produce panic reactions.

   a. ____

   b. ____

   c. ____

   d. ____

4. Researchers have put forth varying theories to explain why the panic-producing brain circuit improperly functions in people who experience panic disorder. Identify two leading theories.

   a. ____

   b. ____

5. Some people may have an inherited biological predisposition to develop panic disorder. Describe one research finding that supports this hypothesis.

   ____

   ____

6. _____ percent of patients who experience panic attacks improve somewhat with drug treatment; about _____ percent improved markedly or fully.

7. Antidepressant drugs and alprazolam seem to be especially helpful in treating panic disorder with agoraphobia. Why?

   ____

   ____

   ____

B. The Cognitive Perspective, 147

Read the following case study of Dave, a 34-year-old male suffering from panic attacks.

Case Study

Dave woke up early one April morning feeling good. While eating his usual breakfast he noticed in the newspaper that a run was being held on Memorial Day to raise money for a charity. Although he hadn't run much in two years, he decided that he would participate in the event and that he would begin training for it that very morning. Dave felt really winded after three miles, but pushed himself to run two more. When he got home, he was sweating profusely, his heart was pounding, and his legs felt shaky and slightly numb. Fearing that he was having a heart attack, Dave began to hyperventilate and had a panic attack that lasted for approximately 20 minutes. Dave went to his doctor and was assured that his heart was very healthy. Two weeks later, he went to a new restaurant with a friend. They both ordered extra spicy dinners. Midway through the meal, Dave and his friend both complained of stomach pain and nausea. Dave became increasingly upset and told his friend that he had to leave right away because he was certain a panic attack was imminent.

1. Briefly describe how Dave's escalating anxiety and panic can be explained by the cognitive perspective of panic disorders.

____

____

____

2. What are some of the factors that may be related to why some people are more prone to misinterpret bodily sensations than others?

____

____

3. What is **anxiety sensitivity,** and how it is related to panic disorders?

____

____

____

4. Cognitive therapists teach clients about the nature of panic attacks, the actual causes of their bodily sensations, and their tendency to _______________ them.

5. In this exercise, (a) define the biological challenge procedure, and (b) state the purpose of such procedures in the context of therapy.

   a. _______________

   ____

   b. _______________

   ____

6. A number of recent studies have shown that _____ percent of subjects with panic disorders significantly improved after receiving cognitive therapy (compared to only 13 percent of control subjects who improved).

7. How did cognitive therapy fare in research comparing it to drug therapies as a treatment for panic disorders?

____

IV. Obsessive-Compulsive Disorder, 149–158

1. Complete the following list of DSM-IV-TR diagnostic criteria for **obsessive-compulsive disorder.** The diagnosis is appropriate when a person's obsessions and compulsions:

   a. feel excessive, _______________;

   b. cause significant _______________;

   c. are very _______________; or interfere with daily functions.

A. What Are the Features of Obsessions and Compulsions?, 150

1. Obsessions are not the same as excessive worries about real problems. They are thoughts that feel both intrusive (ego _______________) and _______________ (ego alien).

2. What may happen when people try to resist their obsessions?

____

Match the numbers 3–7, which list terms clinicians use to distinguish various kinds of obsessions, with the appropriate option from the list a–e, which are examples of these obsessions.

3. _____ obsessive wishes
4. _____ obsessive impulses
5. _____ obsessive images
6. _____ obsessive ideas
7. _____ obsessive doubts

Examples:

a. A student sees himself starting an arson fire in his dormitory.
b. A man dwells on the notion that he should have stayed in the Navy in 1954.
c. A woman incessantly worries that the mosquitoes in her backyard will give her malaria.
d. A girl wishes her older sister would have a car accident.
e. A man worries that one day he will purposely spill hot coffee onto his co-worker's lap.

8. Complete the following table by listing and giving examples of the types of compulsive rituals.

Type	**Example**
cleaning compulsion	washing hands 30 or 40 times a day

9. Most people with an obsessive-compulsive disorder experience _______________ obsessions and compulsions.

10. What is perhaps the greatest fear of people with obsessive-compulsive disorder? Is this fear usually warranted?

____

____

____

B. The Psychodynamic Perspective, 151

1. According to psychodynamic theorists, three ego defense mechanisms are commonly used by people with obsessive-compulsive disorder. Complete the table below by first defining each ego defense mechanism, then giving an example of each relevant to someone with obsessive-compulsive disorder.

Mechanism	Definition	Example
Isolation		
Undoing		
Reaction formation		

Freud explained obsessive-compulsive disorders within the framework of this theory of psychosexual development. Study this diagram of his conceptualization.

Child experiences pleasure and gratification associated with bowel movements.

↓

Parents attempt to toilet train child prematurely. . . | . . .or by using harsh, punitive methods

↓

CONFLICT

Child experiences rage and develops aggressive ID impulses, such as to soil, which are acted upon ⟶ More punishment leads to child feeling shame and guilt ⟶ With help from developing EGO, child tries to retain feces to please parents

↓

In adulthood, id-ego conflict may surface as
Obsessive-Compulsive Disorder

2. In Freud's conceptualization, depicted above, the child's aggressive impulses will now be countered by the child's strong desire to ______________ them.

C. The Behavioral Perspective, 152

1. Give a brief explanation of the behavioral perspective of obsessive-compulsive disorders.

____

____

____

2. In the treatment of obsessive-compulsive disorder, **exposure and response prevention** (or **exposure and ritual prevention**) procedures ask clients to confront dreaded objects or situations that would normally elicit anxiety, ______________ fears, and ______________ behaviors. Clients are then prevented from performing these behaviors.

Read the following case study and complete the exercise that follows.

Case Study

Patricia is obsessed with counting rituals, and specifically with the number 3. Although she is not distressed when, for example, her dishes sit unwashed on the counter, Patricia does feel compelled to order them in groups of three—three plates in a stack, three glasses lined in a row, etc. Patricia answers the telephone only after the third ring, and must buy three of any item on her grocery list. She also checks compulsively, always in increments of three. For example, she is not satisfied that her front door is locked until she turns the key three times, counting "one-two-three" aloud.

3. Complete this exercise by writing three more response prevention homework assignments for Patricia in addition to the one already given.

   a. buy only one of each item on the grocery list

   b. ______

   c. ______

   d. ______

4. Between _____ and _____ percent of obsessive-compulsive clients treated with exposure and response prevention show significant improvement.

5. As many as 25 percent of people with obsessive-compulsive disorder fail to improve at all with exposure and response prevention. What is another limitation of this technique?

______

______

The Media Speaks: Dining Out: The Obsessive-Compulsive Experience, 153

1. In the first-person account in this section, Jeff Bell describes his experience of obsessive-compulsive disorder, and the success he has experienced after receiving exposure and response prevention therapy. Describe how you imagine the course of Bell's therapy.

______

______

D. The Cognitive Perspective, 155

1. The cognitive-behavioral view of obsessive-compulsive disorder begins with the basic premise that everyone has repetitive, unwanted, unpleasant, and intrusive thoughts. List two examples of these thoughts from the textbook.

______

______

2. Compared with most people, how do those with obsessive-compulsive disorder interpret their intrusive, unwanted thoughts?

______

______

3. "Neutralizing" is when a person seeks to eliminate unwanted, intrusive thoughts by thinking or behaving in a way meant to put matters "right" internally. Why is this central to the behavioral explanation of obsessive-compulsive disorders?

______

______

4. Researchers have found that people with obsessive-compulsive disorder have certain characteristics that could be related to why they find normal intrusive thoughts so disturbing. Complete the list of these characteristics.

   People with OCD:

   a. seem to be more ________________ than others,

   b. have unusually high standards of ________________ and ________________,

   c. believe that their negative thoughts can ________________ themselves or others, and must take ________________ for eliminating the "danger" their thoughts pose, and

   d. tend to believe that they should have perfect ________________ over all thoughts and behaviors.

5. What is the underlying rationale of habituation training in the treatment of obsessive-compulsive disorder?

   ____

   ____

   ____

6. Briefly describe the course of treatment that a client with obsessive-compulsive disorder would undergo with a therapist who practices a combination of cognitive and behavioral therapy, which research suggests is often more effective than either cognitive or behavioral therapy alone.

   ____

   ____

   ____

   ____

   ____

   ____

   ____

   ____

E. The Biological Perspective, 156

1. Two sets of findings support the notion that biological factors play a role in obsessive-compulsive disorders. Complete the statements related to them.

   a. Obsessive-compulsive symptoms are reduced with the ________________ drugs clomipramine and fluoxetine, which seem to increase ________________ activity in the brain. The implication of this finding is that obsessive-compulsive disorder is associated with ________________ ________________ activity.

   b. Two areas of the brain—the orbitofrontal cortex and the caudate nuclei—may be functioning abnormally. These parts of the brain control the conversions of ________________ input into thoughts and ________________.

Study the following diagram.

Orbitofrontal region	→	***Caudate nuclei***	→	***Thalamus***
Generates primitive impulses		Filters only strongest impulses		

c. List two of the primitive impulses that the orbitofrontal region generates.

____

d. Researchers believe that the orbitofrontal region or the caudate nuclei may be functioning too _______________, leading to constant "breakthrough" of distressing thoughts and behavior.

2. Research has found that antidepressant drugs such as _______________ help to raise _______________ activity in the brain, thus bringing improvement in 50 to 80 percent of those who suffer from obsessive-compulsive disorder.

V. Putting It Together: Diathesis-Stress in Action, 158–159

1. Increasingly, clinicians and researchers are examining anxiety disorders within the framework of the diathesis-stress model. After reading through this section, create a plausible "scenario" that depicts how an individual might develop GAD. (Be sure to describe both diathesis and stress!)

____

____

____

____

____

____

____

____

MULTIPLE CHOICE

1. The most common mental disorders in the United States are the
   a. anxiety disorders.
   b. conversion disorders.
   c. personality disorders.
   d. dissociative disorders.

2. The Freudian view is that generalized anxiety disorder appears when a person is overwhelmed by
   a. realistic anxiety.
   b. neurotic anxiety.
   c. disintegration anxiety.
   d. an ego defense mechanism.

3. Anxiety disorders develop as a consequence of irrational or maladaptive assumptions or automatic thoughts that influence a person's understanding of life events. This illustrates which perspective?
   a. cognitive
   b. existential
   c. behavioral
   d. psychodynamic

4. The benzodiazepines seem to exert their anti-anxiety effect by
   a. facilitating GABA at receptor sites.
   b. blocking serotonin at receptor sites.
   c. blocking acetylcholine at receptor sites.
   d. facilitating norepinephrine at receptor sites.

5. TJ is terrified of going into crowded stores or anywhere else, unless she is accompanied by her sister. A diagnostician would probably diagnose her behavior as
   a. agoraphobia.
   b. a social phobia.
   c. a general phobia.
   d. generalized anxiety disorder.

6. According to the behavioral view, phobias may develop when a person learns a fear response to a specific object by the process of
   a. repression.
   b. reinforcement.
   c. operant conditioning.
   d. classical conditioning.

7. The most effective treatment of specific phobias seems to be
   a. cognitive therapy.
   b. biological therapy.
   c. behavioral therapy.
   d. psychodynamic therapy.

8. Which of the following is not true of panic disorder?
   a. The diagnosis is half as common in men as in women.
   b. A panic attack always has a specific cause.
   c. The disorder develops between late adolescence and the mid-30s for most people.
   d. In any given year, as many as 2.7 percent of all people suffer from it.

9. The apparent mechanism of action of the drugs useful in treating panic attacks is their ability to
   a. block norepinephrine.
   b. block the action of serotonin.
   c. mimic the action of serotonin.
   d. restore the activity of norepinephrine.

10. Max's physician had him breathe deeply and often until he was lightheaded. Max became very anxious. This procedure describes
    a. meditation.
    b. anxiety sensitivity.
    c. systematic desensitization.
    d. a biological challenge test.

11. Most studies on obsessions and compulsions indicate that
    a. obsessions and compulsions generally occur together.
    b. there is no relation between obsessions and compulsions.

c. obsessions generally occur in the absence of compulsions.
d. compulsions generally occur in the absence of obsessions.

12. Psychodynamic theorists believe that the ego defense mechanisms of isolation, undoing, and reaction formation are particularly common in people with
a. mood disorders.
b. personality disorders.
c. dissociative disorders.
d. obsessive-compulsive disorders.

13. According to the cognitive explanation of obsessive-compulsive disorder, the elimination or avoidance of repulsive and stressful thoughts is known as
a. neutralizing.
b. ego defense reactions.
c. covert-response prevention.
d. constructing a strict code of acceptability.

CHAPTER

6 Stress Disorders

REVIEW EXERCISES

I. Chapter Introduction and Stress and Arousal: The Fight-or-Flight Response, 163–167

1. Whenever we are confronted with situations that require us to change in some way, we experience a state of threat known as **stress.** List and briefly define the two components of a state of stress:

   a. ________________, ____

   b. ________________, ____

2. Complete the following statements, which are paraphrased from the textbook:

   a. The fear response is initiated by the brain structure called the ________________.

   b. The hypothalamus activates the ________________ ________________ ________________

(ANS), which connects the ______ ______ ______ (the brain and the spinal cord) to all the other organs of the body.

c. After a situation is perceived as dangerous, the ______ nervous system increases the heart rate and produces other fear responses; when the danger has passed, the ______ nervous system returns body processes to normal.

d. The hypothalamus also stimulates the ______ gland to release adrenocorticotropic hormone (ACTH) which in turn signals the ______ glands to release the stress hormones ______.

3. Define (a) trait anxiety and (b) state anxiety.

a. ______

______

b. ______

______

II. The Psychological Stress Disorders: Acute and Posttraumatic Stress Disorders, 167–182

1. According to the DSM-IV-TR, acute stress disorders and posttraumatic stress disorders differ primarily in onset and duration. Complete the following table to fit the DSM-IV-TR.

	Acute Stress Disorders	Posttraumatic Stress Disorders
Onset	Symptoms begin within ____ weeks of the traumatic effect.	Symptoms begin anywhere from shortly after to many ______ after the event.
Duration	Symptoms last from 2 to ____ days.	Symptoms have continued for ____ days or more.

Read the following case study and answer the questions pertaining to it.

Case Study

Sarah is a 23-year-old female who works as a pediatric nurse. At 3 AM one night, Sarah finished her shift and walked to her car in the parking garage adjacent to the hospital. As Sarah approached her car, she heard footsteps behind her. Before she was able to react, she was thrown down and pinned to the cement floor by a man with a stocking mask over his face. Brandishing a knife, the attacker threatened to kill Sarah if she made any noise or attempted to fight or run. She was brutally raped and knocked unconscious. When she regained consciousness several minutes later, the perpetrator had fled the scene. Sarah drove home in a state of shock, and managed to call a close friend, who immediately drove her to the emergency room.

2. Four types of symptoms Sarah might manifest if she developed a stress disorder are listed below as a–d. In the spaces provided list two examples of each symptom specific to Sarah's case. (Symptom "a" is provided.)

a. Re-experiencing the traumatic event:
Sarah has nightmares in which she "relives" the rape
Sarah often imagines that she hears the footsteps of her attacker when she goes outside

b. Avoidance:

____

____

c. Reduced responsiveness (also called psychic numbing or emotional anesthesia):

____

____

d. Increased anxiety, arousal, and guilt:

____

____

A. What Triggers a Psychological Stress Disorder?, 169

1. Combat and Stress Disorders, 169

1. This exercise refers to the syndrome involving symptoms of anxiety and depression in soldiers during combat.
   a. At the time of the American Civil War, it was thought that the syndrome was caused by extended absence from home. It was called nostalgia.
   b. During World War I, the syndrome was called ________________ . Clinicians thought its cause was minute brain hemorrhages or concussions triggered by artillery explosions.
   c. During World War II and the Korean War, the syndrome was called ________________ ________________ .
2. After the Vietnam War, approximately _____ percent of all soldiers suffered a stress disorder, and _____ percent still experience posttraumatic symptoms such as flashbacks and nightmares.
3. According to the RAND Corporation's 2008 assessment of the psychological needs of military service members, nearly _____ percent of the 1.6 million Americans deployed to the wars in Iraq and Afghanistan have reported symptoms of posttraumatic stress disorder.

2. Disasters and Stress Disorders, 169

1. Natural disasters and serious accidents actually account for more stress disorders than combat. Why?

____

____

2. List two natural and/or accidental disasters that might lead to a stress disorder.
   a. ____
   b. ____

3. Victimization and Stress Disorders, 170

1. Define *rape*.

____

____

____

2. Complete the following statements related to rape and rape victims:

   a. _____ percent of victims are under age 11, _____ percent are between age 11 and 17, and _____ percent are between age 18 and 29.

   b. Approximately 70 percent of rape victims are assaulted by _______________ or _______________, *not* strangers.

   c. Close to 95 percent of rape victims, when they were examined an average of 12 days after the assault, qualified for a diagnosis of _______________.

   d. Up to _____ percent of rape victims develop a sexually transmitted disease (STD) as a result of the assault, yet the majority do not receive information about testing for exposure to HIV.

3. List some of the psychological aftereffects of rape that can linger for months and years after the assault.

   ____

   ____

   ____

4. Surveys estimate that in the days immediately following September 11, 2001, 90% of people living in the United States experienced at least some level of increased stress; five months later, 25% continued to experience significant symptoms.

   a. How were you, your family, your friends, and/or your community affected by the attacks?

   ____

   ____

   ____

   ____

   b. What kinds of acute or posttraumatic stress symptoms did you see or hear about in the weeks and months after the attacks?

   ____

   ____

   ____

   ____

5. Please give examples of each of the four major types of torture people across the world are subjected to.

   a. Physical torture _______________

   b. Psychological torture _______________

   c. Sexual torture _______________

   d. Torture through deprivation _______________

B. Why Do People Develop a Psychological Stress Disorder?, 173

1. Researchers have focused on five sets of factors in their attempts to answer the question "Why do some people develop stress disorders following a traumatic event and others do not?" Describe these factors in the following table.

Factor	Description/Explanation
a. Biological/genetic factors:	
b. Personality:	
c. Childhood experiences:	
d. Social support:	
e. Multicultural factors:	
f. Severity of trauma:	

2. List three possible reasons why Hispanic Americans may be more vulnerable to posttraumatic stress disorder than other cultural groups.

____

____

C. How Do Clinicians Treat the Psychological Stress Disorders?, 179

1. List the three common goals of all treatment programs for trauma survivors. They all seek to help the survivor:

   a. ____

   b. ____

   c. ____

1. Treatment for Combat Veterans, 179

1. List the symptoms that were successfully minimized in Vietnam veterans by the following treatments: (a) antianxiety drugs, (b) antidepressant drugs, and (c) flooding and desensitization.

   a. ____

   b. ____

   c. ____

2. Describe **eye movement desensitization and reprocessing** (EMDR), a new treatment for stress disorders.

____

____

____

3. Most clinicians believe that trauma survivors cannot fully recover until they gain ________________ into the traumatic experience itself and the continuing ________________ of those experiences on their lives.

4. "________________ groups" provide a safe place for trauma survivors to share experiences and feelings, and to give support to other group members.

5. Write a paragraph describing some of the painful feelings expressed by Vietnam War veterans in the groups mentioned in Exercise 4.

____

____

2. Psychological Debriefing: The Sociocultural Model in Action, 181

1. Many clinicians believe that people who are traumatized by disasters, victimization, or accidents will benefit greatly from immediate community mental health interventions. The leading approach of this sort is ____________ debriefing, or ____________ ____________ stress debriefing.
2. Why is this form of crisis intervention commonly applied to victims who have not manifested any symptoms of stress reactions or trauma? ____________
3. Briefly describe a typical group session of the intervention approach identified in question 1 above.

____

____

3. Does Psychological Debriefing Work?, 182

1. Some studies have suggested that trauma victims who undergo rapid psychological debriefing may experience the same or even higher rates of posttraumatic stress disorder as trauma victims who do not undergo psychological debriefing. Identify three reasons suggested by clinicians why this might be so.

   a. ____________

   b. ____________

   c. ____________

III. The Physical Stress Disorders: Psychophysiological Disorders, 184–198

Physicians and psychologists have long recognized that some physical conditions result from an interaction of physical and psychological/behavioral factors. These disorders, unlike the somatoform disorders, are characterized by actual medical conditions.

In the textbook and workbook, the term "psychophysiological disorders" is used to indicate those medical conditions that are significantly affected by psychological factors, rather than the current "psychological factors affecting medical condition" diagnostic term delineated by DSM-IV-TR.

A. Traditional Psychophysiological Disorders, 184

1. This exercise focuses on the traditional psychophysiological disorders: ulcers, asthma, chronic headaches, hypertension, and coronary heart disease. Complete the table. It was designed to assist in organizing the information in the section.

Ulcers	
Description	lesions that form in the wall of the stomach (gastric ulcers) or in the duodenum (peptic ulcers) cause pain, vomiting, and stomach bleeding
Psychosocial factors	environmental stress, intense anger and/or anxiety, dependent personality traits
Physiological factors	bacterial infections

Asthma	
Description	
Psychosocial factors	generalized anxiety, dependency traits, environmental stress, dysfunctional family relationships
Physiological factors	
Insomnia	
Description	
Psychosocial factors	
Physiological factors	
Chronic Headaches	
Description	muscle contraction (tension): pain to back or front of head or back of neck; migraine: severe or immobilizing aches on one side of the head
Psychosocial factors	
Physiological factors	
Hypertension	
Description	
Psychosocial factors	
Physiological factors	diet high in salt; dysfunctional baroreceptors (nerves in the arteries that signal the brain that blood pressure is too high)
Coronary Heart Disease	
Description	blockage of coronary arteries; myocardial infarction or heart attack
Psychosocial factors	
Physiological factors	

I. Biological Factors, 186

Review pages 164–167 of your text as well as the corresponding workbook exercises regarding how the autonomic nervous system (including the sympathetic and parasympathetic systems) works. Then study the diagram below. It depicts Hans Selye's model describing the relationship between stress and the autonomic nervous system (ANS).

Selye held that people respond to stress with what he called the **general adaptation syndrome,** *composed of three sequential stages.*

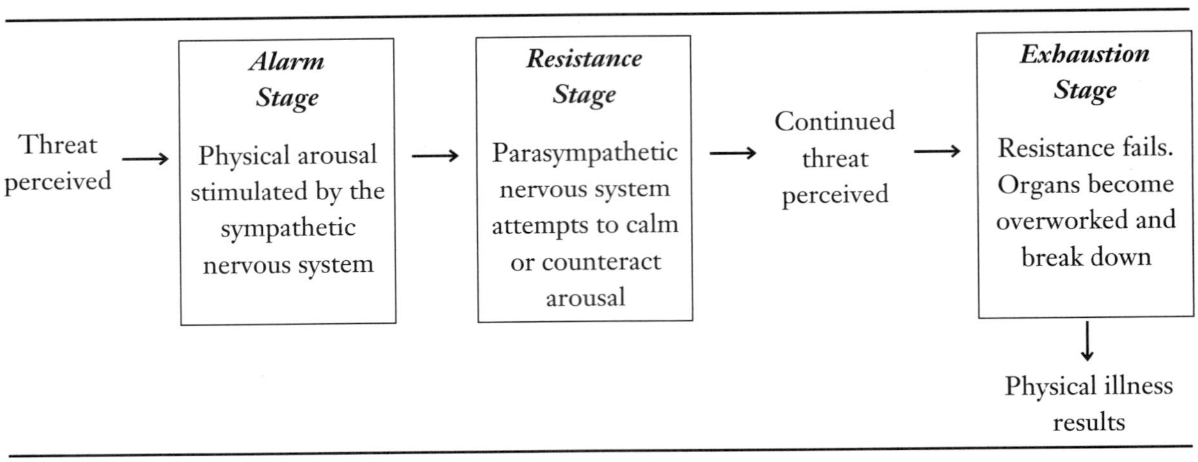

1. The textbook provides several explanations of how biological reactions to stress could lead to psychophysiological illnesses. Complete the following statements, explaining how each factor implicated might be related to a physical disorder.

   a. The ANS is stimulated too easily, which could easily result in certain organs being damaged and a psychophysiological disorder developing.

   b. Specific biological problems, such as "weak" gastrointestinal and respiratory systems, result in

   ____

   c. A psychophysiological disorder may ultimately result from individual biological reactions to stress such as

   ____

2. Psychological Factors, 187

1. Certain needs, ______________, emotions, and coping styles may increase a person's susceptibility to psychophysiological disorders.

2. The link between "______________" coping styles (characterized by pent-up and unexpressed negative emotions) and poor physical health is supported by research.

3. Type _____ personality style is the best known psychological condition that can lead to ______________ ______________ disease.

4. Describe the behaviors of people who exhibit (a) **Type A personality style** and (b) **Type B personality style.**

   a. ____

   ____

   b. ____

   ____

5. Describe (a) the method and (b) the findings of the Friedman and Rosenman study of the relationship between personality style and coronary heart disease.

   a. ____

   ____

   b. ____

   ____

6. What is the Type A characteristic most associated with coronary heart disease?

____

3. Sociocultural Factors: The Multicultural Perspective, 187

1. Give three examples of environmental stressors that may open the door for a psychophysiological disorder:

   a. natural disasters or wars

   b. _______________

   c. _______________

2. For an African American, the inability to successfully hail a cab late at night might be an example of a _______________ stressor, while waiting in line at the post office when late for an appointment might be an example of a _______________ stressor.

B. New Psychophysiological Disorders, 189

Like the textbook, the workbook will study the areas of "new" psychophysiological disorders separately.

1. Are Physical Illnesses Related to Stress?, 190

1. In the late 1960s, researchers _______________ and _______________ developed the _______________ _______________ Rating Scale, which assigned a numerical value to life stressors that people commonly experience (see Table 6–4).

2. In the scale the stressor is assigned a certain number of _______________ _______________ _______________ (LCUs) that corresponds to the degree that both positive and negative life events have an impact on people; the scale allows researchers to estimate the total amount of stress a person has experienced in a given time period.

3. In your own words, describe (with an example) the primary shortcoming of the Social Adjustment Rating Scale.

____

____

____

2. Psychoneuroimmunology, 191

1. _______________ (viruses, bacteria, parasites, etc.) and cancer cells "invade" the body and trigger the immune system to go into action.

2. Lymphocytes are white _______________ _______________ manufactured in the lymph system that help the body overcome antigens.

3. In this exercise, describe the functions of the three groups of lymphocytes in the body's immune system that are described in the textbook.

   a. Helper T-cells identify antigens and then _______________ and trigger the production of other immune cells.

   b. What is the function of natural killer T-cells?

   ____

   ____

   c. B-cells produce _______________, which are protein molecules that recognize and bind to a specific antigen and mark it for _______________.

4. Stress can interfere with lymphocyte activity, which leads to increased ________________ to viral and bacterial infections.

5. Researchers have found compromised lymphocyte activity among people who have experienced stressors such as the recent loss of a ________________ and providing ongoing care for loved ones with ________________ disease.

Questions 6–9 deal with the four sets of factors that can result in a "slowdown" of the immune system: biochemical activity, behavioral changes, personality style, and degree of social support.

6. Biological researchers have discovered that:

   a. Under stress the activity of the sympathetic nervous system increases and results in increased secretion of ________________________ throughout the brain and body.

   b. At low levels or in the early stages of stress, this neurotransmitter "tells" lymphocytes to ________________ activity, but when stress levels become high or prolonged, the same neurotransmitter gives lymphocytes a(n) ________________ message to stop their activity—potentially leading to health problems.

7. In a similar fashion, the so-called stress hormones called ________________ give different messages (to increase or decrease activity) to lymphocytes depending on the level and duration of an individual's stress.

8. Recent research indicates that corticosteroids trigger an increase in the production of __________, proteins that bind to receptors throughout the body. As stress increases and more corticosteroids are released, the spread of these proteins can lead to chronic ________________ throughout the body.

9. Stress can also lead to certain behaviors that are known to suppress immune system functioning. List three of these behaviors.

   ____

   ____

   ____

10. Research indicates that people with "hardy" personality styles are better at fighting off illnesses. Describe this hardy style.

    ____

    ____

    ____

11. Poorer cancer prognoses have been found in people who show a ________________ coping style and who have difficulty expressing emotions such as ________________ .

12. Research findings indicate that the immune system functioning of people who have few social supports and feel ________________ is poorer in times of stress compared to people who do not share these characteristics.

C. Psychological Treatments for Physical Disorders, 194

1. ________________ medicine is the field that combines physical and psychological strategies to treat or ________________ medical problems.

2. Complete the table, which summarizes the most common psychological treatments for the psychophysiological disorders.

Intervention	Description	Illnesses Treated
Relaxation training	Patients taught to relax muscles, which curbs anxiety by reducing sympathetic nervous system activity	Essential hypertension, headaches, insomnia, asthma, effects of cancer treatment and surgery
Biofeedback training		
Meditation		
Hypnosis		
Cognitive interventions		
Insight therapy and support groups		
Combination approaches		

IV. Putting It Together: Expanding the Boundaries of Abnormal Psychology, 198–199

In this chapter you have read about how stress contributes to both psychological disorders and physical illnesses. Researchers have learned the value of considering sociocultural, psychological, and biological factors when treating mental illness. Additionally researchers have learned the value that mental health plays in illness prevention and health promotion. What sorts of coping mechanisms do you use to promote your own physical and mental health? Think of a time when you, or someone close to you, experienced a relatively serious physical or mental illness. Describe psychological and/or environmental influences that you believe played a role in the length or severity of this illness.

____

____

____

____

____

MULTIPLE CHOICE

1. Megan loves riding roller coasters, bungee jumping, skiing, and hang gliding. These activities scare her husband silly. This difference reflects
   a. trait anxiety.
   b. state anxiety.
   c. personality anxiety.
   d. generalized anxiety.

2. If you had forgotten about your abnormal psychology exam on stress disorders and had failed to prepare, you likely would experience such symptoms as a racing heart and sweaty palms. Furthermore, you might not know that the ___________ nervous system is responsible for producing those symptoms.
   a. central
   b. parasympathetic
   c. sympathetic
   d. peripheral

3. Difficulty concentrating, sleep problems, and being easily startled are symptoms in which of the four symptom categories of acute and posttraumatic stress disorders?
   a. reexperiencing the traumatic event
   b. avoidance
   c. reduced responsiveness
   d. increased arousal, anxiety, and guilt

4. Salina was terrified during the San Francisco earthquake of 1989. For a couple of weeks after, she did not sleep well or feel comfortable inside a building. However, gradually the fears diminished and disappeared within a month. Her reaction to the earthquake was
   a. a panic attack.
   b. an acute stress disorder.
   c. a phobic reaction.
   d. a posttraumatic stress disorder.

5. Research after the terrorist attacks of September 11, 2001, found
   a. almost all people living in America experienced severe stress symptoms up to a month after the attacks.
   b. about half of adults in the United States experienced substantial stress symptoms in the first few days after the attacks.
   c. likelihood of developing a stress disorder was unrelated to previous mental health problems.
   d. those individuals who watched less television coverage of the attacks experienced more symptoms because they had less information.

6. The age of a female most likely to be raped is
   a. under 11 years old.
   b. between 11 and 17 years old.
   c. between 17 and 29 years old.
   d. over 29 years old.

7. The rage and guilt that are part of the posttraumatic stress syndrome exhibited by many Vietnam veterans have been successfully treated with
   a. antianxiety drugs.
   b. antidepressant drugs.
   c. a form of group therapy.
   d. the exposure and response prevention procedure.

8. Psychophysiological disorders are different from factitious disorders in that psychophysiological disorders
   a. are caused by hidden needs.
   b. are intentionally produced.
   c. bring about actual physical damage.
   d. are learned through reinforcement.

9. The body's network of activities and cells that identify and destroy antigens and cancer cells is

a. psychoneuroimmunology.
b. the immune system.
c. the psychophysiological response.
d. biochemical activity.

10. What are the characteristics of someone with a Type A personality?
a. calm, patient, and tolerant
b. cold, withdrawn, and intolerant
c. impatient, easily frustrated, and aggressive
d. warm, outgoing, with high frustration tolerance

11. A technique of turning one's concentration inward and achieving a slightly changed state of consciousness is called
a. meditation.
b. self-hypnosis.
c. relaxation training.
d. biofeedback.

CHAPTER

7 Somatoform and Dissociative Disorders

CHAPTER OUTLINE

REVIEW EXERCISES

Stress and anxiety can lead to a wide variety of psychological responses. In the somatoform disorders, unrecognized emotions are expressed as physical symptoms. In the dissociative disorders, stress leads to major losses or changes in memory, conciousness, or identity.

I. Somatoform Disorders, 204–218

A. What Are Hysterical Somatoform Disorders? 204

1. Complete the following table summarizing three types of hysterical somatoform disorders.

Type	Description	Symptoms
Conversion disorder	Expression of psychological problems in the form of one or more motor or sensory symptoms	Called "pseudoneurological": include paralysis, blindness, anesthesia
Somatization disorder		
Pain disorder associated with psychological factors		

2. The textbook discusses several distinctions between symptoms of hysterical somatoform disorders and "true" medical conditions. Provide an example of a hysterical somatoform symptom after each distinction listed.

   a. Symptoms of hysterical somatoform disorders are inconsistent or impossible when compared to the manner in which the nervous system actually functions.

   Example:

   ____

   ____

   b. The physical effects of the hysterical somatoform disorder are very different from the corresponding "true" medical condition.

   Example:

   ____

   ____

3. A person is said to be ______________ when he or she "fakes" an illness in order to achieve an external gain such as financial compensation. (*Note:* This is *not* considered a factitious disorder.)

4. People with factitious disorder ______________ produce symptoms as well, but they are motivated by internal rewards of maintaining a sick role.

5. Describe two ways that people with factitious disorder might create physical symptoms.

   a. ______________________________

   b. ______________________________

6. If people with factitious disorder are "found out," they generally _______________ the charges, quickly _______________ the hospital, and even enter another hospital in the same day.

7. _______________ syndrome is the most chronic form of factitious disorder. *(Be sure to read through "A Closer Look" on page 209 of the text, which describes a variant of this disorder.)*

8. Factitious disorders are most common in people (especially men) who received extensive medical treatment for a true physical condition as _______________, who resent the _______________ profession, who have worked in a medical field, who have dependent, exploitive, or self-defeating personality traits, and who have few _______________ relationships.

B. What Are Preoccupation Somatoform Disorders?, 208

1. People diagnosed with preoccupation somatoform disorders misinterpret and _______________ to bodily _______________ or features.

2. People diagnosed with _______________ become preoccupied with unrealistic misinterpretations of the seriousness of minor or nonexistent physical symptoms.

3. Distinguish between the disorder you identified above and somatization disorder (presented earlier).

____

____

____

4. People suffering from **body dysmorphic disorder,** or _______________, become preoccupied with imagined or exaggerated _______________ in their appearance.

5. List some of the aspects of appearance that are of most concern to people diagnosed with body dysmorphic disorder.

____

____

6. List some of the differences between normal worries about appearance and the experiences of someone suffering from body dysmorphic disorder.

____

____

7. People with body dysmorphic disorder are _______________ likely than others to be unemployed and to have limited academic success.

8. Men with body dysmorphic disorder are primarily preoccupied with their _______________ _______________, _______________, and height.

C. What Causes Somatoform Disorders?, 211

1. Explanations for the preoccupation somatoform disorders are most similar to the cognitive and behavioral theories of _______________ disorders.

2. The ancient Greeks believed that hysterical disorders were experienced when the _______________ of a sexually _______________ woman would wander throughout her body in search of fulfillment, producing a physical symptom wherever it lodged.

1. The Psychodynamic View, 212

1. Complete the statements about Freud's view of hysterical somatoform disorders.

   a. Freud believed that because hysterical somatoform disorders could be treated with hypnosis, these disorders represented a ________________ of underlying ________________ conflicts into physical symptoms.

   b. According to Freud, if parents overreact to a girl's "sexual" feelings toward her father during the ________________ stage, she will not adequately resolve the emotional conflict (or Electra complex).

   c. If the Electra conflict goes unresolved, the girl could experience sexual ________________ throughout her adult life.

   d. Specifically, what did Freud propose would happen when the adult woman's sexual feelings are triggered, which could lead to a hysterical disorder?

   ____

   ____

2. Although today's psychodynamic theorists agree with Freud that hysterical disorders reflect an unconscious, anxiety-arousing conflict that is converted into more tolerable physical symptoms that symbolize the conflict, they now focus on two mechanisms that seem to be involved in the development of the hysterical somatoform disorders. Define the mechanisms (a) **primary gain** and (b) **secondary gain.**

   a. ____

   ____

   b. ____

   ____

2. The Behavioral View, 213

1. The behavioral view of the hysterical somatoform disorders emphasizes the ________________ gained by the patient when he or she displays symptoms of the disorder.

2. A main tenet of the behavioral view is that humans can receive a benefit from being in a "sick" role. Was there ever a time when you benefited in any way from being sick (particularly as a child)? If so, write about it. (*Note: This is not to suggest that you had a hysterical disorder.*)

   ____

   ____

   ____

3. What is the primary difference between the behavioral view and the modern psychodynamic view of hysterical disorder?

   ____

   ____

3. The Cognitive View, 214

1. Cognitive theorists suggest that the hysterical somatoform disorders serve to ________________ distressing emotions such as anger, ________________, guilt, and jealousy in a physical language that is familiar and comfortable to the patient.

2. According to adherents of the cognitive view, people who have difficulty acknowledging their emotions or expressing them to others are candidates for a hysterical disorder. Who else do they believe is susceptible to this disorder?

____

____

4. The Multicultural View, 214

1. Somatization, the development of somatic symptoms in response to personal distress, is generally considered ______________ in Western countries, while it is ____________ in most non-Western cultures. This difference underscores the importance of the influence of culture on an individual's response to stress.

2. Individuals in Latin countries seem to display the ___________ number of somatic symptoms. Even in the United States, people from Hispanic cultures display ______ somatic symptoms while under stress than do other populations.

3. Can you suggest one reason why recent Latin immigrants to the United States may display a lower rate of posttraumatic stress disorder than other people throughout the United States?

____

____

5. A Possible Role for Biology, 215

1. Substances with no known medicinal value, ________________, have relieved the suffering of patients for centuries.

2. While placebos used to be thought of as "magical" treatments, recent research suggests placebos may cause the release of a variety of chemicals in the body. Explain, in your own words, Howard Brody's idea comparing the placebo effect to a visit to a pharmacy.

____

____

D. How Are Somatoform Disorders Treated?, 216

Hysterical somatoform disorder sufferers tend to resist psychotherapy because they believe they have physical rather than psychological ailments. These exercises relate to treatments used when they give up on the medical alternatives.

1. People with body dysmorphic disorders are usually treated with interventions that are also utilized for people suffering from ________________ disorders (especially ________________ disorders); for example, antidepressant (SSRI) drugs and ________________ and ________________ prevention appear to be effective.

Read the following case study.

Case Study

Rita has sought treatment for her mysterious physical symptoms from six medical professionals at four hospitals. Her symptoms include a sensation of numbness that "travels" across her scalp and face, frequent abdominal pain, and paralysis of her legs. The last doctor she visited could find no organic (physical) basis for her condition, even after an extensive series of tests, and finally advised Rita to seek psychotherapy. Although she initially resisted, Rita decided that she had better do what the doctor advised or she might not be able to receive further medical services from the hospital.

2. Complete the following table by writing in the names of the therapeutic techniques used for hysterical somatoform disorder described in the textbook, as well as sample statements you might use for each technique if you were the therapist assigned to treat Rita.

Technique	Sample Therapeutic Statement
Suggestion	
	"Rita, I notice that you walked very quickly into my office today. It's just wonderful that you've been able to suppress the paralysis."

3. Which disorders are more and less likely to benefit from psychotherapy, according to the results of case studies?

____

____

4. Describe the cognitive-behavioral treatment that is offered to those suffering from hypochondriasis.

____

____

II. Dissociative Disorders, 218–236

1. Memory connects our _______________ to our present and _______________.
2. Major changes in memory without any physical causes are called **dissociative disorders**. Complete the following table with brief definitions of the various dissociative disorders.

Disorder	Definition
Dissociative amnesia	Inability to recall important personal events and information
Dissociative fugue	
	The existence of two or more separate identities

A. Dissociative Amnesia, 219

1. People with **dissociative amnesia** manifest an inability to remember important information, usually of a stressful or _______________ event in their lives, which cannot be attributed to _______________ factors.

Read this case study, which is the basis for an exercise following it relating to the different kinds of amnesia.

Case Study

Clara, the proprietor of a popular inn on the beach, was quite busy one fateful June day. The inn was at full capacity with 60 guests—all of whom seemed to be making requests at the same time for more towels and pillows, extra room keys, and use of the fax machine. Clara managed to get through dealing with an angry guest, a Mr. Barnes, who demanded to have a "bigger room facing the ocean," and then decided it would be an ideal time to escape the chaos and obnoxious guests by running to the bank to make a deposit.

Standing in line, Clara became lost in her thoughts about the big dinner that evening at the inn. She heard a scream behind her, and turned to see four men wearing Richard Nixon masks and carrying guns. The gunmen shot out the cameras on the walls and ordered everyone to drop to the floor. One of them threatened to shoot all of the bank tellers if any of them activated the alarm. Face down on the floor, Clara shut her eyes and silently prayed. She was so frightened that she had trouble breathing. Suddenly, more shots were fired and Clara felt a man falling on top of her. She opened her eyes to see the man all bloody and writhing on the floor next to her. Clara screamed, for which she received a sharp kick to the shoulder and a threat that if she didn't "shut the hell up" she would "be next." The next few minutes were a blur. Clara heard the gunmen running shortly before the police swarmed into the bank.

After waiting what seemed like hours, Clara was checked out by a doctor and then interviewed by police. She was finally allowed to return to the inn—six hours after she left for what she thought would be a brief errand. For the next few weeks, Clara felt as if she were in a fog and had difficulty remembering details about the traumatic event she had experienced.

2. Using this case, apply a description of the pattern of forgetting that would illustrate the kinds of amnesia listed.

   a. *Localized amnesia:* Clara is able to recall her hectic day at the inn, including her run-in with Mr. Barnes, but can't remember a thing about being in the bank. She can recall everything after waking up at the inn the day after the robbery.

   b. *Selective amnesia:* ____

   ____

   ____

   c. *Generalized amnesia:* ____

   ____

   ____

   d. *Continuous amnesia:* ____

   ____

   ____

3. People with dissociative amnesia can typically remember abstract or ______________ information, but cannot remember ______________ information; in other words, *semantic memory* is usually intact, but ______________ memory is disrupted in dissociative amnesia.

4. Many cases of dissociative amnesia emerge during ______________ or natural ______________, when people's health and safety are threatened.

5. Give an example of an event more ordinary than military experiences that might precipitate dissociative amnesia.

____

____

Dissociative amnesia has been linked to child sexual abuse as well. This link has stirred considerable controversy over the reality of "repressed" memories, which is examined in "Repressed Childhood Memories or False Memory Syndrome?" on page 223. Read this material and think about your reaction to the controversy.

B. Dissociative Fugue, 221

1. People with **dissociative fugue** forget their personal _______________, flee to a different _______________, and might even establish an entirely new identity.
2. For some people with dissociative fugue, the disorder is relatively brief—lasting only a few hours or days. In others, the fugue is more extensive. List three characteristics of those who have the more extensive fugue state.

   ____

   ____

3. List two ways in which dissociative fugue and dissociative amnesia are similar.

   a. _______________

   b. _______________

4. Complete these questions about the aftereffects of dissociative fugue.

   a. Usually fugues end _______________.

   b. People usually regain most or all of their memories and never experience a _______________.

   c. People away for months or years often have trouble adjusting to _______________ that occurred during their absence.

   d. Some must also face the consequences of illegal acts committed during the fugue.

C. Dissociative Identity Disorder (Multiple Personality Disorder), 224

1. A person with **dissociative identity disorder** manifests _______________ or more distinct subpersonalities, one of which—the primary or _______________ personality—dominates the others and appears more frequently.
2. The transition from one subpersonality to another can be _______________ and dramatic, and is typically precipitated by a _______________ event.
3. Complete these statements relating to the onset and prevalence of dissociative identity disorder.

   a. Most cases of dissociative identity disorder are first diagnosed in late _______________ or young _______________.

   b. However, symptoms of dissociative identity disorder usually appear in childhood before the age of _____, after the child experiences some form of _______________.

   c. For every man diagnosed with dissociative identity disorder, there are at least _______________ women diagnosed with the disorder.

4. Complete the brief descriptions of the characteristics of the three kinds of relationships between subpersonalities in this table.

Type	How the Subpersonalities Relate to Each Other
Mutually amnesic	they have no awareness of each other
Mutually cognizant	
One-way amnesic	

5. Research indicates that the average number of subpersonalities per dissociative identity disorder patient is about _____ for women and _____ for men.

6. The dissociative identity disorder case depicted in the book and movie _______________ illustrates the fact that therapists typically discover increasing numbers of subpersonalities as a patient's therapy progresses.

7. Complete this table by giving examples of the differences between and among the subpersonalities in people who suffer from dissociative identity disorder.

Types of Differences	Examples of Differences
Personality characteristics	one subpersonality might be fun-loving, spontaneous, and optimistic; another might be hostile and aggressive; a third might be shy, withdrawn, and passive
Vital statistics	
Abilities and preferences	
Physiological responses	

8. Some researchers suggest that cases of dissociative identity disorder are actually **iatrogenic,** or unintentionally caused by therapists. Complete the list of ways in which they say therapists create dissociative identity disorder during therapy.

   a. Therapists subtly _______________ the existence of alternate personalities.

   b. While the patient is under _______________, therapists elicit the personalities.

   c. Therapists may _______________ multiple personality patterns by becoming more interested in a patient when he or she displays symptoms of dissociation.

9. Although a diagnosis of dissociative identity disorder is still rare, its prevalence rate has risen dramatically in the past several decades. What two factors might account for this increase?

   a. ____

   ____

b. ____

____

D. How Do Theorists Explain Dissociative Disorders?, 227

Explanations for dissociative disorders have been offered by psychodynamic and behavioral theorists. Newer theories that explain these disorders in terms of state-dependent learning and self-hypnosis combine aspects of the cognitive, behavioral, and biological perspectives. Each of these views will be covered separately.

1. The Psychodynamic View, 227

1. The psychodynamic view posits that people with dissociative disorders use ________________ excessively in order to prevent painful memories from reaching conscious awareness.
2. According to psychodynamic theorists, people with dissociative amnesia and fugue unconsciously use a ________________ episode of repression to avoid confronting a very traumatic event.
3. Dissociative identity disorder is a style of coping characterized by continuous use of repression that is triggered by extremely ________________ childhood experiences, according to psychodynamic theory.
4. In order to escape an abusive and dangerous world, children take to flight symbolically by regularly ________________ to be another person who is ________________ looking on from afar.

Study this diagram relating to the psychodynamic view of dissociative identity disorder.

Abused children try to be "good" and repress the "bad" impulses, which they believe cause the abuse →	When the "bad" impulses break through, the child tries to disown them by . . . →	. . . unconsciously assigning all unacceptable thoughts, impulses, and emotions to other personalities

5. The bulk of support for the psychodynamic view of the dissociative disorders is provided by________________ ________________ .

2. The Behavioral View, 227

1. Complete these questions about the behavioral view of dissociative disorders.
   a. The view holds that dissociation is a response acquired through ________________ ________________ .
   b. Those affected have learned that momentarily forgetting a horrible event leads to a reduction of ________________ .
   c. The relief resulting from this reduction ________________ the act of forgetting and increases the likelihood of more forgetting in the future.
2. Here is a statement representing a belief of the psychodynamic theorists about dissociative disorders. Explain the difference between this statement and the behavioral view of these disorders.

   A hardworking unconscious is keeping the individual unaware that he or she is using dissociation as a means of escape.

   ____

   ____

3. What is one significant limitation of the behavioral view of dissociative disorders?

____

____

3. State-Dependent Learning, 229

1. What are the central processes underlying state-dependent learning?

____

____

2. One explanation for state-dependent learning phenomena is that a certain ______________ level has a set of remembered thoughts, events, and skills "attached" to it.

Study this diagram that depicts an example of the state-dependent learning explanation of dissociative identity disorder.

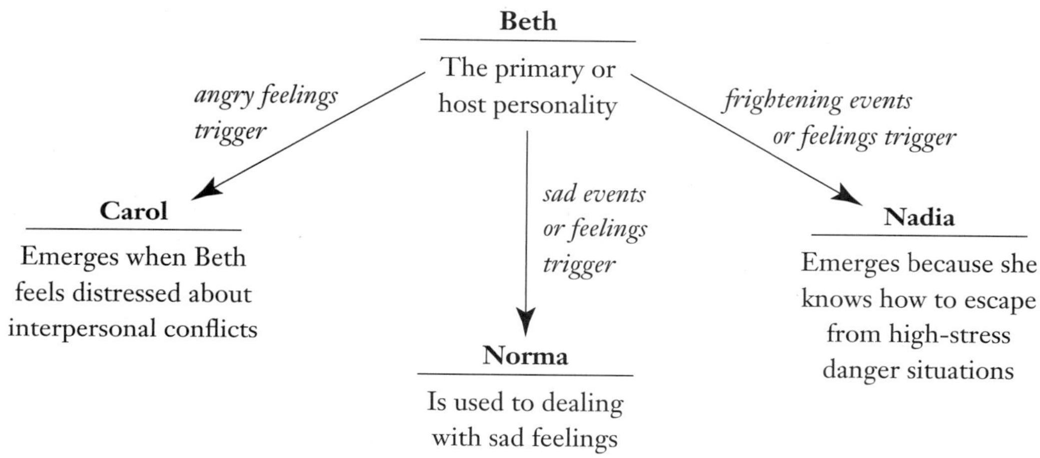

3. People prone to dissociative disorders may have very rigid and ______________ state-to-memory links in which certain thoughts, memories, and skills are tied ______________ to certain arousal states.

4. Self-Hypnosis, 229

1. Hypnosis is defined as the deliberate induction of a sleeplike state in which the person shows a very high degree of ______________ .
2. Complete this description of the three-step process that many researchers use to examine the effects of hypnosis on memory and recall.
   a. Subjects are asked to memorize certain material (such as a list of words).
   b. ____
   c. ____
3. Complete this list of the three parallel features of hypnotic amnesia and dissociative disorders that provide support for the hypothesis that dissociative disorders represent a form of self-hypnosis.
   a. ____
   b. ____

c. In both, personal events are more readily forgotten than basic knowledge or abilities.

4. The self-hypnosis view of dissociative identity disorder is supported by the fact that the disorder usually begins at a time when children are excellent hypnotic ________________ and are very ________________; perhaps they learn self-hypnosis very early as an attempt to cope with a threatening world.

5. Two different schools of thought about the nature of hypnosis have generated two distinct explanations of how "hypnosis" might be involved in the development of dissociative disorders. Complete the following table that summarizes these contrasting views.

School of Thought	Nature of Hypnosis	Explanation of Dissociative Disorders
Special process	Hypnosis is an out-of-the-ordinary, special trance state of consciousness	
Common social and cognitive process		

E. How Are Dissociative Disorders Treated?, 231

1. How Do Therapists Help People with Dissociative Amnesia and Fugue?, 231

1. The primary goal of psychodynamic therapy in treating dissociative disorders is to guide patients to ________________ their unconscious in the hope of bringing repressed experiences back to the level of consciousness.

2. In **hypnotic therapy** or ________________ for dissociative disorders, therapists hypnotize patients and then guide them to recall the forgotten events.

3. Less common treatments involve injections of ________________ drugs that may help some people recall forgotten events because of their calming and disinhibiting effects.

2. How Do Therapists Help Individuals with Dissociative Identity Disorder?, 232

1. As you have done before, this exercise calls upon you to imagine that you are a clinician. This time you have been called upon to create a treatment plan for a patient named Maggie N., who suffers from dissociative identity disorder.

City Hospital Department of Psychiatry

Treatment plan for: Maggie N.
Diagnosis: Dissociative Identity Disorder

Treatment Phase I: Recognizing the Disorder

Goals and Strategies

Treatment Phase II: Recovering Memories	
Goals and Strategies	

Treatment Phase III: Integrating the Subpersonalities	
Goals and Strategies	

Treatment Phase IV: Postintegration	
Goals and Strategies	Through continuing therapy, help Maggie develop the social and coping skills she needs so that she won't have to dissociate in order to function in the world.

The Media Speaks: Homeward Hound: A Case of Dog Fugue?, 233

1. Read the media account of the lost dog's return in this section. Although the reasons for Bear's six-year disappearance are completely unknown, list several ways in which the circumstances of his case are similar to those of the average human case of dissociative fugue, and then list several ways in which Bear's case is different.

____

____

____

____

F. Depersonalization Disorder, 235

1. Depersonalization disorder is quite different from the other dissociative disorders in that the key symptom involves an alteration in one's ________________ of self such that one's ________________ or body feels ________________ or foreign.
2. Define the following potential symptoms of depersonalization disorder.
   a. *Doubling*: ____

   ____

   ____

   b. *Derealization*: ____

   ____
3. While very few people develop a depersonalization disorder, many people experience brief episodes of depersonalization. For example, many people in auto accidents describe the events as "moving very slowly" during the seconds before or during the crash. Other people experience depersonaliza-

tion during meditation. Think of a time when you or someone you know experienced a depersonalization episode. Describe the event and the accompanying sensations.

4. What is the primary difference between most peoples' depersonalization experiences and depersonalization disorder?

5. Depersonalization symptoms are also seen in other disorders such as ______________ or PTSD.

III. Putting It Together: Disorders Rediscovered, 237

1. While somatoform and dissociative disorders were among the first identified psychological disorders, the clinical field began to ignore these disorders. In fact, some questioned the existence of such disorders. In the last 25 years, however, interest in the somatoform and dissociative disorders has increased again. Certainly, the increased interest will be beneficial in finding explanations of and treatments for these disorders. Unfortunately, gains are rarely without costs. What are some potentially problematic side effects of the new interest in and focus on the somatoform and dissociative disorders?

MULTIPLE CHOICE

1. The psychogenic disorders called hysterical disorders include:
   a. malingering.
   b. factitious disorder.
   c. conversion disorder.
   d. Munchausen syndrome.

2. Which of the following is a correct pairing?
   a. conversion disorder—heart disease
   b. factitious disorder—somatization disorder
   c. somatoform disorder—conversion disorder
   d. psychophysiological disorder—"glove anesthesia"

3. A person who interprets minimal symptoms as signs of serious physical problems and suffers significant anxiety and depression as a result might be diagnosed with a
   a. conversion disorder.
   b. somatoform pain disorder.
   c. hysterical somatoform disorder.
   d. preoccupation somatoform disorder.

4. People who feign illness because they like "being sick" are diagnosed with a _____ disorder.
   a. factitious
   b. somatoform
   c. psychogenic
   d. psychophysiological

5. Preoccupation somatoform disorders are usually explained by theorists in the same way that they explain
   a. mood disorders.
   b. anxiety disorders.
   c. personality disorders.
   d. dissociative disorders.

6. Teresa was examined for her arm paralysis (conversion disorder). Her physical brought her into his consultation room and carefully explained the etiology of her paralysis (he made it up). He told her that this serious disorder would run its course and "heal itself" in about a month. This therapy was based on
   a. insight.
   b. suggestion.
   c. confrontation.
   d. reinforcement.

7. Karen experienced a mugging and robbery in which her prized Siamese cat was kidnapped. Eventually the cat was found and returned. However, she was able to recall only certain events that occurred between the attack and the safe return of her cat, such as conversations with friends and phone calls from the police. This is a classic example of
   a. selective amnesia.
   b. localized amnesia.
   c. continuous amnesia.
   d. generalized amnesia.

8. Cameron had the traumatic experience of seeing his wife run over by a truck. Two days later, he doesn't remember this event or who he is. He ends up in another town working in a fast-food restaurant under a new name and identity. His overall reaction would probably be diagnosed as
   a. amnesia.
   b. displacement.
   c. dissociative fugue.
   d. dissociative identity disorder.

9. What event most often precipitates the onset of dissociative identity disorder?
   a. head trauma
   b. physical and/or sexual abuse
   c. personal stress
   d. natural disasters

10. What has been found out about the subpersonalities of people with dissociative identity disorder?
    a. They have similar abilities to one another.
    b. They differ in age and family history but not gender or race.
    c. They rarely exhibit a unique pattern of physiological responses.
    d. They differ from one another in age, sex, race, and family history.

11. Glenda experiences a horrifying event. She lets her mind drift to other subjects, reducing her anxiety. She does this more often, and each time the behavior is reinforced by the reduction in anxiety. This pattern may be used by behaviorists to describe the development of
    a. mood disorders.
    b. anxiety disorders.
    c. personality disorders.
    d. dissociative disorders.

12. Self-hypnosis has been offered as an explanation for
    a. personality disorders.
    b. dissociative disorders.
    c. schizophrenic disorders.
    d. impulse control disorders.

13. Which class of drugs has been used to treat dissociative amnesia and fugue?
    a. barbiturates
    b. antipsychotics
    c. antidepressants
    d. antianxiety drugs

14. The following cultures all exhibit high rates of somatization except:
    a. Chinese culture.
    b. Latin cultures.
    c. Arab cultures.
    d. American culture.

CHAPTER

8 Mood Disorders

CHAPTER OUTLINE

REVIEW EXERCISES

I. Unipolar Depression, 242–246

A. How Common Is Unipolar Depression?, 242

1. Complete the following statements about the prevalence of unipolar depression.
   a. Each year, almost 7 percent of adults in the United States suffer from a severe unipolar pattern of depression, and another 5 percent suffer mild forms.
   b. As many as _____ percent of adults worldwide experience a severe depressive episode during their lifetime.
   c. It appears that the risk of experiencing depression has _______________ in the last 100 years.

d. ________________ are two times more likely to suffer depression than the other gender.

e. Few differences in prevalence have been found among ethnic or age groups.

f. While ________________ of severely depressed people recover within six weeks and ________________ within a year, those who have been depressed are more likely to become depressed again.

2. The median age for the onset of unipolar depression in the United States is _______ years.

B. What Are the Symptoms of Depression?, 242

Complete the table below by giving three key words or phrases that describe the symptoms of depression in the listed areas of functioning.

Area of functioning	Key words or phrases
Emotional	miserable, loss of pleasure, anxiety
Motivational	
Behavioral	
Cognitive	
Physical	

The Media Speaks: The Crying Game: Male vs. Female Tears, 245

1. Describe how the results of the Penn State research study support the theory that men who cry in public are taken more seriously than women who cry.

____

____

2. Reflect on the media coverage of Hillary Clinton's moments of public emotion during the 2008 Democratic Presidential primary season. Do you feel that this coverage supports the idea that women who cry publicly are not taken seriously?

____

____

C. Diagnosing Unipolar Depression, 246

1. DSM-IV-TR specifies that the diagnosis of a major depressive episode is made when a person experiences at least _____ symptoms of depression that last _____ weeks or more. Furthermore, psychotic symptoms may be present in extreme cases.

People experiencing a major depressive episode are usually assigned a diagnosis of "major depressive disorder." A clinician may clarify this diagnosis by indicating the specific type of depression. This part of a diagnosis will use the following terms: recurrent, seasonal, catatonic, melancholic, and postpartum.

2. Complete this exercise by putting yourself in the place of a clinician clarifying a diagnosis of "major depressive disorder." Match each of the following examples with one of the terms listed in the preceding paragraph.

Example	Diagnosis
Although he feels fine most of the year, Clark feels extremely depressed from Thanksgiving until well past New Year's Day.	
Sherrie has been experiencing symptoms including excessive crying, loss of appetite, feelings of hopelessness, and insomnia since the birth of her son three weeks ago.	
Over the last 10 years, Debbie has experienced seven depressive episodes. She fears that she will never have a "normal" life.	
Marjorie's primary and most debilitating symptom is that she feels unable to move. Her face shows no emotion whatsoever, and she does not speak, even when spoken to. She stays in bed for days on end.	
Until recently, Richard loved to go to basketball games and socialize with friends. Now, Richard takes no interest in any activity. He states that he feels like a robot going through the motions. Richard feels most depressed in the very early morning; he typically wakes up at 3:00 or 4:00 A.M. and is unable to fall back asleep because he feels so terrible.	

3. Complete the following statements regarding dysthymic disorder (see p. 246 in the textbook).
   a. It is a more chronic but less _______________ pattern of unipolar depression.
   b. Typically, a depressed mood and only two or three other symptoms are present and the depression persists for at least _______________ in adults.
   c. If the dysthymic disorder leads to major depression, it is called _______________.

II. What Causes Unipolar Depression?, 247–263

1. Researchers have discovered that across cultures, depressed people experience more _______________ life events just before the onset of their disorder than do nondepressed people.
2. Define (a) reactive (exogenous) depression and (b) endogenous depression.
   a. _______________
   b. _______________

A. The Biological View, 247

1. Genetic Factors, 247

1. Complete the following statements relating to studies examining the role of genetic factors in the development of unipolar depression.

a. ________ ________ studies have shown a higher rate of depression in close relatives of depressed people (20 percent) than in the population at large (less than 10 percent).

b. A recent twin study found that out of 200 pairs of twins, the concordance rate for depression among monozygotic (identical) twins was ____ percent, whereas the concordance rate in dizygotic (fraternal) twins was only ____ percent.

c. ________ parents of adoptees hospitalized for severe depression had a much higher occurrence of severe depression than ________ parents of nondepressed adoptees.

Psych Watch: Sadness at the Happiest of Times, 248

1. Postpartum depression, in which symptoms of clinical depression can last up to ________ following the birth of a child, is experienced by ____ to ____ percent of new mothers.

2. Identify four factors that may, according to various theorists, play important roles in causing postpartum depression.

   a. ________

   b. ________

   c. ________

   d. ________

3. Why do many women suffering from postpartum depression shy away from seeking treatment that could prove very beneficial?

   ____

   ____

   ____

2. Biochemical Factors, 249

1. In the 1950s, two sets of research findings suggested that reduced activity of the neurotransmitters **norepinephrine** and **serotonin** were implicated in unipolar depression. Complete the following diagram.

Some high blood pressure medications cause depression → These medications also ________ ________ ________ → Therefore, depression may be related to low serotonin and norepinephrine activity

Discovery of drugs that alleviated depression → Researchers discovered the reason these drugs worked was that ________ ________ → Therefore, depression may be related to low serotonin and norepinephrine activity

2. Studies have suggested that the explanation depicted in exercise 1 above may be too simplistic. What are three more recent theories about the relation of neurotransmitters to depression?

   a. ________

   ____

   ____

b. ______________________________

____

____

c. ______________________________

____

____

3. Researchers have found that depression may be related to endocrine system functioning. As you have read, endocrine glands release hormones that affect the activity of various organ systems in the body. What are the two hormones that have been implicated in depression?

   a. ______________________________

   b. ______________________________

4. Give one limitation of research conducted on the biological theories of depression.

____

____

____

3. Brain Anatomy and Brain Circuits, 250

1. Name four brain areas believed to be part of the brain circuit responsible for unipolar depression.

   a. ______________________________

   a. ______________________________

   b. ______________________________

   d. ______________________________

2. The brain's ______________ ______________ is involved in many important brain functions, such as mood, attention, and immune functioning.

3. The hippocampus is one of the few brain areas to perform an activity called ______________, producing new neurons throughout adulthood.

4. PET and fMRI scans indicate that blood flow and activity in the ______________, which is believed to be involved in expression of negative emotions and memories, is 50 percent greater in depressed persons than nondepressed persons.

5. Describe the findings that have caused researchers to believe Brodmann Area 25 is involved in unipolar depression.

____

____

____

B. Psychological Views, 251

1. The Psychodynamic View, 251

Freud and Abraham's psychoanalytic theory of depression was based on the observation that people's grief reactions are very similar to symptoms of major depression.

1. Study and complete the following chart based on Freud and Abraham's formulation.

A loved one dies or is lost in some way, and a series of unconscious processes is set in motion

↓

People regress to the oral stage of development in order to fuse their own identity with that of the person they lost

↓

That is, they introject the loved one and experience feelings toward the loved one as feelings toward themselves

↓

THE LENGTH OF THE REACTION PERIOD DIFFERS AMONG PEOPLE

For some, the mourning period lasts a relatively short time	For others, the reaction worsens, and they feel empty and avoid social contact
↓	↓
These people reestablish a separate identity and resume social relationships	Introjected feelings of anger create self-hatred, self-blame, and DEPRESSION

The two kinds of people who are most susceptible to depression following the loss of a loved one are:

a. ____________________

b. ____________________

---

2. Which Freudian concept is illustrated in the following scenario? A *teenager fails to gain admittance to his father's college and becomes depressed because he unconsciously believes that his father will no longer love him.*

____

3. Object relations theorists suggest that people whose parents pushed them toward excessive ____________ or excessive ____________ are more likely to become depressed when faced with the loss of a relationship.

Several tenets of the psychodynamic perspective of depression have been generally supported by empirical investigations. The next three exercises concern three hypotheses within the perspective and research findings that support them.

4. Complete the following statements regarding research findings that support the hypothesis *Depression is related to early loss.*

   a. Infants and children under age 6 who are separated from their mothers can experience a reaction called ____________ depression.

   b. One study found that depressed medical patients were more likely to have lost a ____________ during childhood, compared to nondepressed patients.

5. Complete the following statement regarding a finding that supports the hypothesis *People whose needs were not adequately addressed in childhood are more likely to become depressed when they experience loss as adults.*

Compared to nondepressed people, depressed people were more likely to say that their parents raised them with a(n) "________________ control" style, which is defined as a mixture of low care and high ________________ .

6. One limitation of psychodynamic research on depression is that findings do not establish that early loss and inadequate parenting are *typically* responsible for the development of depression. List other limitations.

   a. ____

   b. Many components of the psychodynamic view of depression are impossible to test empirically.

2. The Behavioral View, 255

Peter Lewinsohn's behavioral explanation of unipolar depression suggests that some people engage in fewer positive behaviors when the rewards for their positive behaviors start to diminish, and that this is the basis for the development of a depressed style of functioning. Read the following case study relating to Lewinsohn's theory of depression.

Case Study

Saul is a 59-year-old grocery store owner, who through 40 years of hard work has made his store the biggest in town. He has accomplished this in spite of stiff competition from national chain stores. He has always taken great pride in beating them. Saul has earned the respect of his customers and employees alike. But profits have been down for a few years—a situation he blames on his advancing age. He decides to sell his store when one of the chains offers him a good price. He and his wife retire to the coast of Maine.

Saul enjoys retirement for about a week, then starts to complain of feeling "empty." He tries improving his golf game, but quits when he is consistently beaten at the sport by his wife and others. He finds himself drinking more alcohol than ever before. He had wanted to take up sailing, but decides not to, figuring he is too old. Within six months of retirement, he is doing little more than watching television, drinking, and going to bed early every night.

1. Apply Lewinsohn's explanation of unipolar depression to the case study.

   a. List some of the rewards for positive behavior Saul received as a store owner.

   ____

   ____

   ____

   b. Saul's eventual depressed style of functioning results from a downward spiral. Which of Saul's activities could be seen as evidence of this spiral?

   ____

   ____

   ____

2. Lewinsohn suggests that ________________ rewards decrease as a person becomes more depressed; some studies have indicated that ________________ characteristics contribute to the loss of these rewards.

3. Cognitive Views, 255

a. *Negative Thinking, 255*

You should recall from Chapter 3 that theorist Aaron Beck is closely associated with the cognitive perspective. His theory of depression rests on the notion that maladaptive attitudes, the cognitive triad, errors in thinking, and automatic thoughts combine to produce the negative thinking patterns that are characteristic of depression. In this part of the workbook, each of these components will be covered in succession.

1. Beck suggests that some people develop maladaptive attitudes as children. Come up with two original examples of maladaptive attitudes.

   a. ______________________________

   b. ______________________________

2. When people who hold maladaptive attitudes face an upsetting event later in life (such as a failure at work or in a relationship), a series of ______________ thoughts are triggered. According to Beck, these thoughts take the form of the "cognitive triad."

3. In this exercise, complete the following figure by supplying the missing "forms" in Beck's cognitive triad.

Negative view of self

Negative view of ______________

Negative view of ______________

4. Beck's theory of depression states that depressed people commonly use illogical or erroneous logic that results in an even stronger (depressive) cognitive triad. Define each type of error below, then complete the example that illustrates each error.

   a. arbitrary inference: ______________________________

   ____

   Example: The host of an elegant restaurant tells a woman that it will be at least one hour before she can be seated for dinner. The woman concludes that:

   ____

   b. minimization/magnification: ______________________________

   ____

   Example: A man gets an unexpected promotion at work and concludes that:

   ____

   When he accidentally calls his new boss by the wrong name, he concludes that:

   ____

5. According to Beck, people experience (or manifest) the cognitive triad in the form of automatic thoughts, a steady train of unpleasant, "reflexive" thoughts that remind depressed people of their assumed ______________ and the ______________ of their situation.

Examine the following flow chart and be sure you understand it. It depicts the feedback system that incorporates all the components of Beck's cognitive theory of depression. Note that Beck believes that the emotional, motivational, behavioral, and somatic aspects of depression all follow from the cognitive process he has described.

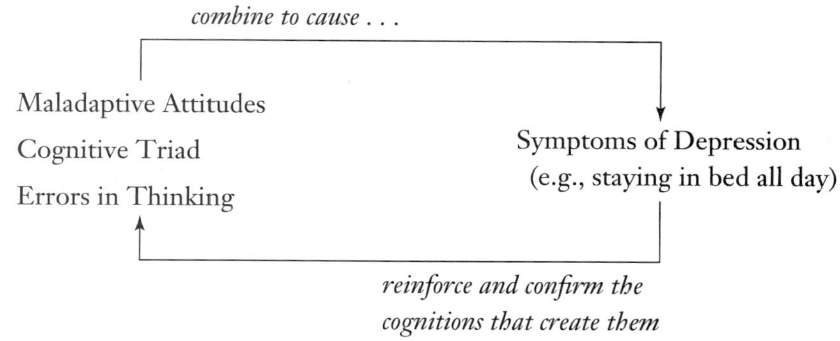

6. Complete the following table summarizing the empirical support for Beck's theory of depression. Provide one example of a research finding that provides evidence for each tenet of the theory listed.

Tenet	Supportive Finding
Depressed people hold maladaptive attitudes	The number of maladaptive attitudes correlates strongly with the degree of depression
Depressed people exhibit the cognitive triad	
Depressed people show errors in logic	
Depressed people experience negative automatic thoughts	

b. Learned Helplessness, 257

1. What are the two primary components of Martin Seligman's cognitive-behavioral view of depression?

   a. ____________________

   b. ____________________

2. Complete the following exercises relating to Seligman's **shuttle box** experiments on dogs, which were the basis for his original theoretical framework.

   a. Dogs were strapped into hammocks and given ____________ electric shocks from which they could not escape.

   b. The dogs were placed in the shuttle box, which had a "shock" compartment and a "safe" compartment.

   c. How did the dogs react when they were placed in the "shock" area?

   ____

   ____

3. Specifically, how did Seligman explain his findings?

   ____

   ____

4. Complete the following table summarizing one of Seligman's studies of learned helplessness in people:

Subjects	***Nondepressed People***		
Condition	*Group I* Exposed to loud noise, which subjects could stop by pushing a button	*Group II*	*Group III*
Procedure	***After subjects were "pretreated" in each condition, all subjects were given a control shuttle box and exposed to loud noise. The control box was "rigged" so that the noise would stop if subjects moved the handle from one side to another.***		
Results	*Group I*	*Group II*	*Group III* Subjects quickly learned to move the handle and stop the loud noise

5. List two research findings that have provided empirical support for the hypothesis that receiving uncontrollable negative reinforcements can result in depressive symptoms.

a. ______________________________

____

b. ______________________________

____

6. A revision of the learned helplessness theory of depression suggests that when people believe events are beyond their control they ask themselves "why?" In other words, they make **attributions** about why they lost control in a particular situation. There are three basic dimensions of these attributions:

Internal vs. External Attributions: Is the cause of this event located within myself (internal) or elsewhere (external)?

Global vs. Specific Attributions: Is the cause of this event relevant to many situations (global) or just this one situation (specific)?

Stable vs. Unstable Attributions: Is the cause of this event enduring (stable), or is it short-lived (unstable)?

After you have studied the text material related to attributions, try the next exercise. The following table depicts eight possible attributions made by Russell, who has just lost an important tennis match. From the list of Russell's statements after the table, choose the one that best fits each "cell" of the table.

Event: "I just lost an important tennis match."

	Internal		**External**	
	Stable	**Unstable**	**Stable**	**Unstable**
Global		a.		h.
Specific	d.		g.	

a. "I really didn't feel well today."

b. "I felt especially nervous for this match because so many people were watching."

c. "This sort of competition doesn't prove whether you're a good tennis player or not."

d. "I am a horrible tennis player. I simply have no talent at all."

e. "That line judge really made some lousy calls today; he must not have been paying attention to what was happening."

f. "I am unable to cope with any high-pressure situation no matter what it is."

g. "That line judge has always had it in for me. Every time I play with him up there I lose, no matter how well I play."

h. "No one can play well on a court like this; there are cracks and bumps everywhere!"

7. The combination of attributions that seems to indicate a person is most likely to be depressed is ____________, ____________, and ____________.

8. Yet another revision of the learned helplessness theory suggests that only attributions that produce a sense of ____________ lead to depression.

9. One problem with the learned helplessness theory is that studies reveal mixed findings regarding the relationship between depression and internal, stable, and global attributions. List two other problems with the theory.

   a. ________________________

   b. ________________________

C. Sociocultural Views, 259

1. Sociocultural theorists believe that social factors such as culture, gender and race, and social support are linked to depression. After reading through this section of the text, complete the following table by summarizing at least two research findings that support the link between depression and each factor listed.

Factor	Research Findings
Culture	
Gender and race	
Social support	

1. The Family-Social Perspective, 259

1. Discuss the ways in which the connection between declining social rewards and depression is considered "a two-way street."

____

2. The study mentioned on textbook page 260 regarding the correlation between marital satisfaction and depression found that the participants who were in unsatisfying relationships were ___________ times ___________ likely to experience a major depressive episode.

3. The researchers in the same study mentioned in question 2 estimated that eliminating marital stress could prevent ___________ of the cases of major depression.

2. The Multicultural Perspective, 261

1. Women around the world are at least ___________ as likely as men to be diagnosed with unipolar depression.

2. Name and briefly explain the seven theories mentioned in your textbook for the disparity in diagnoses of unipolar depression between men and women.

   a. ____

   b. ____

   c. ____

   d. ____

   e. ____

   f. ____

   g. ____

3. Depressed people in non-Western countries are more likely than their Western counterparts to be troubled by ___________ symptoms, less often experiencing ___________ symptoms like self-blame, low self-esteem, and guilt.

III. Bipolar Disorders, 263–271

A. What Are the Symptoms of Mania?, 263

1. Rather than feeling sad and apathetic, people in a state of mania experience dramatic and ___________ elevations in mood.

2. Complete the table below by giving three key words or phrases that describe the symptoms of mania in the listed area of functioning.

Area of Functioning	Evidence
Emotional	elation, euphoric joy, irritability
Motivational	
Behavioral	
Cognitive	
Physical	

B. Diagnosing Bipolar Disorders, 264

1. DSM-IV-TR criteria for a manic episode include experiencing an abnormally ____________ or ____________ mood, as well as at least ____________ other symptoms of mania, for a minimum of one week.
2. If symptoms of mania are less severe and of shorter duration, the diagnosis would be a ____________ episode.
3. DSM-IV-TR distinguishes between two types of bipolar disorders. Briefly describe (a) bipolar I, and (b) bipolar II.

   a. ____

   ____

   b. ____

   ____

4. Complete the following statements regarding the prevalence of bipolar disorders.

   a. The prevalence of bipolar disorders is the same for men and women, at all socioeconomic levels, and in all ____________ groups.

   b. The age of onset is usually between ____ and ____ years.

5. A diagnosis of ____________ disorder would be assigned to a person who experienced alternating periods of hypomanic and mild depressive symptoms for a period of two or more years.

C. What Causes Bipolar Disorders?, 267

The most promising clues for an explanation of bipolar disorders comes from three areas of the biological realm—neurotransmitter activity, ion activity, and genetic factors. Each of these is covered separately in this part of the workbook.

1. Describe one of the two findings that led researchers to believe that mania is related to abnormally high levels of norepinephrine.

   ____

   ____

2. Contrary to the expectations of theorists, research has shown that mania, like depression, is associated with a low supply of ____________ .
3. Complete the following diagram, which depicts the permissive theory of mood disorders.

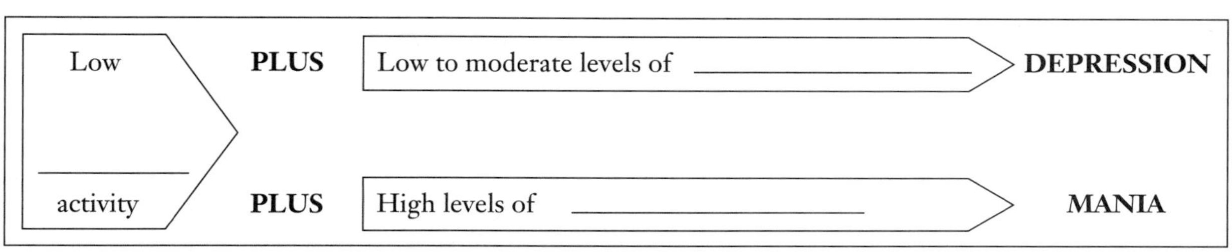

4. Complete the following sequence of events that describe how a neuron "fires" its message to other neurons in the brain.

   a. At rest, the outside of a neuron is positively charged because more ____________ ions are outside vs. inside the cell membrane.

b. The neuron's receptor sites are stimulated, resulting in a "wave" of electrochemical activity down the neuron.

c. As sodium ions flow *into* the neuron, ______________ ions flow *out* of the neuron.

d. The neuron returns to its resting state.

5. Some researchers believe that improper sodium ion transport that causes neurons to fire too easily results in ______________, while that which causes neurons to resist firing results in ______________.

6. Name six brain structures that have been shown to display abnormalities in people with bipolar disorders.

____

____

____

7. Studies involving close relatives and twins of those with bipolar disorders indicate that the more similar the ______________ ______________ of two people, the more similar their tendency to develop a bipolar disorder.

8. Complete the following description of the method used by researchers in genetic linkage studies.

a. They select families that have high rates of bipolar disorder over several ______________.

b. They observe the pattern of distribution of bipolar disorder in family members.

c. They determine whether the bipolar pattern follows the distribution patterns of other family (inherited) traits such as:

____

IV. Putting It Together: Making Sense of All That Is Known, 271–272

1. Identify and briefly describe four possible relationships between major contributing factors to unipolar depression (such as biological abnormalities, reduction in positive reinforcements, negative thinking, perceived helplessness, life stress, and sociocultural influences) and unipolar depression itself.

____

____

____

____

____

____

2. Clinicians and researchers have come to believe that bipolar disorders can be best explained by a focus on one kind of variable: ______________ factors.

MULTIPLE CHOICE

1. What role does gender play in the incidence of depression?
   a. Gender is unrelated to the incidence of depression.
   b. Men are twice as likely to suffer from depression as women.
   c. Women are twice as likely to suffer from depression as men.
   d. Depression is more frequent in women but more severe in men.

2. Which of the following would be a cognitive symptom of depression?
   a. lack of desire to eat
   b. a negative view of oneself
   c. experiences of sadness and anger
   d. staying in bed for hours during the day

3. To receive a diagnosis of major depressive episode, seasonal, the individual must display
   a. repeated episodes of depression.
   b. mood fluctuation during the year.
   c. motor immobility or excessive activity.
   d. onset within four weeks of giving birth.

4. What structure is responsible for secreting cortisol?
   a. pineal gland
   b. hypothalamus
   c. adrenal glands
   d. pituitary gland

5. Which theoretical perspective employs the concept of "symbolic loss" to explain depression?
   a. cognitive
   b. humanistic
   c. existential
   d. psychodynamic

6. What disorder do psychodynamic therapists believe that unconscious grieving over real or imagined loss produces?
   a. conversion disorder
   b. unipolar depression
   c. countertransference
   d. schizotypal personality disorder

7. Who developed a behavioral theory of depression based on insufficient positive reinforcement?
   a. Beck
   b. Freud
   c. Seligman
   d. Lewinsohn

8. Every time Sophie's homework is not done her teacher punishes her. When she does it, she gets a low grade. If she complains about never being recognized for trying, she is given detention. This is an example of a set of conditions that, over time, is most likely to lead to
   a. depression.
   b. schizophrenia.
   c. anxiety disorder.
   d. bipolar disorder.

9. What critical feature does bipolar II have that is different from bipolar I?
   a. hypomania
   b. mild depression
   c. major depression
   d. full manic episodes

10. Some researchers believe that symptoms of mania can be due to
    a. excessive serotonin.
    b. depleted levels of norepinephrine.
    c. sodium ions increasing a neuron's resistance to firing.
    d. abnormal function of proteins that transport sodium ions.

11. Within the United States, differences in overall depression rates between minority groups are
    a. high.
    b. minimal.
    c. nonexistent.
    d. different at different times of the year.

CHAPTER

9 Treatments for Mood Disorders

CHAPTER OUTLINE

REVIEW EXERCISES

I. Treatments for Unipolar Depression, 276–297

A variety of treatment approaches are available for persons suffering from unipolar depression. In the following section, exercises will cover three general categories of treatments: psychological approaches (psychodynamic, behavioral, and cognitive therapies), sociocultural approaches (culture-sensitive, interpersonal and couple therapies), and biological approaches (electroconvulsive therapy and antidepressant drugs). Additionally, exercises addressing trends in treatment are included at the end of this section.

A. Psychological Approaches, 276

1. Psychodynamic Therapy, 278

1. Complete the following chart regarding psychodynamic therapy for unipolar depression.

Psychodynamic therapists believe

That unipolar depression results from unconscious grief over real or imagined loss compounded by ______________________

↓

This leads them to

↓

Try to help depressed clients bring those processes to conciousness, so they can understand the source of their pain and learn to leave it behind

↓

The Procedures They Use to Do This

- Encourage clients to associate freely.
- Suggest interpretations of the client's associations, dreams, and displays of ______________________
- Help clients ______________________

2. List two aspects of psychodynamic therapy described in the textbook that could explain its limited effectiveness in the treatment of depression.

   a. ______________________

   b. ______________________

The Media Speaks: How Well Do Colleges Treat Depression?, 277

Read the article in this section regarding mental health services provided by colleges to their students. Reflect on the mental health services provided by your own school. Do you know if the school offers unlimited therapy, or a full-fledged staff therapist? How accessible would mental health services be to you if you required them?

2. Behavioral Therapy, 279

1. Complete the following table by listing and describing each of the components of Peter Lewinsohn's influential behavioral treatment of depression.

Component	Description
1. Reintroducing pleasurable events	
2.	Contingency management approach that ignores depression behaviors and rewards positive behaviors
3.	

2. Therapies that ______________ several of Lewinsohn's strategies seem to reduce symptoms of ______________ levels of depression.

3. Cognitive Therapy, 280

1. Complete the following table summarizing the four phases of Beck's **cognitive therapy** of depression.

Phase	Description
1. Increasing activities and elevating mood	Preparation of a detailed weekly schedule that includes behavioral "assignments" designed to gradually involve the client in more activities
2.	
3.	
4.	

2. Hundreds of studies have concluded that ______________ to ______________ percent of depressed people show a total elimination of depressive symptoms.
3. Although Beck calls his treatment approach cognitive therapy, many theorists really consider it a __________ __________ therapy.
4. Many of the new wave cognitive-behavioral therapists do not agree with Beck's proposition that people must completely __________ their negative cognitions to overcome depression. Some, including those who practice ________________ (ACT), see their role as guiding depressed clients to __________ their negative thoughts for what they are and then work around them in their lives.

B. Sociocultural Approaches, 283

1. Many of today's therapists offer ___________ therapy for depressed minority clients in combination with a culture-sensitive focus on their economic pressures and related cultural issues.
2. In the United States, minority clients are ___________ likely than European Americans to receive helpful antidepressant medication.
3. Complete the following table by first describing the key problem areas addressed in **interpersonal psychotherapy** (IPT), then by giving examples of the therapist's tasks in each of these areas.

Problem Areas	Description	Therapist's Tasks
Interpersonal loss	Feelings of grief and sadness after the loss of a loved one (e.g., through death or divorce)	Explore relationship with lost person, help client express feelings toward lost person, encourage development of new relationships

Problem Areas	Description	Therapist's Tasks
Interpersonal role dispute		
Interpersonal role transition		
Interpersonal deficits		

4. Depressive symptoms were relieved in approximately _____ to _____ percent of clients treated with IPT, according to research findings.
5. Interpersonal psychotherapy appears to be the most effective treatment for what kinds of clients?

____

6. Research has indicated that as many as _____ percent of all depressed clients are in a dysfunctional relationship.
7. Describe the central goals of the behavioral marital therapist.

____

____

C. Biological Approaches, 285

1. Electroconvulsive Therapy, 285

1. Complete the following list of characteristics of ECT.
   a. In _________________ electroconvulsive therapy (ECT), electrodes carrying 65 to 140 volts of an electrical current are placed on both sides of the patient's head, whereas in _________________ ECT, electrodes are placed on only one side of the head.
   b. The electrical current causes a brain _________________ that lasts from 25 seconds to a few minutes.
   c. ECT programs consist of _____ to _____ treatments over the course of two to four _________ .
2. Inducing convulsions as a treatment for depression has historical origins in an accident that occurred over 70 years ago. Provide the missing information in the following statements regarding the path that led from this accident to ECT.
   a. Believing that epileptic convulsions prevented psychosis, Joseph von Meduna used the camphor derivative _________________ to induce convulsions in psychotic patients.
   b. _________________ _________________ therapy, a related and very dangerous technique, was developed at about the same time by Manfred Sakel, a Viennese physician.
   c. A few years later ECT was developed by _________________ and his colleague Lucio Bini.

3. Describe the purpose of (a) barbiturates and (b) muscle relaxants in ECT.

   a. ______________________________

   b. ______________________________

4. Describe the most disturbing side effect observed in some patients after they undergo ECT.

   ____

   ____

5. Approximately 60 to 80 percent of patients improve with ECT. What are some of the symptoms of the patients with the best improvement rates?

   ____

2. Antidepressant Drugs, 290

The primary classes of drugs that are used to treat depression are the MAO inhibitors, the tricyclics, and the second-generation antidepressant drugs. Each of these kinds of drugs will be examined separately in the following exercises.

a. MAO Inhibitors, 290

1. Complete the following exercises related to how researchers believe MAO inhibitors alleviate depression.

   a. Recall (from Chapter 8) that in some people, depression seems to be associated with decreased activity of the neurotransmitter norepinephrine.

   b. The enzyme MAO, which stands for ______________________________, interacts with norepinephrine and breaks it down so that it is no longer effective.

   c. When the antidepressant drug MAO inhibitor is introduced into the system, what is prevented?

   ____

   ____

   d. Summarize why MAO inhibitors act to alleviate depressive symptoms.

   ____

   ____

2. Explain how tyramine can present a danger to people using MAO inhibitors.

   ____

   ____

b. Tricyclics, 290

1. Before it was found to be effective in treating depression, the tricyclic drug ______________________ was used unsuccessfully in the treatment of schizophrenia.

2. About _____ to _____ percent of mildly to severely depressed patients who take tricyclic antidepressant drugs improve (although the drugs must be taken for at least _____ days before improvement is observed).

3. Complete the following statements related to relapse among depressed patients who take tricyclic drugs.

   a. If they stop taking the drugs immediately after they experience relief, they are at high risk of ______________________ within 1 year.

b. The risk of relapse decreases significantly if patients continue to take the drugs for a period of approximately ________________ after depressive symptoms disappear (this is called "________________ therapy").

c. Some studies have indicated that patients who take full dosages of the drugs for _____ or more years after initial improvement—a strategy called "__________________________ therapy"—reduce their risk for relapse even more.

4. When neurons release neurotransmitters into the synapse, they simultaneously "recapture" some of the neurotransmitter by way of a pumplike mechanism in the nerve ending. Answer the following questions about this process.

   a. What is the purpose of this reuptake process?

   ____

   ____

   b. What might be "going wrong" in the reuptake process of depressed people?

   ____

   ____

   c. How are tricyclics thought to alleviate depressive symptoms?

   ____

   ____

5. This question has two parts: (a) What observation did researchers make about the action of tricyclics on the reuptake mechanism that led them to question how these drugs alleviate depression? and (b) What do researchers now believe about how tricyclics work?

   a. ____

   b. ____

   ____

c. *Second-Generation Antidepressants, 292*

1. Some second-generation antidepressants such as Prozac (fluoxetine) are classified as selective ________________ ________________ ________________ (SSRIs) because they alter serotonin activity specifically but do not affect other neurotransmitters in the brain.

2. List some of the (a) strengths and (b) weaknesses of the second-generation antidepressants compared to older tricyclics.

   a. ____

   b. ____

3. Brain Stimulation, 293

a. *Vagus Nerve Stimulation*

1. Vagus nerve stimulation was first developed by depression researchers who were trying to mimic the positive effects of ____________ without the accompanying undesired effects and trauma.

2. Briefly describe the procedure of vagus nerve stimulation.

   ____

   ____

3. Why was vagus nerve stimulation approved by the U.S. Food and Drug Administration?

____

____

b. Transcranial Magnetic Stimulation, 294

1. In transcranial magnetic stimulation (TMS), an electromagnetic coil placed on the patient's head sends a current into the ____________________.

2. Why has TMS not yet been approved by the U. S. Food and Drug Administration, despite encouraging test results?

____

____

c. Deep Brain Stimulation, 295

1. In deep brain stimulation, tiny holes are drilled into the patient's skull and electrodes are implanted into ____________ in the patient's brain. These electrodes are connected to a battery that sends a stream of low-voltage electricity to this brain region.

2. Although the early test results on deep brain stimulation have been very encouraging, why is it important for scientists to do much more research before assuming that this technique will prove effective and safe for most patients?

____

____

D. How Do the Treatments for Unipolar Depression Compare?, 295

1. In comparative outcome studies, ________________, ________________, interpersonal (IPT), and ________________ therapies appear to be equally and highly effective at alleviating mild to severe depressive symptoms.

Below is a diagram relating to the ambitious National Institute of Mental Health outcome study of treatments for depression.

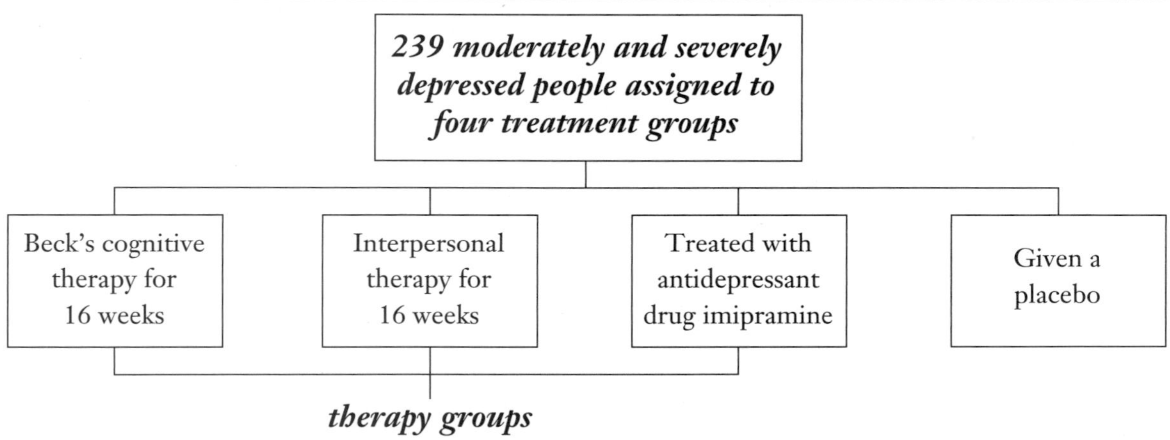

2. Answer the questions below relating to the findings of the National Institute of Mental Health outcome study of antidepressant therapy.

   a. Describe improvements in the three therapy groups.

   ____

   ____

   b. Describe the improvement in the placebo group.

   ____

   ____

   c. What were the differences in how quickly the treatments worked in relieving depression?

   ____

   ____

   d. ____________ and ____________ therapy may be more effective than ____________ therapy at preventing relapses in depression, except when the latter therapy is continued for an extended period.

3. Because as many as _____ percent of depressed patients treated with cognitive or interpersonal therapies relapse, clinicians are now encouraging "continuation" or "____________" cognitive or IPT sessions to prevent relapse among successfully treated patients.

4. Depressed people who experience marital conflict are treated effectively with ____________ therapy (with improvement rates similar to cognitive, IPT, and biological treatment rates).

5. ____________ therapy is less effective in treating depression (particularly severe depression) than cognitive, interpersonal, or biological therapies.

6. A much disputed finding is that ____________ therapy does not appear to be very effective in treating depression.

7. A combination of ____________ and ____________ therapy may be more helpful to depressed people than any single treatment, although the evidence for this is not consistent.

8. Complete the following statements that relate to biological treatments of unipolar depression.

   a. ECT seems to act more ____________ than antidepressant drugs.

   b. Clinicians usually treat depressed people with ____________ first, and only if that treatment is unsuccessful will they consider ____________ .

   c. Research findings have indicated that _____ to _____ percent of people who do not respond to drug therapy are helped by ECT.

Eye on Culture: First Dibs on Antidepressant Drugs?, 293

1. According to a 2005 Medicaid study, depressed individuals who were African American, Hispanic American, or Native American were ____________ as likely as white Americans to be prescribed antidepressant medication on their initial therapy visit.

2. List three other trends indicating unequal treatment of white and nonwhite depressed individuals that were identified by this study.

   ____

   ____

II. Treatments for Bipolar Disorders, 298–303

A. Lithium and Other Mood Stabilizers, 300

Researchers are not certain about how lithium relieves symptoms of bipolar disorder, but several possible explanations exist. The two most prominent theories involve second-messenger systems and sodium ion transport.

1. Lithium therapy requires that patients undergo regular analyses of ____________ and ____________ in order for doctors to determine the correct dosage.
2. If the lithium dosage is too low, the drug will be ineffective; however, if the dosage is too high, what are the potential results?

   ____

   ____
3. Improvement rates for people with manic symptoms are ______ percent and higher.
4. One study found that the risk of relapse is ______ times greater if patients stop taking mood stabilizers, suggesting that mood stabilizers may be a ________________ drug (one that actually *prevents* symptoms from developing).
5. Study this diagram of the role of second messengers in neuronal firing, then complete the exercise that follows.

   Neurotransmitter binds to receptor sites on the receiving neuron → Second messengers (chemicals) are produced in the neuron → Second messengers "trigger" the firing mechanism of the neuron

   a. Lithium appears to affect second-messenger chemicals called ________________ which in turn alter the way certain neurons—presumably implicated in bipolar disorder—function.
6. To the extent that bipolar disorder is triggered by ion instability across the membranes of certain neurons, lithium may work by ________________ for sodium ions themselves, or by changing the way that ions are transported across the neuronal membranes.

B. Adjunctive Psychotherapy, 302

1. Most clinicians agree that neither ________________ alone nor ________________ therapy alone is effective in treating bipolar disorders. In light of these beliefs, some clinicians utilize ________________, ________________, or ________________ as adjuncts to lithium treatment.
2. What are some of the reasons patients give for why they stop taking mood stabilizers?

   ____

   ____
3. List three objectives of therapies in the treatment of bipolar disorder.

   a. ____

   b. ____

   c. ____
4. Clinical reports suggest that combining psychotherapy with drug treatment for patients with bipolar disorder leads to reduced ________________, better social functioning, and higher ________________ rates.

III. Putting It Together: With Success Come New Questions, 303

1. Summarize two explanations for the somewhat surprising finding that a number of **very** different approaches (e.g., cognitive therapy, electroconvulsive therapy, interpersonal therapy, etc.) have been effective in the treatment of unipolar depression.

   a. ______________________________

   ____

   ____

   ____

   b. ______________________________

   ____

   ____

   ____

MULTIPLE CHOICE

1. Why was the use of insulin, camphor, or metrazol to induce convulsions or comas in mentally ill people discontinued?
   a. It did not work.
   b. It was expensive.
   c. It was dangerous.
   d. The treatment was too difficult to manage.

2. What disorders are monoamine oxidase (MAO) inhibitors and tricyclics most effective in treating?
   a. agoraphobia
   b. schizophrenia
   c. bipolar disorders
   d. unipolar depression

3. There is some evidence that tricyclic antidepressant medications help depressed people feel better by
   a. raising monoamine oxidase (MAO) activity.
   b. lowering norepinephrine and serotonin activity.
   c. increasing the level of norepinephrine and serotonin synthesis.
   d. increasing the availability of norepinephrine and serotonin in the synapse.

4. Johnny has recently entered a large university and lately has been feeling depressed. He came from a very small high school with 35 seniors in his graduating class. He knew everyone and was a class leader. He feels lost in the crowd here. According to the premises of interpersonal psychotherapy, his depression stems from
   a. a grief reaction.
   b. an interpersonal conflict.
   c. an interpersonal role transition.
   d. unrealistic expectations regarding his place in his new school.

5. Which intervention is the single most effective current treatment for bipolar disorder?
   a. ECT
   b. lithium and other mood stabilizers
   c. tranquilizers
   d. antidepressant medication

6. George is depressed and has sought therapy. His cognitive therapist is most likely to
   a. test the reality behind his thoughts.
   b. reinforce him only when he says positive things.
   c. ask him to talk about conflicts he had with his parents as a child.
   d. question whether he is actually depressed.

7. The primary goal of the psychodynamic therapist in treating a patient who is depressed is
   a. to challenge depressive styles of thinking.
   b. to explore disputes and conflicts with significant others.
   c. to bring unconscious grief and dependency issues into conscious awareness.
   d. to reward active, non-depressed behavior and punish apathetic, depressed behavior.

8. Monoamine oxidase (MAO) serves the function of
   a. relieving depressive symptoms.
   b. breaking down tyramine in the liver.
   c. relieving manic symptoms.
   d. preventing the reuptake of serotonin.

9. One of the risks associated with the contemporary use of ECT is
   a. memory loss.
   b. death.
   c. stroke.
   d. fractures of limbs.

10. Approximately how many days after a person starts taking tricyclic antidepressant will he/she experience a reduction of depressive symptoms?
    a. 2
    b. 5
    c. 10
    d. 20

CHAPTER

10 Suicide

CHAPTER OUTLINE

REVIEW EXERCISES

1. Statistics show there are ________________ suicides each year in the United States and ________________ more unsuccessful attempts, called ________________ .
2. The textbook suggests that the actual number of suicides could be much higher than the official total. Give two reasons for the difficulty in obtaining accurate suicide statistics.
   a. Suicide is ________________ by society, so relatives and friends might not acknowledge that suicide was the actual cause of death.
   b. ____

I. What Is Suicide?, 310–315

1. Edwin Shneidman defines **suicide** as a self-inflicted death in which the person makes an ________________ , direct, and ________________ effort to end his or her life.
2. Complete the following table by describing the characteristics of Shneidman's four categories of people who attempt or commit suicide. Then, read through the case examples provided and match each with the most appropriate category.

Category	Description of Characteristics	Example
Death seekers		
Death initiators		
Death ignorers		
Death darers		

Cases:

a. Sheldon repeatedly engages in high-risk activities such as drinking and driving, and mixing alcohol and drugs. When his girlfriend pleads with him to stop the dangerous behavior, Sheldon usually retorts with statements like "You wouldn't care if I died, anyway" and "It would serve you right if I did kill myself one of these days."

b. After her suicide attempt by drug overdose, Jackie stated the following to a hospital psychiatric nurse: "I had thought about killing myself on and off for weeks. I would have a really bad day and almost do it, but then I'd feel a little better the next day and decide not to. Today was a really, really bad day—the worst."

c. Six-year old Marianne is devastated after seeing her family dog, Jo-Jo, killed by a car in front of her house. Her parents try to comfort her by telling her that Jo-Jo is happy in heaven, but later she runs into the busy street and is nearly hit by an oncoming truck. When Marianne's parents ask why she did what she did, she replies, "I wanted to go to heaven to make sure Jo-Jo is okay."

d. Antonio is a 72-year-old man who is suffering from advanced bone cancer. Certain that his last days will be filled with intolerable pain, Antonio asphyxiates himself in his car.

3. The terms **subintentional death** and **chronic suicide** describe similar patterns of behavior. Describe these patterns in your own words, then come up with an original example.

a. Description: ____________________

____

b. Original example: ____________________

____

A. How Is Suicide Studied?, 312

1. Complete the following statements regarding some of the sources of information used by researchers for **retrospective analyses** of suicide, and the limitations of those sources.

a. Relatives and friends may remember past statements, conversations, and behavior that can be revealing. Unfortunately, grieving and perhaps guilt-ridden friends and relatives may be incapable of objective and accurate recollections.

b. About half of all suicide victims have never been in ____________, which limits this potential data source.

c. Likewise, less than one-third of victims leave ____________ ____________.

d. Because of these limitations, many researchers rely on a useful, albeit imperfect, study strategy. Describe that strategy.

____

____

B. Patterns and Statistics, 312

1. The United States and Canada have annual suicide rates of about 12 per 100,000 persons. List (a) three countries with *higher* rates and (b) three countries with *lower* rates.

a. ____________________

b. ____________________

2. ____________ affiliation, in particular the extent to which people are devout in their beliefs, could account for national differences in suicide rates.

3. The male: female ratio for suicide *attempts* is roughly ____ : ____, whereas the male: female ratio for suicide *completions* is roughly ____ : ____.

4. Write a brief response to the question "Why do completed suicide rates differ between men and women?"

____

____

5. According to research on marital status and suicide, which groups of people are

a. at highest rate for suicide? ____________________

b. at moderate risk for suicide? ____________________

c. at lowest risk for suicide? ____________________

6. The suicide rate of white Americans is ______________ as high as the suicide rate for ______________ Americans and members of most other nonwhite racial groups. (Be sure to examine Figure 10–1 in the textbook.)

7. The suicide rates of some Native Americans is an exception to the usual rule that white Americans have a higher suicide rate than nonwhite Americans. What are some of the factors that might account for the high suicide rate among Native Americans?

____

II. What Triggers a Suicide?, 315–321

A. Stressful Events and Situations, 315

1. Give examples of immediate and long-term stressors that might precipitate suicide.

   Immediate stressors: ______________________________

   Long-term stressors: ______________________________

2. Complete the following table by describing research evidence of the association between suicide and the delineated long-term stressors.

Long-Term Stressor Linked to Suicide	Research Evidence
Serious illness	
Abusive environment	High suicide rates seen for prisoners of war, Holocaust victims, abused spouses and children, and prison inmates
Occupational stress	

B. Mood and Thought Changes, 317

1. Increased sadness is one mood change that is associated with suicide. List some others.

____

2. Describe the most salient cognitive changes (shifts in patterns in thinking) that seem to precipitate suicide.

____

____

____

C. Alcohol and Other Drug Use, 317

1. Evidence gained from autopsies of suicide victims indicate that about _____ percent of them drank alcohol just before the act, and that one-fourth of these people were legally intoxicated at the time of death.

2. Alcohol may allow suicidal people to overcome their ______________ of committing suicide, lower inhibitions against ______________ and the expression of underlying aggression, and/or impair their ability to make ______________ and solve problems.

Psych Watch: Abnormality and the Arts: Can Music Inspire Suicide?, 318

1. *Reread this section on page 318 of your textbook and reflect on whether you think music should be held accountable for inspiring some teenage suicides, or whether there are inevitably other factors at play. Do you think parents should be concerned about whether their children are listening to music that might inspire them to commit suicide? Explain.*

D. Mental Disorders, 318

1. The majority of all suicide attempters meet DSM-IV-TR diagnostic criteria for a mental disorder. Which mental disorders are most often linked with suicide?

   ____

   ____

2. Why might psychiatric staff continue to monitor a patient for suicide risk even after his or her depression seems to be lifting?

   ____

   ____

3. Although the link between substance-related disorders and suicide is not well understood, there are two distinct possibilities that could explain the relationship. The first possibility is provided. What is the second?

   a. The substance user's tragic lifestyle may lead to a sense of hopelessness that triggers suicidal thinking.

   b. ____

      ____

4. Among people with schizophrenia, suicide is most often associated with feelings of ______________, rather than being a response to hallucinations or delusions.

E. Modeling: The Contagion of Suicide, 320

1. List the three kinds of models that most often seem to trigger suicide attempts.

   ____

2. Can you think of people you know or have read about that have modeled suicides or suicide attempts? Write a paragraph describing the effects of that model on others' behavior.

   ____

   ____

   ____

   ____

III. What Are the Underlying Causes of Suicide?, 321–325

A. The Psychodynamic View, 321

1. Many psychodynamic theorists believe that suicide results from ______________ and anger toward another person that is ______________ toward oneself.

2. Freud and others felt that through introjection, extreme ________________ feelings toward a lost loved one could lead to unrelenting ________________ toward oneself. Suicide could be yet a further expression of this self-________________ .

3. Freud suggested that human beings have a basic "death instinct," called ________________ , that most people direct toward ________________ and suicidal people toward ________________ .

4. Describe research findings supporting the psychodynamic theory of suicide in relation to (a) childhood losses and (b) the "death instinct."

   a. ____

   ____

   b. ____

   ____

B. Durkheim's Sociocultural View, 323

1. Emile Durkheim proposed that a person's likelihood of committing suicide is strongly influenced by his or her involvement in social institutions and structures. Complete the following chart by providing the missing information on social structures and Durkheim's three categories of suicide.

Category of Suicide	Relationship with Society	Characteristics or Examples of People in This Category
Egoistic Suicide		Isolated, alienated, nonreligious
Altruistic Suicide	So well integrated into the social structure that they sacrifice their lives for the well-being of society	
Anomic Suicide		Displaced by economic depression, social disintegration, and great changes in wealth/status

C. The Biological View, 324

The exercises in this subsection together represent an interesting "story" of how the biological view of suicide has evolved with continual research.

Until the 1970s, researchers using family pedigree studies consistently found evidence of higher than normal rates of suicidal behavior among the parents and close relatives of suicidal people. On the basis of this evidence, it was supposed that biological factors contributed to suicide.

1. Twin studies have supported the notion that genetic factors might contribute to suicide. Complete this exercise that relates to one Denmark study that examined suicide rates among the surviving twin in fraternal and identical twin pairs in which one of the pair had previously committed suicide.

   a. Out of the 19 identical twin pairs, ______ of the surviving twins also committed suicide.

   b. Out of the 58 fraternal twin pairs, ______ of the surviving twins also committed suicide.

2. Researchers have found evidence that low activity of the neurotransmitter serotonin is linked to suicide. Describe the results of these studies.

   ____

   ____

   ____

3. Some researchers speculate that low serotonin levels might increase the likelihood of suicide (regardless of the presence or absence of depression) by causing ________________ feelings and ________________ behavior.

4. Recent PET scan studies have revealed that people who contemplate or attempt suicide display abnormal activity in areas of the brain that are comprised of many ____________-using neurons.

IV. Is Suicide Linked to Age?, 325–332

A. Children, 327

1. Circle the correct answer in the following statements related to suicide among children.
   a. Of the children under the age of 14 who commit suicide each year in the United States, (boys/girls) are five times more likely to be suicide victims than the other gender.
   b. It is (true/false) that most children who attempt suicide do not understand death and do not really wish to die.

2. List some of the behaviors that commonly precede suicide attempts among children.

3. What does recent research say about how common suicidal thinking is among "normal" children?

B. Adolescents, 327

1. Suicide ranks ________________ among causes of death in people between the ages of 15 and 24 in the United States.

2. Although white American teenagers are more likely to attempt suicide than are African American teenagers, the suicide rates of these two groups have become more similar in recent years. One reason for this trend may be that African American and white American youths increasingly are facing similar pressures to achieve academically. What are other possible reasons for this trend?

3. Compared to other teenagers, teenagers who attempt suicide seem to be more angry and ________________, and have deficient problem-solving abilities.

4. Suicidal behavior in teenagers has been linked to depression, low self-esteem, and feelings of hopelessness, as well as to experiences of both long-term and immediate stress. List some of the (a) long-term and (b) immediate stressors that have been identified.
   a. ________________
   b. ________________

5. Describe some of the ways in which the period of adolescence itself produces stress that could increase the risk of suicide.

6. The ratio of suicide attempts to fatalities among teenagers is about 200:1, suggesting that teenagers may be more ________________ about killing themselves than people from other age groups.

7. Complete the following list of the four perceived societal changes discussed in the textbook that could explain the recent dramatic rise in suicides among adolescents and young adults.

   a. Competition for jobs, college positions, and academic and athletic honors is steadily increasing—leading to high levels of frustration and desperation in some.

   b. Recently weakened ties in the family structure have resulted in alienation and rejection among the young, fitting Durkheim's notion of ________________ suicide.

   c. A propensity toward suicide may be increased by the availability of drugs and

   ____

   d. ____

   ____

8. Identify two possible reasons for the closing trend in teenage suicide rates between African and Hispanic Americans and white Americans. (Thirty years ago, the white American suicide rate was far greater, now that gap is closing.)

   a. ____

   b. ____

9. List three or four possible reasons why Native Americans display the highest rates of teenage suicide of any ethnic group in the United States.

   ____

   ____

   ____

A Closer Look: The Black Box Controversy: Do Antidepressants Cause Suicide?, 329

1. Identify several advantages to the mental health field stemming from the controversy over the FDA issuing black box warnings regarding a potential link between antidepressants and suicide in children and young adults.

   ____

   ____

   ____

C. The Elderly, 330

1. Suicide rates among the elderly are higher than in any other age group; in fact, elderly persons committed _____ percent of all suicides in the United States during the 1980s but accounted for just _____ percent of the U.S. population.

2. This subsection in the textbook discusses many factors and events that seem to contribute to the high rate of suicide among the elderly. In this workbook you have been presented with several case studies that depict people experiencing a range of problems. Now you will write a case study: one that fits the textbook's discussion of characteristics of the suicidal elderly. Describe the suicide of an 87-year-old woman. Be sure to include information on the victim's *recent life events, particular thoughts and feelings,* and *method of suicide.* (*Note:* Writing your own case study will help you to remember the "profile" that is characteristic of elderly persons who attempt suicide.)

Case Study

3. Briefly describe explanations for the lower suicide rates (relative to elderly white Americans) of (a) elderly Native Americans and (b) elderly African Americans.

   a. ____________________

   ____

   b. ____________________

   ____

V. Treatment and Suicide, 332–337

A. What Treatments Are Used after Suicide Attempts?, 332

1. Studies indicate that most suicidal people do not receive continued ____________________ after a suicide attempt.

2. The first goal of therapy for people who have attempted suicide is to keep the client alive. What are two other primary goals?

   a. ____________________

   b. ____________________

3. About _____ percent of suicide attempters who receive treatment attempt suicide again, compared with _____ percent who do *not* receive treatment, suggesting that psychological intervention following a suicide attempt is effective.

4. List four ways in which cognitive-behavioral therapies, including mindfulness-based cognitive therapy, are found to be particularly helpful for suicidal people.

   a. ____________________

   b. ____________________

   c. ____________________

   d. ____________________

B. What Is Suicide Prevention?, 333

1. List two programs or services that have developed as a result of the growing emphasis on suicide *prevention* rather than suicide treatment.

____

____

2. List some of the characteristics of a person who is "in crisis."

____

____

3. Complete the following table by putting yourself in the place of a crisis-line counselor at the Los Angeles County Suicide Prevention Center. List your primary tasks to accomplish when taking a crisis call. Then match the task with the statement on the next page that is most indicative of that particular task. The first is given.

Task	Statement
1. Establishing a positive relationship	d.
2.	
3.	
4.	
5.	

Statements:

a. "Do you have a suicide plan at this point? Do you have access to a gun or pills?"

b. "What is going on in your life right now that feels difficult to handle? Did something happen that made you think about killing yourself?"

c. "Instead of hurting yourself, I want you to come to the crisis center now. Will you agree to do that?"

d. "I can hear how overwhelmed you feel. I want you to know that I am here to listen to you and help you."

e. "Do you have a friend or family member who you feel you can talk to and trust? Who is that person?"

C. Do Suicide Prevention Programs Work?, 336

Assessing the effectiveness of suicide prevention centers is difficult. The findings of such studies have not been consistent. While some studies indicate that in some communities, centers have had no effect on suicide rates—or even that rates have gone up after centers were established—these findings are not conclusive.

1. It appears that only a small percentage of suicidal people contact prevention centers; furthermore, whereas the highest rate of suicides is among elderly ______________ ______________, the typical caller to a suicide prevention center is young, ______________, and ______________.

2. A study of the Los Angeles Suicide Prevention Center indicated that among ______________ people who did call the center, a much higher than expected number were averted from committing suicide.

3. One certain implication of effectiveness studies of suicide prevention centers seems to be that they need to be more ________________ to and ________________ for people who are harboring thoughts of suicide.

4. If you or someone you know were suicidal, what kinds of professionals probably are most knowledgeable about suicide and could provide you (or your friend) with the most effective help?

____

____

5. Edwin Shneidman has called for broader and more effective ________________ ________________ about suicide as the ultimate form of prevention.

VI. Putting It Together: Psychological and Biological Insights Lag Behind, 337–338

1. Which of the models of abnormality has made the most progress in terms of shedding light on the dynamics of suicide?

____

2. The identification of effective ________________ strategies for people who are suicidal continues to evade clinicians and researchers, but it is clear that public ________________ about suicide will be an important component of any successful intervention program.

MULTIPLE CHOICE

1. In Edwin Shneidman's taxonomy of people who end their own lives intentionally, those who do not believe that their self-inflicted death will mean the end of their existence are called
   a. death darers.
   b. death seekers.
   c. death ignorers.
   d. death initiators.

2. A suicide note expresses hostility directed at the self and interpersonal problems. The writer is most likely
   a. younger than 40.
   b. 40 to 49 years old.
   c. 50 to 59 years old.
   d. over 60 years of age.

3. About what percent of people who successfully commit suicide leave suicide notes?
   a. 5%–10%
   b. 20%–30%
   c. 40%–45%
   d. 55%–60%

4. Why do more men than women commit suicide?
   a. Men use more lethal means.
   b. Men make more attempts at suicide.
   c. Men are more likely to be death initiators.
   d. Women are more likely to be death ignorers.

5. What is the term for the belief that a current negative mood and situation cannot be changed?
   a. anxiety
   b. sadness
   c. hopelessness
   d. dichotomous thinking

6. According to Durkheim's sociological theory of suicide, egoistic suicide occurs when
   a. persons sacrifice themselves for their society.
   b. persons have a close friend who commits suicide.
   c. persons have a history of few ties to their society.
   d. individuals experience a sudden change in their relationship to society.

7. Which neurotransmitter has been linked to suicidal behavior when levels are low?
   a. GABA
   b. serotonin
   c. dopamine
   d. norepinephrine

8. The arguments in favor of a person's right to commit suicide generally focus on the issue of
   a. role conflict.
   b. serious illness.
   c. occupational stress.
   d. abusive environment.

9. Which of the following persons is in a group at highest risk for suicide?
   a. female, African American, single
   b. elderly Native American male, married
   c. adolescent white female
   d. elderly white male, divorced

CHAPTER

11 Eating Disorders

CHAPTER OUTLINE

REVIEW EXERCISES

I. Anorexia Nervosa, 342–345

Until recently, anorexia nervosa and bulimia nervosa were viewed as very distinct disorders with different characteristics and causes that required different kinds of treatment. Although it is true that the varieties of eating disorders do have important differences, clinicians now realize that the similarities are significant as well.

1. According to the DSM-IV-TR, the central features of anorexia nervosa are:
   a. a refusal to maintain more than ____85____ percent of normal body weight,
   b. intense fear of becoming ____overweight____,
   c. a ____dysmorphic____ view of body weight and shape, and
   d. the cessation of ____menstruation____.
2. In ____restrictor____ type anorexia, people move from cutting out sweets and fattening foods to eating very little food at all. *(Note the difference between this type and the binge-eating/purging type.)*
3. Complete the list of facts concerning anorexia nervosa.
   a. ___90___ to ___95___ percent of people with anorexia nervosa are female.
   b. The average age of onset is between ___14___ and ___18___ years.
   c. About ___2___ percent of the Western female population develops the disorder.
   d. The disorder often develops following a particularly ____traumatic____ event in the person's life.
   e. Between ___2___ and ___2___ percent of people with anorexia nervosa die, typically from medical problems associated with ____malnutrition____ or from suicide.

A and B. The Clinical Picture and Medical Problems, 344

1. In the following table complete the summary of the central features of anorexia nervosa by providing an example of each feature.

Features	Examples Illustrating Features
Drive for thinness	The patient fears she will not be able to control her eating and that she will become obese
Preoccupied with food	obsessed with food + what she/he can eat + when

Cognitive distortions	
Psychological problems	
Medical problems	

II. Bulimia Nervosa, 345–351

1. Bulimia nervosa is also known as ___binge___-___purge___ syndrome.
2. Define the following two terms as they relate to bulimia nervosa:

   Binge: excessive/uncontrolled intake of food, usually in secret

   Compensatory behavior: exercise, purge, abuse of laxatives

3. Write the appropriate subtype of bulimia next to each description below.
   a. Jessie binges regularly, then does not eat for days and exercises at least four hours each day that she "fasts". ___non purging/compensatory___
   b. Michelle, after consuming huge amounts of food very quickly forces herself to vomit.
   ___purging___
4. Unlike those who suffer from anorexia nervosa, the weight of people with bulimia nervosa usually fluctuates in the ___normal___ range.
5. ___binge___-___eating___ disorder, which does not involve compensatory behaviors, has been identified by clinicians but is not an official category of the DSM-IV-TR.

A. Binges, 347

1. Complete the following table by giving a description of the typical aspects of a binge that are listed.

Features	Examples Illustrating Features
Setting of binge	In secret
Types of food chosen	fatty, soft
Feelings at start of binge	Unbearable tension, irritability, removed, powerless
Feelings during binge	uncontrollable, primal
Feelings after binge	guilty

B. Compensatory Behaviors, 348

1. Describe the results of the following kinds of compensatory behaviors: (a) self-induced vomiting and (b) laxative abuse.

   a. ______________________________

   ____

   b. ______________________________

   ____

C. Bulimia Nervosa vs. Anorexia Nervosa, 350

1. List five similarities between anorexia nervosa and bulimia nervosa.

   a. ______________________________

   b. ______________________________

   c. ______________________________

   d. ______________________________

   e. ______________________________

2. In the table below, certain features that seem to distinguish the "typical" person with anorexia nervosa from the "typical" person with bulimia nervosa are presented. Decide which disorder is being described in each column, then write the name of the disorder in the box above the column.

Which disorder is described?	______________	______________
Physical features	Weight fluctuation, dental and gastrointestinal problems, potassium deficiencies	Very underweight, amenorrhea
Personality and mood	Impulsive, dramatic, mood swings, trusting, need to please others	Less trusting, emotionally over-controlled, obsessive
Behavior	More antisocial behavior, more alcohol and drug use, more likely to be sexually experienced/active	Less antisocial behavior, less likely to be sexually active

III. What Causes Eating Disorders?, 351–363

1. Today's theorists usually apply a ________________ ________________ perspective to eating disorders—a view that identifies several key factors that place a person at risk for developing them.

A. Psychodynamic Factors: Ego Deficiencies, 352

1. Eating disorders pioneer Hilde Bruch proposed a theory of eating disorders that is in line with the ________________ perspective.

2. Study the completed diagram that shows how Bruch proposed children of "effective" parents were raised. Then give the missing information in the diagram below it showing how eating disorders can develop in the children of "ineffective" parents.

Effective parents accurately attend to their children's expressions of biological and emotional needs	⟶	Children develop a sense of self-control and are able to differentiate between internal need states	⟶	Children become autonomous, confident, and self-reliant individuals

Ineffective parents: ________________ ________________ ________________ ________________ ________________ ________________	→	Children fail to develop cohesive self-concept and are unable to differentiate between internal need states—children rely on other people (parents) to tell them what they need and when they need it	⟶	As adolescents, children feel ________________ because they are unable to establish ________________	→	To overcome these feelings, children try to achieve extreme ________________ over their body size and shape, and their ________________

3. Research and clinical reports support Bruch's tenet that parents of adolescents with eating disorders define their children's needs for them. List two other tenets relating to people with eating disorders that have been supported.

   a. ____
   ____

   b. ____
   ____

B. Cognitive Factors, 352

1. Cognitive theorists believe that a broad cognitive distortion, or "________________," lies at the center of disordered eating.
2. Explain the ways in which cognitive theorists believe this type of disordered thinking is on display in:

   a. anorexia nervosa ____

   b. bulimia nervosa ____

C. Mood Disorders, 353

1. In the following table, summarize the research findings that support the notion that people who suffer from mood disorders are predisposed to develop eating disorders.

Research Topic	Findings
Major depression	
Close relatives	
Neurotransmitter activity	
Medications	The dysfunctional eating patterns of those with eating disorders are often helped significantly by antidepressant drugs

D. Biological Factors, 353

1. Research findings that support the contention that genetic factors contribute to the development of eating disorders. Fill in the missing statistics below.
   a. Compared to the general population, relatives of those with eating disorders are up to ______ times more likely to develop the disorders themselves.
   b. The concordance rate for bulimia nervosa among identical twins is ______ percent, whereas the concordance rate for fraternal twins is only ______ percent.
2. Recently, researchers found a link between abnormally low levels of the neurotransmitter ______ and eating disorders; the specific relationship between these variables is still being studied.

Biological researchers are also interested in the role that specific brain areas might play in eating disorders. In particular, the ***hypothalamus****— a part of the brain that regulates the endocrine system—has been implicated. Complete the following questions related to the ways in which hypothalamic functioning might be related to eating disorders.*

3. The ______ hypothalamus (LH) and the ______ hypothalamus (VMH), the two parts of the hypothalamus that control eating, have become the focus of biological researchers studying eating disorders.
4. Researchers think that the LH, the VMH, and the natural appetite suppressant called GLP-1 set up a "weight______" in the body that predisposes people to maintain a stable body weight, called the weight set point.
5. What are the two things that happen when a person's weight falls *below* his or her weight set point? The ______ is activated and seeks to ______ the lost weight by (1) ______ hunger, and (2) ______ the body's metabolic rate.
6. What are the two things that happen when a person's weight *rises above* his or her weight set point? The ______ is activated and seeks to ______ the excess weight by (1) ______ hunger, and (2) ______ the body's metabolic rate.

E. Societal Pressures, 355

1. The textbook describes several pieces of evidence that since the 1950s, Western culture's image of the "perfect" female form has steadily become thinner. Describe the findings related to "Miss America," "Playboy," or "thin subcultures."

______

______

______

2. Describe the research findings of one of the studies in the textbook that point to Western society's prejudice against overweight people.

____

____

____

F. Family Environment, 358

1. Research findings suggest that about half of the people with eating disorders come from families who seem to emphasize _______________, physical appearance, and _______________.

*Theorist Salvador Minuchin believes that **enmeshed family patterns** can lead to eating disorders. Study the chart on enmeshed family patterns below, then complete the following exercises.*

Characteristics of Enmeshed Family "Set the Stage" for Eating Disorders
• family members are overinvolved with each other's affairs • family members are overconcerned about each other's welfare • little room for family members' individuality and autonomy • parents too involved in the lives of their children • family members are discouraged from speaking about their own ideas and feelings • families can be clinging and foster dependency
Conflict Arises During Adolescence
During adolescence, these characteristics come into conflict with the natural tendency toward independence among adolescents
As a Result, Problems Can Develop
The family responds to the conflict by subtly forcing the child to take on a "sick" role (to develop an eating disorder or some other problem)

2. The chart lists negative characteristics of the enmeshed family. List any aspects of the pattern that could be viewed as positive.

____

3. _______________ studies and empirical studies have sometimes, but not always, lent support to this family systems explanation.

G. Multicultural Factors: Racial and Ethnic Differences, 360

1. Briefly compare the attitudes toward their own body image and beauty of young African American women and young white women revealed in a 1995 study at the University of Arizona, and then briefly describe the clinical picture that has been unfolding since then. Suggest some possible reasons for the changes.

   a. Pre-1995 _______________

   ____

   ____

   ____

b. Post-1995 ____

____

____

____

H. Multicultural Factors: Gender Differences, 361

1. Males account for ______ to ______ percent of all cases of eating disorders.
2. Give two possible reasons for the disparity in eating disorder rates between males and females.

   a. ____

   b. ____
3. Give two reasons men develop eating disorders.

   a. ____

   b. ____
4. There is a new eating disorder emerging, found almost exclusively among men, known as ______________, or ______________ .

IV. How Are Eating Disorders Treated?, 363–369

Current treatments for eating disorders vary depending on the symptoms, behaviors, and circumstances of each client. However, all treatments are comprised of two broad components, or dimensions: (1) correcting the eating pattern that is endangering the client's health and (2) addressing the psychological and situational factors that led to and maintain the eating disorder.

A. Treatments for Anorexia Nervosa, 363

Read the following case study to be used in an exercise relating to the treatment of anorexia nervosa.

Case Study

Josie S. is a 15-year-old female who was referred to the City Hospital's Department of Psychiatry because she is believed to be suffering from anorexia nervosa. Josie is 5 feet 6 inches tall. In the last six months, her weight has dropped 59 pounds, from 142 to 83 pounds. She appears emaciated and is physically weak. Josie reached menarche at age 11 but has not had a period in 16 weeks. Her parents state that although they really wanted Josie to lose some weight "because she was too big to wear all the nice clothes" they bought for her, they are now concerned because she is refusing to eat meals at home. Josie reports that she feels fine and "doesn't understand all the fuss because I am still a fat pig."

1. This exercise is designed to give you a thorough understanding of some of the important concepts and issues involved in the treatment of eating disorders. Be sure that you have carefully read pages 363–366 in the textbook before attempting this exercise.

   In this exercise, you will put yourself in the place of the therapist assigned to treat Josie's anorexia nervosa by completing the "treatment plan" on the following pages. For both of the treatment dimensions listed, describe the specific treatment strategies that you might employ as Josie's therapist.

City Hospital—Department of Psychiatry	
Treatment Plan for:	Josie S.
Diagnosis:	Anorexia nervosa, restrictive type
Treatment dimension: Weight restoration and resumption of normal eating patterns	
Treatment Strategy #1:	**Medical/biological approaches:** If Josie's life is threatened, use tube and intravenous feedings and/or antidepressant drugs to help restore her weight.
Treatment Strategy #2:	**Behavioral approach:**
Treatment Strategy #3:	**Supportive nursing care:**
Treatment dimension: Address broader psychological and family issues	
Treatment Strategy #1:	**Self-exploration/insight approach:** Help Josie express her need for independence and control in more appropriate ways; help Josie learn to recognize and trust her internal sensations and feelings.
Treatment Strategy #2:	**Cognitive-behavioral approach:**
Treatment Strategy #3:	**Family therapy:**

2. This exercise summarizes some of the positive and negative outcomes of people who have been treated for anorexia nervosa. Complete the statements below.

Posttreatment Positive Outcomes

When patients are evaluated several years after treatment:

a. _____ percent are fully recovered and _____ percent are considerably improved.

b. ________________ returns and other medical problems improve.

Posttreatment Negative Outcomes

When patients are evaluated several years after treatment:

a. Up to _____ percent continue to show significant anorexic symptoms and behaviors.

b. Approximately _____ percent continue to show emotional difficulties, such as depression, social anxiety, and obsessiveness.

3. This exercise focuses on the recovery rates of people who have been treated for anorexia nervosa and addresses information contained on pages 366–367 of the textbook. In the following paragraph, create a profile for the "ideal" patient with anorexia nervosa from the standpoint of the characteristics that seem to indicate the best chances for recovery. Draw a line through the option within each set of parentheses that represents the *poorer* prognosis or recovery rate.

Before treatment, the patient lost (a lot of/relatively little) weight. The patient suffered with the disorder for a (long/short) period without successful clinical intervention. (He/She) was a (young adolescent/older person) at the time of treatment. The patient (did/did not) experience pre-onset psychological and sexual problems.

B. Treatments for Bulimia Nervosa, 367

Treatment programs for bulimia nervosa emphasize education as well as therapy. Specific treatment strategies are addressed in the following exercise.

1. Complete this table summarizing treatment strategies for bulimia nervosa. Find two examples of strategies for each type of treatment approach (from the list below the table), and then summarize the effectiveness of each approach.

Treatment Approach	Examples	Effectiveness
Individual insight therapy	b.	Pschodynamic, cognitive, and combined approaches effective
Group therapy	a	
Behavioral therapy	d	Decrease in eating anxiety; decreased binging and purging
Antidepressant medications	g.	

Examples

a. Group meals in which clients plan and eat a meal together, while discussing thoughts and feelings

b. Free association and interpretation of clients' underlying conflicts about lack of self-trust and need for control

c. Exposure and response prevention

d. Teaching that having an eating disorder is not "strange" or shameful

e. Evaluation and alteration of maladaptive beliefs toward food, eating, and weight (e.g., "I must lose weight in order to be happy")

f. Keeping diaries of eating behavior, body sensations, thoughts, and feelings

g. Use of Prozac or other similar drugs

2. Complete the following statements regarding the aftermath of bulimia nervosa.

a. Of clients treated for bulimia, _____ percent almost immediately stop their binge-purge behaviors and stabilize their eating habits, 40 percent show a moderate response to treatment, and the remaining _____ percent show no improvement in bulimic behaviors.

b. By 10 years after treatment, _____ percent of people with bulimia had recovered, according to recent studies.

c. As with anorexia, relapses are usually precipitated by new ______________ in the person's life.

d. One study showed that almost one-third of recovered bulimic clients relapsed within _____ years of treatment.

V. Putting It Together: A Standard for Integrating Perspectives, 369–370

1. Describe the multidimensional risk perspective on eating disorders.

____

____

____

____

2. As stated in your text, one person who had recovered from bulimia nervosa made a very intriguing comment: **"I still miss my bulimia as I would an old friend who has died"** (Canwels, 1983). Discuss possible meanings of this statement, and explain why it is so important for clinicians to understand feelings like these if they want to provide effective treatments for patients with eating disorders.

____

____

____

____

____

____

MULTIPLE CHOICE

1. The relentless pursuit of thinness by starving to lose weight is called
   a. obesity.
   b. obsession.
   c. anorexia nervosa.
   d. bulimia nervosa.

2. The person who will be anorexic usually starts out
   a. underweight.
   b. quite a bit overweight.
   c. just to lose a little weight.
   d. always with normal weight.

3. One reason men are less likely to suffer from anorexia than women is the cultural stereotype that the "perfect" male body is
   a. thin.
   b. tall.
   c. muscular.
   d. much more variable than for women.

4. People who display anorexia nervosa usually display
   a. mania.
   b. a clinical depression.
   c. a preoccupation with food.
   d. generalized anxiety disorder.

5. For people with bulimia nervosa, binge episodes are often preceded by feelings of
   a. mania.
   b. control.
   c. high tension.
   d. guilt and depression.

6. In contrast to people suffering from anorexia nervosa, individuals suffering from bulimia nervosa
   a. are less concerned with food.
   b. don't struggle with anxiety and depression.
   c. tend to be more interested in pleasing others.
   d. feel conflicted about what, when, and how much to eat.

7. According to a survey of women in sports, the weight-control method that is most likely to be used/abused by female athletes in general is
   a. using diet pills.
   b. using a diuretic.
   c. using a laxative.
   d. inducing vomiting.

8. Activation of the ________________ appears to produce hunger.
   a. thalamus
   b. lateral hypothalamus
   c. anterior hypothalamus
   d. ventromedial hypothalamus

9. The prognosis for recovery from anorexia nervosa is worse as a function of
   a. the length of time in treatment.
   b. amount of weight lost before treatment.
   c. the weight of the patient at the onset of treatment.
   d. the amount of weight gained by the patient during treatment.

10. Parents who incorrectly interpret their children's actual conditions are:
    a. enmeshed.
    b. ineffective.
    c. dysfunctional.
    d. anticipatory.

11. What is the *first* goal of most treatment plans for anorexia?
    a. weight gain
    b. changing misperceptions about the body
    c. changing eating habits
    d. changing purging habits

CHAPTER

12 Substance-Related Disorders

CHAPTER OUTLINE

REVIEW EXERCISES

The following exercises cover Chapter 12's introductory material on pages 373–375.

Match numbers 1–6 below with the appropriate letter from the list a–f.

1. ______ Intoxication
2. ______ Hallucinosis
3. ______ Substance abuse
4. ______ Substance dependence
5. ______ Tolerance
6. ______ Withdrawal

a. Condition in which a person needs increasing doses of a substance in order to keep obtaining the desired effect.

b. A state of perceptual distortions and hallucinations.

c. Condition in which people experience unpleasant symptoms when they suddenly stop taking or reduce their dosage of a drug.

d. Addiction—physical dependence on a drug.

e. A temporary syndrome in which the person exhibits impaired judgment, mood changes, irritability, slurred speech, and loss of coordination.

f. An excessive and chronic reliance on drugs, in which the drugs occupy a central place in a person's life.

7. Research indicates that in any given year in the United States, 9.2 percent of all adults have a substance-related disorder, but only about ______________ percent of these individuals receive treatment.

8. The highest rate of substance abuse or dependence in the United States is found among ______________ Americans, while the lowest is among ______________ Americans.

I. Depressants, 375–383

A. Alcohol, 375

1. Almost 7 percent of all persons over 11 years of age are heavy drinkers, which means that they consume at least ______ drinks on at least ______ occasions each month.
2. The ratio of male heavy drinkers to female heavy drinkers is about ______________ to one.

Ethyl alcohol consumption affects the physiological, cognitive, and emotional states of people who consume progressively more amounts of it. Study the diagram, which illustrates these progressive effects.

All alcoholic beverages contain ethyl alcohol, which is . . .

↓

Rapidly absorbed into the blood through the lining of the stomach and the intestines

↓

Alcohol is taken by the bloodstream to the central nervous system (CNS)

↓

In the CNS, alcohol acts to depress functioning by binding to GABA receptors

---

Alcohol first affects the higher centers of the CNS, which control judgment and inhibition

- People become less constrained, more talkative, and often more friendly
- As inner control breaks down, they may feel relaxed, safe, self-confident, and happy
- Impairment of fine motor skills, increased sensitivity to light, feeling warm, and having a flushed face and neck also occur

These effects increase, and other CNS areas are depressed, as more alcohol is ingested

- People become still less restrained and more confused
- The ability to make rational judgments declines, speech becomes less guarded and less coherent, and memory falters
- Many become loud, boisterous, and aggressive, and emotions become exaggerated
- Motor impairment increases, reaction times slow, people become unsteady, and vision and hearing problems occur

---

3. The concentration of ethyl alcohol in the ____________ determines its effect on body chemistry.
4. Women have significantly ____________ of the stomach enzyme called alcohol ____________, the enzyme that breaks down alcohol before it enters the blood.
5. The effects of alcohol decline as it is ____________ by the liver; this rate differs among people, so rates of "____________" varies as well.
6. What are the only two things that can help a person sober up?

____

I. Alcohol Abuse and Dependence, 377

1. About 3 percent of high school ____________ say that they use alcohol daily, and approximately 10 percent of those in ____________ school say that they have consumed alcohol.
2. At some point in their lives, about 13 percent of all adults in the United States will experience a pattern of alcohol abuse and/or dependence. The male to female ratio of these patterns in adults is at least ____________ to 1.
3. Each of the following case studies illustrates one of three broad patterns of alcohol abuse described in the textbook. Make up a name for each pattern that will help you remember it (if your instructor has given names, use those). Then underline the parts of each description that are typical for that pattern.

Case Study

Name of pattern:

Almost every day of Alan's life in the last six years has been built around alcohol. This is his fourth year in college, but he hasn't progressed much since he rarely makes it through the entire term of a class. Alan usually blames "rotten" professors. Most days Alan gets up at lunchtime (he's learned not to attempt morning classes) and meets friends at a fast-food restaurant. Invariably he orders just a jumbo soft drink, which he proceeds to spike with alcohol. If he hasn't drunk too much, and if he isn't too hungover, he might then go to a class or two. Often, however, Alan goes straight from "lunch" to a bar, where he nibbles on the buffalo wings they put out at happy hour and drinks copious amounts of beer until he stumbles home and passes out.

Name of pattern:

There are over 20 times as many people attending Rebecca's college as there are living in her hometown. She is the first member of her family to go to college, and she wants to make everyone proud of her. Rebecca gets excellent grades because she works very hard, never missing a class and spending a good part of the evenings in the library. After a long day of studying, though, she usually goes to her room and drinks alone for at least a couple of hours. Rebecca gets up early on Saturdays to go to the library. However, her Saturday afternoons and Sundays are spent just like her weekday evenings—drinking alone in her room.

Name of pattern:

Ric is probably the most intelligent and hardest working undergraduate in his college's math department. He loves his classes, and he pushes himself tremendously to maintain a near-perfect academic record. Whenever a big test is approaching, he vanishes for several days so he can devote himself entirely to studying. The results are always the same—an A+. Once the test is over, Ric makes up for lost time by partying every bit as hard as he studies. If a test falls on a Thursday, he probably won't draw a sober breath from that night until Monday morning. Stories of these episodes and of his drunken exploits during school vacations have become legendary among his friends. Ric is glad for this, since he himself often remembers little of what he does while drunk.

4. For many, the pattern of alcoholism includes physical dependence. Complete these questions relating to the effects of physical dependence.
   a. As they use alcohol repeatedly, many build up a ___tolernce___, which forces them to drink more to feel any effects.
   b. Describe some of the withdrawal symptoms people dependent on alcohol experience when they stop drinking.
   ___shakie nausea sweats aches___
   ____
   c. Alcohol withdrawal delirium, or ___delerium___ ___tremens___ (the DT's), is characterized by great mental confusion, clouded consciousness, and terrifying visual ___hallucinatio___.
   d. Like most other alcohol withdrawal symptoms, the DT's usually run their course in two to three days.

2. What Is the Personal and Social Impact of Alcoholism?, 379

1. List some of the social costs of alcoholism.

____

____

2. Write a paragraph about the impact of alcoholism on the 30 million children of alcoholic parents.

____

____

____

____

____

Take a few moments to consider some of the damaging physical effects of chronic and excessive alcohol consumption. Make sure you understand how alcohol consumption can lead to each of the following physical problems:

- Cirrhosis of the liver
- Heart failure, irregularities of heart functioning
- Immune system impairment, susceptibility to certain diseases
- Malnutrition, Korsakoff's syndrome (see below)

3. Chronic alcohol use can result in malnutrition, since alcohol contains no nutritional value, but lowers a person's desire for food. Furthermore, alcohol-related vitamin and mineral deficiencies can result in mental disorders, such as Korsakoff's syndrome. Complete this diagram relating to these disorders.

Alcohol-related vitamin B deficiency → *can lead to* → Korsakoff's syndrome

vitamin B is also called: ______________________

Characteristics

____

____

4. Alcohol during pregnancy can result in miscarriage and **fetal alcohol syndrome.** What are some of the characteristics of fetal alcohol syndrome?

____

____

B. Sedative-Hypnotic Drugs, 380

1. Sedative-hypnotic drugs produce a sedative or ______________ effect at low doses and at high doses are ______________ inducers.

1. Barbiturates, 380

1. Low doses of barbiturates reduce anxiety by binding to ______________ of the inhibitory neurotransmitter ______________ .
2. Complete these statements relating to the results of higher doses of barbiturates on the reticular formation.
   a. The reticular formation is responsible for keeping people awake and alert, and barbiturates ______________ its functioning.
   b. Overdoses can result in ______________ failure and ______________ blood pressure, leading to coma and even death.
3. List some parallels between alcohol dependence and barbiturate dependence.

____

____

4. One of the great dangers of barbiturate dependence is that the ______________ dose of the drug remains the same even while the body is building up to a ______________ for its other effects.

2. Benzodiazepines, 381

1. Complete these items relating to benzodiazepines, the antianxiety drugs discovered in the 1950s that are now the most popular hypnotic drugs available.

   a. What are some of the trade names of benzodiazepines?

   ____

   b. Reasons for their popularity include the fact that, compared to other kinds of sedative-hypnotic drugs, they relieve anxiety while causing less ________________, and their use is less likely to lead to death by an ________________.

   c. Approximately 1 percent of the adults in the United States abuse or become dependent on antianxiety drugs at some point in their lives.

C. Opioids, 381

Be sure to read the material about the many uses and misuses of opioids from the use of opium in ancient times through the development of synthetic opioids in our day.

1. Write in the correct term that is associated with the following definitions.

Term	*Definition*
a. ________________	Used in the past as a cough medicine and pain reliever, this highly addictive, illegal substance is derived from morphine.
b. ________________	This is the name for all natural and synthetic opioids that include both illegal and medically prescribed substances.
c. ________________	A natural substance that comes from the sap of poppies.
d. ________________	A synthetic opioid manufactured in laboratories that is sometimes used in the treatment of heroin addiction.
e. ________________	A substance that is derived from opium that is medically prescribed for pain relief but that can lead to addiction.

2. Narcotics may be smoked, inhaled, injected just beneath the skin, or "________________," which means it is injected directly into the ________________.

3. Name and describe the two phases people experience when they use narcotics.

   a. ________________, ____

   b. ________________, ____

4. Opioids generate their effects because they stimulate neuron receptor sites that usually receive ________________, neurotransmitters that help to relieve ________________ and ________________ tension.

1. Heroin Abuse and Dependence, 382

1. Most heroin abusers develop a dependence on it, quickly building up a tolerance and experiencing withdrawal symptoms when they abstain. Complete these statements relating to heroin withdrawal symptoms.

   a. Initial withdrawal symptoms include ________________, restlessness, ________________, and rapid breathing.

b. Symptoms become progressively more serious for two or three days and can be accompanied by twitching, constant aches, fever, vomiting and diarrhea, loss of appetite, higher blood pressure, dehydration, and weight loss.

c. Unless the person takes more heroin, the withdrawal distress usually peaks by the ____________ day and disappears by the ____________ day.

2. What Are the Dangers of Heroin Abuse?, 383

1. During a heroin overdose, the drug depresses the ____________ center of the brain, virtually paralyzing it.

2. List two major health risks other than overdosing to which heroin users are particularly susceptible.

____

____

II. Stimulants, 383–389

Cocaine and amphetamine use stimulates activity of the central nervous system, resulting in effects such as increased blood pressure and heart rate, as well as intensified behavioral activity, thought processes, and alertness.

A. Cocaine, 383

1. Cocaine is the most powerful ____________ stimulant known and is derived from the ____________ plant found in South America.

2. Processed cocaine is most commonly snorted through the nose, but it is also intravenously injected, or ____________ .

Be sure to read about the dramatic surge in the number of people in the United States who have tried cocaine over the course of the last few decades. Today 2.4 million people are using cocaine. Many users are young; 6 percent of all high school seniors have used cocaine in the past year.

3. Describe the high experienced by those who use cocaine.

____

4. Cocaine produces its effects because it overstimulates the central nervous system by releasing excessive amounts of which three neurotransmitters?

____

5. What are the symptoms of cocaine intoxication?

____

6. If a person with a physical dependence for cocaine decides to stop, what are the withdrawal symptoms that may result from abstinence?

____

____

7. Newer forms of cocaine have produced an increase in abuse and dependence on the drug. Complete the statements regarding these recent forms.

a. In the technique called ________________, the pure cocaine basic alkaloid is chemically separated from processed cocaine, vaporized by heat from a flame, and inhaled with a pipe.

b. Almost 2 percent of high school seniors say they have used ________________ (a form of freebase cocaine that is smoked) in the past year.

Take some time to consider the many ways in which cocaine can be an extremely dangerous drug to one's health. Be sure you understand how cocaine use can lead to each of the following physical problems:

- Cocaine overdose (effects on the brain and body)
- Irregular heart functioning
- Fetal cocaine syndrome

B. Amphetamines, 387

1. Unlike substances such as opium and cocaine, amphetamines are stimulant drugs that are ________________ in the laboratory.

2. List some of the uses and misuses of amphetamines since they were first synthesized in the 1930s.

   ____

   ____

   ____

3. Amphetamines are taken in the form of ________________, can be injected, or are ingested in such forms as "ice" and "________________."

4. Complete the list of physiological and psychological similarities between the effects of amphetamines and cocaine.

   a. They both increase energy and alertness and reduce appetite in low doses.

   b. Both cause an emotional ________________ as they leave the body.

   c. Both stimulate the central nervous system by increasing the release of the neurotransmitters ________________, ________________, and ________________.

Read the following case study relating to amphetamine abuse.

Case Study

Margaret is a full-time college student, holds a part-time job, and is also on the cross-country team. While competing in a track meet one week ago, Margaret started her race feeling good and full of energy. At the 1-mile mark, however, she felt a wrenching pain in her hamstring muscle. She pushed herself to run, but had to drop out of the race as she approached the 2-mile mark. Margaret felt exhausted, and the pain in her leg was excruciating. After being examined by a physician, Margaret learned that in addition to tearing several ligaments, she had tested positive for amphetamines. She confessed to her coach that she had been using increasing amounts of Dexedrine in order to maintain the energy she needed to keep up with the demands of her life.

5. Using the concepts of tolerance and dependence, how would you explain Margaret's increased amphetamine use and subsequent injuries?

____

____

____

6. Almost ________ percent of all Americans over the age of 11 in the United States have used methamphetamine at least once.

7. Compared to men, women are ________ likely to use methamphetamine.

8. One particular health concern associated with methamphetamine use is ____________, which damages nerve endings.

C. Caffeine, 388

1. List the most common forms in which caffeine is consumed.

   coffee energy drinks

2. Caffeine affects the central nervous system by stimulating the release of which three neurotransmitters?

   ____

3. The possible physiological effects of caffeine include disruption of the performance of complex motor tasks and interference with both duration and quality of sleep. Listed below are several physiological processes. Put an "I" before those that caffeine increases, and a "D" before those it decreases.

I	Arousal	D	Fatigue
I	General motor activities	I	Rate of breathing
I	Heart rate	I	Secretion of gastric acid by stomach

4. Describe (a) the method and (b) results of Silverman and colleagues' study on the effects of caffeine withdrawal.

   a. ____

   ____

   b. ____

   ____

III. Hallucinogens, Cannabis, and Combinations of Substances, 389–397

A. Hallucinogens, 389

1. **Hallucinogens** (a.k.a. psychedelics) are chemical substances that affect sensory experiences, producing sensations that are sometimes called "hallucinations."

2. Psychedelics include **LSD** (lysergic acid diethylamide), mescaline, psilocybin, and MDMA (also called ecstasy).

3. LSD was derived by the Swiss chemist Albert Hoffman in 1938 from a group of naturally occurring drugs called ergot mold.

4. Describe hallucinogen intoxication, or hallucinosis.

   ____

   ____

5. If a person using LSD has sensations that he or she can "see" musical vibrations in the air, that person is experiencing ______________.
6. The immediate effects of LSD wear off in about ______ hours.

Study this diagram that shows how LSD produces the characteristics of a "trip."

Normal Process		***LSD-Influenced Process***
Serotonin released	***Neurons***	LSD binds to serotonin receptor sites, preventing release of serotonin
↓		↓
Serotonin helps filter incoming sensory information	***The Brain***	Brain is flooded by sensory input
Undistorted Sensory Perception		***Distorted Sensory Perception*** (e.g., hallucinations)

7. Even though LSD use does not result in significant tolerance or withdrawal, it poses serious risks—even to first-time users. Complete the following questions relating to the three primary risks related to LSD.

   a. LSD is so remarkably ______________ that a dose of any size is likely to elicit powerful perceptual, emotional, and behavioral reactions—which are sometimes extremely unpleasant (i.e., a "bad trip").

   b. ______________ sensory and emotional changes that recur long after the LSD has left the body—called ______________—are experienced by about a quarter of LSD users.

B. Cannabis, 391

1. Cannabis is harvested from the leaves and flowers of the ______________ plant, and its main active ingredient is **tetrahydrocannabinol,** or ______________.
2. The most powerful of the cannabis drugs is ______________, whereas the most common is ______________.
3. Complete this exercise by describing some of the characteristics of cannabis intoxication as they relate to the categories below.

   a. *Mood changes:* Most people feel joyful and relaxed and become contemplative or talkative. Others become anxious, suspicious, apprehensive, or irritated.

   b. *Perceptual distortions:* Many report sharpened perceptions and preoccupation with sounds and sights. ______________ seems to slow down, and distances and ______________ seem greater than they actually are.

   c. *Physical changes:* ____

   ____

4. The effects of cannabis last about ______ to ______ hours, although mood changes can persist.
5. What is the main reason why increased patterns of marijuana abuse and dependence have emerged since the early 1970s?

   ____

6. Researchers have become more aware of the potential negative effects of chronic marijuana use, such as how it induces panic attacks in some. Describe other negative effects.

____

____

____

Read through the material on "Cannabis and Society" on pages 394–395, and consider how you feel about the medical legalization of marijuana and the 2005 United States Supreme Court ruling on the subject.

C. Combinations of Substances, 395

1. Define **cross-tolerance.**

tolerance of one drug causes a tolerance of another drug with similar effects

2. A synergistic effect occurs when different drugs are in the body at the same time and they enhance each other's effect. Complete these questions about the two types of synergistic effects.

   a. One type of synergistic effect called **similar actions** is when one or more drugs have the same effects, or similar actions, on the brain and body.

   b. Physiologically, how can the similar actions of alcohol, antianxiety drugs, barbiturates, and opioids lead to death even when mixed in small doses?

   Supress breathing/heartrate/blood pressure to dangerous levels

   c. The other type of synergistic effect is called **opposite** (or ______________) **actions.**

   d. Physiologically, why is it dangerous to combine barbiturates or alcohol with cocaine or amphetamines?

   they cause toxins to build up

3. Often, drugs are mixed in ignorance of the dangerous consequences. However, increasingly this kind of multiple drugs use, or ______________ use, seems to be done knowingly because the user enjoys the synergistic effects.

IV. What Causes Substance-Related Disorders?, 397–401

A. The Sociocultural View, 397

The sociocultural theories of drug abuse and dependence propose that the people most likely to develop problems are those whose societies create an atmosphere of stress and those whose families value, or at least tolerate, drug taking.

1. Complete the following statements regarding research that has tended to support sociocultural theories regarding substance abuse.

   a. Higher rates of addiction have been found in regions of the United States where Poverty is more common.

   b. People in lower Socioeconomic classes have higher substance abuse rates than other classes.

c. Problem drinking is more common among teenagers whose parents and peers drink than among those whose parents and peers do not.

d. Lower rates of alcohol abuse were found among ethnic and religious groups in which drinking is acceptable *and* the __rules__ of drinking are clearly defined.

B. The Psychodynamic View, 397

1. Psychodynamic theorists suggest that people who abuse substances were not __attended to__ enough during childhood, and that they subsequently try to meet their need for comfort and support by relying on others, or on drugs.
2. The psychodynamic hypothesis that some people develop a "substance abuse personality" is supported by research findings indicating that, compared to others, people who abuse substances are more likely to have what kinds of personality characteristics?

   ____

3. What is the major problem with studies that have purported to identify personality traits of people with or prone to substance abuse problems?

   ____

   ____

C. The Cognitive-Behavioral Views, 398

There are three primary behavioral theories that attempt to explain substance-related disorders: the operant conditioning theory, the opponent-process theory, and the classical conditioning theory. Read the following case study. The exercise after the case will ask you to apply it to each of these three theories.

Case Study

Glenn started using alcohol at age 15. Always rather shy and socially awkward, he found that drinking helped him "loosen up" enough to interact with his peers, who he had avoided in the past. By age 18, Glenn was known as a real "partyer." He drank nearly every day and often experienced blackouts. Glenn managed to get into college but dropped out at the end of his first semester because his grades were so poor. He got a job at a convenience store but was fired for coming to work intoxicated. Depressed and broke, Glenn asked an acquaintance if he could "crash" at his place until he found another job. It turned out that the acquaintance sold heroin. Glenn continued his heavy drinking, and within three months of moving in, he was also hooked on heroin. He tried to quit, but whenever his roommate brought out his drug paraphernalia, Glenn would succumb to an overpowering urge to shoot up. The fact that he would become depressed, anxious, and physically ill after going without heroin for even a day or two, made it even more difficult to quit.

1. How would each of the following behavioral theories explain Glenn's increasing heroin and alcohol use?

   a. Operant conditioning theory: ____

   ____

   ____

   ____

b. Opponent process theory: ____

____

____

____

c. Classical conditioning theory: ____

____

____

____

D. The Biological View, 400

1. Genetic Predisposition, 400

1. There are several lines of research that have implicated genetic factors in the development of substance abuse and dependence. Complete this table by summarizing the findings from each area of research.

Research area	Study or studies	Summary of findings
Twin studies	Kaij, 1960	In 54% of cases where one identical twin abused alcohol, so did the other, compared to a 28% concordance rate among fraternal twins.
Adoption studies	Walters, 2002; Cadoret, 1995; Goldstein, 1994	
Genetic linkage	Connor, et al. 2002; Preuss et al., 2007 Blum et al., 1996, 1990	

2. Biochemical Factors, 400

Recent advances in technology have enabled researchers to explore the biochemical underpinnings of drug dependence. The diagram below relates to a line of study that has pinpointed some of the biological processes that produce drug tolerance and withdrawal symptoms.

The normal process . . .	The brain normally produces particular kinds of neurotransmitters, which produce certain reactions (i.e., to sedate, alleviate pain, lift mood, increase alertness)		
When on a drug . . .	A particular drug produces the same reaction as the neurotransmitter, making the neurotransmitter less necessary—excessive and chronic ingestion of the drug causes the brain to produce fewer neurotransmitters		
This leads to . . .	***Tolerance*** As the drug is taken increasingly, the body's production of the corresponding neurotransmitter decreases, leaving the person in need of more of the drug to achieve its initial effects	***and***	***Withdrawal*** Relying on the drug to feel good rather than on neurotransmitters means that discontinuing drug use will lead to a deficient supply of the neurotransmitter for a while; this means the user will feel terrible

1. The diagram on previous page lists neither specific drugs nor specific neurotransmitters. Complete the table below by providing the names of the neurotransmitters that become deficient when a person abuses the identified substance.

Drug(s)	**Neurotransmitter(s)**
Alcohol, benzodiazepines	
Opioids	
Cocaine or amphetamines	
Marijuana	

2. One reason why drugs are so rewarding is that they seem to trigger (either directly or indirectly) the _________________ center, or "_________________ pathway" in the brain, by increasing _________________ activity in those areas of the brain.

3. Some theorists believe that people who abuse drugs may suffer from _________________ _________________ syndrome, which might involve a reward center that is not easily activated by usual events in their lives (so they use drugs to activate it).

V. How are Substance-Related Disorders Treated?, 402–410

A. Psychodynamic Therapies, 402

1. Psychodynamic therapies help clients discover and work through underlying needs and _________________ in order to foster change in their substance-related lifestyles, but research has not found these approaches to be very _________________ .

B. Behavioral Therapies, 402

Match the numbers 1–3 below with the appropriate option from the list a–c below the numbers. Numbers 1–3 are widely used behavioral treatments for substance-related disorders. Options a–c represent examples of these treatments.

1. _____ Aversion therapy.
2. _____ Covert sensitization
3. _____ Contingency management

   a. A man who is alcohol dependent is given a nausea-producing chemical injection at the same time he drinks alcohol.

   b. Whenever she takes a drink, a woman who is alcohol dependent imagines gruesome scenes of the carnage after a terrorist bombing.

   c. A woman addicted to cocaine gets rewards whenever she submits drug-free urine samples to her treatment program manager.

4. In general, behavioral strategies appear to be most effective in treating people who are very _________________ to continue despite the work these strategies require.

C. Cognitive-Behavioral Therapies, 404

1. Complete this exercise that summarizes central steps in **behavioral self-control training (BSCT),** a technique used by clinicians whose aim is to help clients control (but not abstain from) alcohol use.

a. Clients monitor and record certain aspects of their drinking behavior. Name three of these aspects.

____

b. Why is it so important for clients to become aware of the aspects noted above?

____

c. Clients are then taught how to set and recognize ____________ on how much alcohol they will drink to control their ____________ of drinking, and to apply coping strategies in situations that might otherwise lead to drinking.

d. What are the two client characteristics that predict success in BSCT treatment programs?

____

2. Although **relapse-prevention training (RPT)** is similar to BSCT in many respects, RPT teaches clients additional skills. What are these skills?

____

____

D. Biological Treatments, 404

1. **Detoxification** is the ___System___ and medically supervised ___withdrawl___ from a drug.
2. Briefly describe one method or strategy of detoxification.

   ___withdrawn gradually___

3. The relapse rates of people who fail to pursue ___help___ after withdrawal tend to be high.

Antagonistic drugs *are used to avoid a relapse of drug abuse and dependence after a successful withdrawal from drugs.*

4. Antagonist drugs ___Stop___ or ___negate___ the effects of an addictive drug.
5. Complete the following statements regarding various antagonist drugs.

   a. Disulfiram, or ____________, is given to people being treated for alcohol problems and produces a terrible physical reaction when taken with alcohol.

   b. Although narcotic antagonists are sometimes used for people who are dependent on ___narcotics___, they are more often considered too dangerous because they result in very severe ___withdrawl___.

6. Summarize key points in the current debate (pros and cons) over the usefulness of **methadone maintenance programs.**

   Pros: ____

   ____

   ____

   Cons: ____

   ____

   ____

E. Sociocultural Therapies, 407

1. **Alcoholics Anonymous (AA)** was founded in 1935 and today has over 2 million members worldwide. Describe two or three of the features and emphases of AA.

____

____

2. Culture-sensitive treatment programs pay attention to the special pressures faced by people in lower socioeconomic status and ethnic minority groups. Likewise, women might benefit from gender-sensitive treatment programs for several reasons. List two of these reasons.

   a. ____

   ____

   b. ____

   ____

3. Community drug-prevention programs offer education and intervention to people whose lives are affected by substance abuse. Give an example of one strategy that such prevention programs might employ with the following groups.

   a. *Individual:* Provide education about the risks associated with drug use

   b. *Family:* ____

   c. *Peer group:* ____

   d. *Community:* ____

The Media Speaks: In Real Time, Amy Winehouse's Deeper Descent, 408

Read the article in this section regarding Amy Winehouse's alleged drug problems. Reflect on the ways that the era of the Internet and cell phone cameras has affected the public's perceptions of celebrities who abuse alcohol and/or drugs. Do you think images, such as the hidden-camera video of Amy Winehouse supposedly using drugs, glamorize or deglamorize substance abuse in the eyes of the public?

VI. Putting It Together: New Wrinkles to a Familiar Story, 410–411

1. Summarize two things that researchers and clinicians have learned about the causes and treatments of substance-related disorders that have come about as a result of **integrated** efforts to understand these disorders.

   a. ____

   ____

   ____

   b. ____

   ____

   ____

MULTIPLE CHOICE

1. Which of the following is not a characteristic of simple substance abuse?
   a. excessive reliance on a drug
   b. physical dependence on a drug
   c. excessive and chronic use of a drug
   d. the possibility of damage to family and social relationships

2. How long does it take to fully sober up, that is, to get all the alcohol out of your body, after a single beer?
   a. about 1 hour
   b. about 3 hours
   c. the same for a 200-pound man as for a 120-pound woman
   d. it depends on the metabolism of the individual.

3. The legal limit for blood alcohol in the operator of a motor vehicle is .10 in most states. How many cans of beer would a 100-pound female need to consume in an hour to be legally drunk (for purposes of driving)?
   a. a little over 1
   b. a little over 2
   c. a little over 4
   d. at least 4

4. Guessing to fill in memory lapses is a symptom of the condition called
   a. delirium tremens.
   b. alcohol intoxication.
   c. Korsakoff's syndrome.
   d. withdrawal from opioids.

5. Death by heroin overdose is often due to
   a. respiratory failure.
   b. neuronal breakdown.
   c. cirrhosis of the liver.
   d. a drop in blood sugar levels.

6. Which of the following are associated with the action of cocaine?
   a. endorphins and dopamine
   b. GABA and norepinephrine
   c. endorphins and norepinephrine
   d. dopamine, norepinephrine, and serotonin

7. Gina was sitting in her living room when she suddenly began experiencing the same pretty wavy visions as she did in her last trip two years ago. This is an example of
   a. a memory.
   b. a flashback.
   c. LSD psychosis.
   d. a withdrawal symptom.

8. According to psychodynamic theory, substance abuse develops when parents fail to fulfill a child's need for
   a. discipline.
   b. nurturance.
   c. dependence.
   d. independence.

9. Research on the efficacy of psychodynamic therapy for substance use disorders has found it to be
   a. detrimental to patients.
   b. not particularly effective.
   c. more effective than Alcoholics Anonymous.
   d. effective in encouraging alternatives to drug taking.

10. The reason there has been a reawakening of interest in methadone maintenance as a means of managing heroin addiction is
    a. that nothing else seems to work.
    b. fear of AIDS from shared needles.
    c. the development of a new, "less addictive" substitute drug.
    d. the increase in support for such programs because of federal grants.

CHAPTER

13 Sexual Disorders and Gender Identity Disorder

REVIEW EXERCISES

I. Sexual Dysfunctions, 415–428

1. What is the definition of sexual dysfunction given in your textbook?

____

____

2. DSM-IV-TR categorizes sexual dysfunctions according to the **phase of the sexual response cycle** that is most affected by specific dysfunction. The table below will help you to organize basic information about each phase of the sexual response cycle, as well as dysfunctions that occur in each phase. Information on each of the phases and dysfunctions is scattered throughout the first half of the chapter (pages 416–428). As you read material on each of the cycles and associated dysfunctions, come back to this table and fill in the symptoms and prevalence rates of each dysfunction listed.

Phase: Desire	
Phase characteristics:	
Dysfunction name	**Dysfunction symptoms (and prevalence)**
Hypoactive sexual desire:	lack of interest in sex
Sexual aversion:	revulsion, disgust, and fear regarding sex (rare in men, more common in women)
Phase: Excitement	
Phase characteristics:	increased heart rate, muscle tension, blood pressure, and respiration; pelvic vasocongestion leads to male erections and female vaginal lubrication and genital swelling.
Dysfunction name	**Dysfunction symptoms (and prevalence)**
Male erectile disorder:	lack of erection 10 %
Female arousal disorder:	(formerly called frigidity) failure to lubricate and swell (10 percent prevalence rate)
Phase: Orgasm	
Phase characteristics:	
Dysfunction name	**Dysfunction symptoms (and prevalence)**
Rapid, or premature ejaculation:	
Male orgasmic disorder:	inability to reach orgasm despite adequate stimulation (8 percent prevalence rate)
Female orgasmic disorder:	

Note that the resolution phase has no associated disorders.

A. Disorders of Desire, 416

Go back to the table that you have just worked on and fill in symptoms and prevalence rates of each dysfunction associated with the ***desire phase.***

1. In defining **hypoactive sexual desire,** DSM-IV-TR refers to a "deficient" level of sexual desire without specifying what a "deficient" level is. The statements given in boxes in this exercise illustrate some of the problems that can arise from this lack of specificity. Below each boxed statement, see if you can formulate a counterstatement that shows its limitations.

> The average frequency of sex for married couples is two to three times per week, so anything less is "deficient."

a. ____

____

> Frequency of intercourse is a good estimator of sexual desire.

b. ____

____

> When partner A complains that partner B does not want to have sex enough, it is a good indication that partner B has hypoactive sexual desire.

c. ____

____

2. In both men and women, a (high / low / either high or low) level of prolactin, a (high / low / either high or low) level of testosterone, and a (high / low / either high or low) level of estrogen are associated with low sex drive.

3. List three illicit drugs that can interfere with sex drive.

alcohol, cocaine, heroin

4. Complete the following table by giving two examples of each psychological and/or sociocultural factor that could interfere with sex drive or cause sexual aversion.

Psychological or Sociocultural Factors	Examples
Emotional factors	increase in anxiety
Personal attitudes and beliefs	
Psychological disorders	
Situational factors	

Psychological or Sociocultural Factor	Examples
Relationship issues	feeling powerless and very dominated by the other in a relationship
Cultural factors	
Sexual trauma	fears about/aversion to sex

B. Disorders of Excitement, 420

Go back to the table on page 182 of the workbook and fill in symptoms and prevalence rates of each dysfunction associated with the ***excitement phase.***

1. Female Sexual Arousal Disorder, 420

1. Female sexual arousal disorder is usually associated with ______________ disorder, so it will be covered in the section related to the latter disorder *(on page 185 of this workbook).*

2. Male Erectile Disorder, 420

Traditionally, the causes of male erectile disorder were assumed to be either psychological or organic. Currently, clinicians believe that this problem is a result of interacting biological, psychological, and sociocultural factors.

1. ______________ abnormalities—which are abnormalities in the structure of the penis and blood flow through the penis—are more commonly the cause of erectile failure than are hormonal problems.

2. List four factors that could lead to erectile failure related to abnormality in the structure of and blood flow through the penis.

   ____

   ____

3. Complete the following statements related to techniques used to identify causes of erectile failure.

   a. Evaluation of ______________ ______________ ______________ (NPT), or erections during sleep, in a laboratory is useful in assessing physical factors related to erectile problems.

   b. Healthy men typically have two to three hours of erections, during the usual two to five ______________ periods each night.

   c. Abnormal or absent NPT usually indicates some ______________ basis for erectile failure.

4. Certain sociocultural issues such as ______________ loss and extreme ______________ stress are often associated with erectile failure.

5. Two relationship patterns seem to be associated with erectile disorder among men. The first is provided. What is the second pattern?

   a. An aging man (who very naturally requires more intense and direct stimulation to achieve erection) is not provided enough stimulation by his partner.

   b. ____

   ____

Examine this diagram, which depicts a primary psychological mechanism that can result in erectile failure: ***performance anxiety and the spectator role.*** *According to the performance anxiety theory of erectile failure, whatever the initial reason for the erectile failure, the resulting anxious, self-evaluative spectator role becomes the reason for the ongoing problem.*

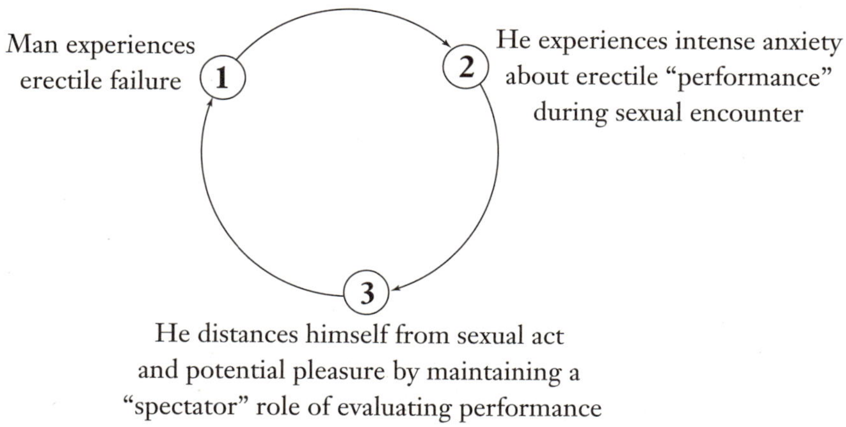

C. Disorders of Orgasm, 422

Go back to the table on page 182 of the workbook and fill in symptoms and prevalence rates of each dysfunction associated with the ***orgasm phase.***

1. Rapid, or Premature, Ejaculation, 422

1. Young men who are sexually ____________, and who have not learned to slow down and control their ____________, appear to be most prone to premature ejaculation.
2. List three other factors that seem to be related to premature ejaculation among men.

   ____

   ____

   ____
3. List three theories that have been put forward as biological explanations for rapid ejaculation.

   a. ______________________________

   b. ______________________________

   c. ______________________________

2. Male Orgasmic Disorder, 424

1. List (a) three biological factors and (b) three psychological factors that can inhibit ejaculation—i.e., contribute to *male orgasmic disorder*—among men.

   a. ______________________________

   ____

   ____

   b. ______________________________

   ____

3. Female Orgasmic Disorder, 424

1. Studies indicate that women who are more sexually ________________ and who feel comfortable ________________ have more frequent orgasms.
2. Whereas early ________________ theorists held that the failure to achieve orgasm from vaginal intercourse alone was an indication of pathology in women, contemporary clinicians and researchers agree that not only is orgasm *not* a criterion of ________________ sexual functioning, but that women who rely on stimulation of the ________________ to reach orgasm are completely normal and healthy.
3. A variety of biological causes can affect arousal and orgasm among women. Describe examples in each of the three categories listed below:
   a. physical illness or injury: ________________________________
   b. postmenopausal changes: ________________________________
   c. drugs and medications: ________________________________
4. In one study, several factors that were associated with a lack of orgasm among women emerged, including memories of an unhappy childhood and loss of a parent during childhood. List three factors that seem to be *positively* related to orgasm among women.
   a. ________________________________
   b. ________________________________
   c. ________________________________
5. The traditional explanation for the causes of female arousal and orgasmic dysfunction held that these difficulties result from cultural messages that demand women suppress and deny their ________________ .
6. Describe two characteristics of the upbringing of many women with arousal and orgasmic problems that lend support to the theory described above.
   ____
   ____
7. What is the flaw in the theory described above? ________________________________
   ____
8. Many women who were victims of ________________ suffer from arousal and orgasm dysfunction.

D. Disorders of Sexual Pain, 426

Note that sexual pain disorders are not associated with a particular phase in the sexual response cycle.

1. Complete the following statements regarding **vaginismus.**
   a. In this condition, the ________________ around the vagina involuntarily ________________ to prevent penile penetration.
   b. Most clinicians agree that it is a ________________ fear response that is triggered by the fear that vaginal penetration will be ________________ and damaging.
2. List three psychological factors that can lead to the fears described above.
   ____
   ____
3. List three biological factors that might be associated with vaginismus.

____

____

4. Describe the symptoms of **dyspareunia.**

____

____

5. List four causes of dyspareunia.

   a. _______________

   b. _______________

   c. _______________

   d. _______________

6. Psychogenic dyspareunia usually reflects an underlying condition of _______________ _______________ _______________.

II. Treatments for Sexual Dysfunctions, 428–435

A. What Are the General Features of Sex Therapy?, 428

In 1970, Masters and Johnson published the book Human Sexual Inadequacy. *It described a revolutionary approach to the treatment of sexual dysfunction that came to be called "sex therapy." Although the approach has been modified, the original components remain intact. In some ways, you can think of this approach as a generic program, and not necessarily focused on any one dysfunction.*

1. This exercise calls for a summary of each component of modern sex therapy. For each component, be sure to include a brief statement regarding the specific issues being addressed and the therapist tasks and/or techniques. The first is done for you.

Component 1

Assessment and conceptualization of the problem

a. Understanding past and current factors that might have caused or maintain the patient's problem is the emphasis. Along with a thorough medical examination, the therapist gathers information on the patient's "sex history" through in-depth interviews and tests.

Component 2

Mutual responsibility

b. _______________

____

____

Component 3

Education about sexuality

c. _______________

____

____

Component 4

Attitude change

d. ______________________________

Component 5

Elimination of performance anxiety and the spectator role

e. ______________________________

Component 6

Increase sexual communication skills

f. ______________________________

Component 7

Change destructive lifestyles and interactions

g. ______________________________

Component 8

Address physical and medical factors

h. ______________________________

Be sure to read A Closer Look: Common Sex-Role Myths, on textbook page 427. The myths about sexuality that are discussed pervade our culture in the form of media messages, themes in books and movies, and generational legacies of unchallenged stereotypes of men and women. Try to pick out the myths that you may have heard—or even that you may have believed in the past to the detriment of an intimate relationship. You might also want to consider how society can move beyond these stereotypes and their destructive power on relationships.

B. What Techniques Are Applied to Particular Dysfunctions?, 431

1. Clinicians employ several kinds of strategies and specific interventions to treat clients with *hypoactive sexual desire* and *sexual aversion.* In the table below, describe the purpose of each set of strategies, then write a specific example of the technique.

Strategy	Purpose	Specific Techniques
Affectual awareness	Uncover negative feelings about sex	
Self-instruction training		
Behavioral approach		
Approach for sexual aversion due to assault	Work through feelings associated with trauma	

2. Complete the following descriptions of techniques used to treat *erectile disorder.*
   a. During ________________ focus exercises, the *tease technique* is taught. One partner ________________ the other until he achieves an erection, then stops when he loses his erection.
   b. The recent development of the popular drug ________________ (sildenafil) increases blood flow to the penis within ________________ hour of ingestion, leading to erection.
   c. The ________________ ________________ device (VED) is a hollow cylinder that is placed over the penis; when air is pumped out of the cylinder, ________________ is drawn into the penis, causing an erection.
   d. A penile ________________ is a semi-rigid rod made of rubber and wire or an inflatable hollow cylinder that is implanted into the patient's penis. This approach is now extremely rare.
3. Describe one technique used in the treatment of *male orgasmic disorder.*

   ____

   ____

4. In one treatment for *rapid ejaculation,* the stop-start or ________________ procedure gradually increases the man's ejaculation threshold through repeated stimulation to ________________, but not to ejaculation.
5. The primary components of treatment for *female arousal and orgasm dysfunction* emphasize ________________, enhancement of body ________________, and directed masturbation training.
6. Complete the statements about directed masturbation training's success rates.
   a. Over 90 percent of women learn to have orgasms during masturbation.
   b. Eighty percent of women learn to have orgasms . . .

   ____

   c. Thirty percent of women learn to have orgasms . . .

   ____

7. Sex therapists emphasize that women who are able to reach orgasm in some, but not all, situations should be reassured that they are ________________ and probably need ________________ rather than treatment.

8. Complete the following statements regarding the treatment of *vaginismus.*
   a. Women who suffer from vaginismus learn to contract and relax their ________________ muscles at will until they have gained ________________ control over them.
   b. The vaginal insertion of gradually larger ________________ helps these women overcome their fear of ________________ .
   c. Most women treated are able to have pain-free intercourse.

9. What strategies can be recommended by a sex therapist when a medical examination reveals that a patient's *dyspareunia* is caused by scars or lesions?

   ____

C. What Are the Current Trends in Sex Therapy?, 434

1. Complete the following list of new directions in sex therapy:
   a. Partners who ________________________ but are not married are regularly treated.
   b. Sexual dysfunctions that arise from psychological disorders such as ________________ , mania, and schizophrenia are treated.
   c. Sex therapists are more likely to provide treatment to clients with severe ________________ ________________ , the elderly, the mentally ill, or the physically ________________ .
   d. People with a ________________ orientation, those with no ongoing sex partner, and people with sexual ________________ are also provided sex therapy.

III. Paraphilias, 435–443

1. According to DSM-IV-TR criteria, to be diagnosed with a paraphilia, a person must:
   a. have recurrent, intense sexual urges and sexually arousing fantasies involving either ________________ objects, children, ________________ adults, or experiences of suffering or ________________ .
   b. have experienced these urges, fantasies, or behaviors for at least 6 months.

2. Relatively few men (and almost no women) are ever formally diagnosed with a paraphilic disorder. So why do clinicians suspect that the disorder is actually quite prevalent?

   ____

3. Complete the following chart that summarizes the descriptions, causes, and treatments for the paraphilias.

Fetishism	
Description	recurrent, intense sexual urges that involve the use of nonliving objects (e.g., women's undergarments, shoes) that may be smelled or touched
Causes	*psychodynamic:* these are defense mechanisms against anxiety of normal sexual contact; *behavioral:* acquired through classical conditioning

Treatment	*behavioral:* aversion therapy, covert sensitization, masturbatory satiation (which is designed to produce boredom in clients who are told to masturbate for long durations to fetishistic fantasies), and orgasmic reorientation (teaching more appropriate sexual responses)
Transvestic Fetishism (Transvestism, Cross-Dressing)	
Description	those with disorder (almost exclusively heterosexual males) have a recurrent need to dress in clothes of the opposite sex in order to become sexually aroused
Causes	*behavioral:* as children, those with the disorder were operantly conditioned, or reinforced, for cross-dressing
Treatment	no specific treatment described in textbook
Exhibitionism	
Description	
Causes	no specific cause described in textbook; individuals act on exhibitionistic urges when they have free time or are under stress.
Treatment	
Voyeurism	
Description	recurrent and intense sexual urges to spy on people as they undress or have sex; usually begins before age 15 and is chronic
Causes	
Treatment	no specific strategies described in textbook; however, typical strategies used for treatment of paraphilias could be applied (e.g., covert sensitization, masturbatory satiation, orgasmic reorientation)
Frotteurism	
Description	
Causes	no specific cause described in textbook; however frotteurism frequently develops after observing another engage in similar behaviors.
Treatment	no specific treatments described in textbook; usually disappears after the age of 25
Pedophilia	
Description	

Causes	
Treatment	*behavioral:* orgasmic reorientation, in which clients are conditioned to become sexually aroused by other stimuli; aversion therapy; and masturbatory satiation; *cognitive-behavioral:* relapse prevention training focuses on identifying triggering situations and the development of healthier coping strategies
Sexual Masochism	
Description	recurrent sexual urges and fantasies that involve being made to suffer (e.g., through pain, humiliation)
Causes	
Treatment	no specific treatments described in textbook
Sexual Sadism	
Description	
Causes	*behavioral:* as children, the sexually sadistic might have been classically conditioned to become aroused when inflicting pain, or may have seen models engaging in sexual sadism; *cognitive, psychodynamic:* may feel sexually inadequate and insecure; *biological:* evidence of abnormal endocrine functioning
Treatment	aversion therapy, relapse prevention training

4. Briefly explain why some clinicians argue that, except when people are hurt by them, many paraphilic behaviors should not be considered disorders at all.

____

____

____

IV. Gender Identity Disorder, 443–449

1. In ________________, people feel that they have been assigned the wrong sex.
2. The ratio of males to females with this disorder is _____ to 1.
3. List some of the characteristics of people who have gender identity disorder.

____

____

____

4. People with gender identity disorder do not have ________________ ________________. In other words, they do not cross-dress in order to achieve sexual arousal.

5. Many adults with this disorder had a gender identity disorder as children, but most children with a gender identity disorder . . .

   ____

6. Findings of a study on the autopsied brains of six people who changed their sex from male to female suggest that biological factors may play a role in gender identity disorder. Complete the following statements related to this study.

   a. Compared to a control group of autopsied brains of "normal" males, the autopsied brains of six males with gender identity disorder had cells in the ______________ called the *bed nucleus of stria terminalis* (BST) that were only ______________ as large as in the control group of male brains.

   b. In effect, the brains of men with gender identity disorder seem to have "______________-sized" BST cells.

   c. Although the function of human BST cells is not known, researchers have discovered that in rats, BST cells help control ______________ behavior.

Although hormone therapy and psychotherapy are effective in helping many with gender identity disorder lead satisfying lives that reflect their "true" gender role, some such individuals undergo sex-reassignment surgery. Approximately 6,000 such surgeries have been performed in the United States. Sex-reassignment surgery is a highly controversial procedure, and research has not been able to settle the debate regarding its long-term effectiveness.

7. Complete the following statements regarding sex-reassignment procedures.

   a. Surgery is preceded by one or two years of ______________ therapy.

   b. For men, the surgery consists of ______________ of the penis, creation of an artificial ______________, and plastic surgery.

   c. For women, the surgery consists of bilateral ______________, hysterectomy, and sometimes ______________ (the surgical creation of a functioning penis) or the implantation of a silicone prosthesis.

8. The long-term psychological outcome of sex-reassignment surgery is not well established. Some believe sex-reassignment surgery is a "humane solution," whereas others view it as a "drastic nonsolution." What do you think?

   ____

   ____

   ____

   ____

   ____

   ____

9. Briefly define the three patterns of gender dysphoria identified by Richard Carroll.

   a. female-to-male gender dysphoria ______________________________

      ____

   b. male-to-female gender dysphoria: androphilic type ______________________________

      ____

   c. male-to-female gender dysphoria: autogynephilic type ______________________________

      ____

The Media Speaks: Battling a Culture of Shame, 448

Read the article about Lena, who was formerly a man and is now living as a woman. Reflect on Lena's description of the prejudice those with gender identity disorder encounter, as well as the public's lack of knowledge about the condition. How does Lena's experience relate to the controversy over whether gender identity disorder should be classified as a disorder?

V. Putting It Together: A Private Topic Draws Public Attention, 449

1. Describe three pieces of knowledge, or insight, with regard to the explanation and treatment of sexual disorders that have emerged over the last three decades.

   a. ______________________________

   ____

   b. ______________________________

   ____

   c. ______________________________

   ____

MULTIPLE CHOICE

1. Sexual dysfunction can occur during all of the following phases except
   a. desire.
   b. orgasm.
   c. arousal.
   d. resolution.

2. Hypoactive sexual disorder is a disorder of which phase of the sexual response cycle?
   a. excitement phase
   b. orgasm phase
   c. resolution phase
   d. desire phase

3. Which of the following drugs increases sexual drive at a low level and decreases it at higher levels?
   a. alcohol
   b. antidepressants
   c. antianxiety drugs
   d. antipsychotic drugs

4. Samuel experienced a period of high stress during which he was unable to perform sexually. Thereafter, he was detached and apprehensive during sexual activity and unable to perform. Samuel is displaying
   a. sexual frustration.
   b. performance anxiety.
   c. hypoactive sexual desire.
   d. organically induced male erectile disorder.

5. In a study of female orgasm, women who had higher rates of orgasm
   a. were more aggressive than other women.
   b. behaved in a stereotypically "feminine" way.
   c. had more affectionate parents than other women.
   d. were more passive in their behavior than other women.

6. A major component of sex therapy is
   a. hormone therapy.
   b. elimination of performance anxiety.
   c. relieving depression about the symptoms.
   d. identifying who is responsible for the problem.

7. Paraphiliacs treated by clinicians are usually
   a. male.
   b. young.
   c. female.
   d. ordered into treatment by the court.

8. During which period does frotteurism typically develop?
   a. adolescence
   b. early adulthood
   c. middle adulthood
   d. late adulthood

9. Which of the following used to be, but is no longer, considered a sexual disorder?
   a. transvestism
   b. sexual masochism
   c. homosexuality
   d. pedophilia

10. One characteristic of people with gender identity disorder is that they often feel
    a. heterosexuality is abnormal.
    b. angry and exploited by others.
    c. they were born the wrong sex.
    d. they underwent a sex-change operation during childhood.

CHAPTER

14 Schizophrenia

CHAPTER OUTLINE

REVIEW EXERCISES

The following items cover chapter introductory material on pages 453–454.

1. In 1911, the Swiss psychiatrist Eugen ________________ first used the term **schizophrenia** (meaning ________________ ________________) to describe this group of disorders.
2. Although the term *schizophrenia* is often misused for multiple personality disorder, it actually denotes these three points:

   a. a ________________ of thought processes,

   b. a split between ________________ and ________________, and

   c. a withdrawal from ________________ .

3. Approximately _____ percent of the world's population meets DSM-IV-TR criteria for schizophrenia.

4. Figure 14–1 on page 454 illustrates the fact that people in lower socioeconomic groups are more likely to suffer from schizophrenia than wealthier groups. Complete this list of possible reasons for this fact.

   a. The stress of _______________ could lead to schizophrenia.

   b. Schizophrenia could cause people to:

   ____

   ____

5. For this exercise, complete the paragraph describing the prevalence of schizophrenia by drawing a line through the incorrect option within each set of parentheses.

   Schizophrenia prevalence rates are higher among people in (lower/higher) socioeconomic groups. Neither gender appears to be at higher risk, but the age of onset is earlier among (men/women). Although divorced people have (higher/lower) rates than either married or single people, the exact reasons for this are not clear.

I. The Clinical Picture of Schizophrenia, 454–464

1. DSM-IV-TR classifies schizophrenia as a single disorder with different "faces." A number of clinicians hold a contrary view. Describe that view.

   ____

   ____

A. What Are the Symptoms of Schizophrenia?, 456

Symptoms of schizophrenia can be grouped into three categories: positive symptoms, so named because they represent bizarre "additions" to or "excesses" of normal behavior; negative symptoms that represent "deficits" of normal behavior; and psychomotor symptoms that reflect unusual or bizarre motor behaviors.

Exercises in this subsection are broken down into one part for each of the three categories of symptoms. Within these category parts, exercises are broken down further into specific symptoms.

1. Positive Symptoms, 457

a. Delusions, 457

1. Delusions are ideas that schizophrenic people believe fervently, but that have no basis in _______________ .

2. Complete this exercise by describing the type of delusion and then by matching the example that best illustrates each type.

Type of delusion	Description	Example
Persecution	irrational belief that one is being threatened, plotted against, spied upon, etc.	
Reference		
Grandeur		
Control		

Examples:

a. Lowell eats at a Chinese restaurant every day. At the end of each meal, he reverently reads the message in the fortune cookie and carefully writes it down in a notebook. He believes that the messages are written specifically for him.

b. [Excerpt from a letter to a newspaper] Beware of the plot of destruction orchestrated by so-called door-to-door salesmen. They come to my home 20 or 100 times a day, always snooping around and wanting to kill me. They say they are selling things, but they lie! They carry guns and knives and explosives. Beware! You could be the next victim!

c. Over the past two years, Lea has become convinced that thoughts are being put in her brain by alien life forms conducting mind-control experiments. Lately she has become certain that the aliens want her to disguise herself as Madonna and appear on television.

d. While watching the national college basketball championship on television, Margaret becomes convinced that she is determining the outcome of the game by manipulating the players with her mind.

b. *Disorganized Thinking and Speech, 458*

3. Many people with schizophrenia display positive formal ________________ disorders that are manifested in the form of peculiar ________________ and illogical patterns of thinking.

Match the numbers 4–7 below with the appropriate option from the list a–d below the numbers.

4. _____ loose associations
5. _____ neologisms
6. _____ perseveration
7. _____ clang

a. Made-up words that have meaning only to the person using them
b. Using rhyme as a guide to formulating thoughts and statements
c. Repeating words and statements over and over again
d. Rapidly shifting from one topic to another, making inconsequential and incoherent statements, and apparently believing them to make sense (also called derailment)

c. *Heightened Perceptions and Hallucinations, 459*

8. People with schizophrenia often report a heightened sensitivity to ________________ and ________________, making it difficult for these individuals to attend to relevant stimuli.

9. One study demonstrated that, compared to nonschizophrenic subjects, subjects with schizophrenia were less able to pick out a target ________________ when they listened to a recording that also contained distracting ________________ speech.

10. Attention problems in people with schizophrenia may be related to smooth ________________ eye movement (the ability to keep one's head still and track a moving object back and forth with one's eyes.

11. Define the term **hallucination.**

____

12. ________________ hallucinations are the most common form of hallucination and may be experienced as voices talking, or giving ________________ or warnings.

13. Research has suggested that people with schizophrenia actually "hear" sounds that they attribute to ________________ sources; the area of the brain that is most active during an auditory hallucination is ________________ area (the area associated with speech production).

Match the numbers 14–19, representing the types of hallucinations, with the example from letters a–f that best illustrates each type of hallucination.

14. _____ auditory
15. _____ tactile
16. _____ somatic
17. _____ visual
18. _____ gustatory
19. _____ olfactory

a. While on a cross-country flight, Norman starts to see his fellow passengers as grotesque, green-colored monsters.

b. Lil, an office worker, quits her job when she can no longer bear the "stench of death" that she can smell coming from her vent. No one else can smell the odor.

c. While at the mental health clinic, Phil tells the counselor taking information from him that she will have to get rid of her wristwatch if she wants him to be able to answer the questions. "It's ticking so loud that I can't hear your voice," he shouts.

d. Much to the consternation of her family and doctor, Bernadine insists against all medical evidence to the contrary that she has "grapefruit-sized" tumors throughout her body.

e. Roger, a guest at a nice hotel, calls the front desk to say that his room is "crawling with spiders." When the hotel investigates and finds no spiders, Roger contends that he could feel the spiders running over his body all night long.

f. At her nephew's wedding, Fay stands by the punch bowl and warns the other guests not to drink the punch because she tasted poison in it.

d. Inappropriate Affect, 461

20. In some cases, inappropriate affect may come about as a result of another positive symptom of schizophrenia. Give one explanation for this example:

Jerry, a man with schizophrenia, shows extreme anger at the same time he wins $500 playing the state lottery.

____

____

2. Negative Symptoms, 461

a. Poverty of Speech, 462

1. Complete these exercises relating to the forms of poverty of speech.

a. **Alogia** is a reduction in ________________ and ________________ of speech characterized by brief and meaningless statements.

b. After reading the diary entry of Vaslav Nijinsky on page 462 of the text, identify one statement that best illustrates alogia, in your opinion.

____

____

____

b. Blunted and Flat Affect, 462

2. What is the difference between blunted affect and flat affect?

____

3. Blunted or flat affect may reflect ________________, a general lack of pleasure and enjoyment.

c. Loss of Volition, 462

4. Schizophrenic people who display **avolition,** or ________________, feel drained of energy and ________________ in normal goals, are unable to initiate or complete a normal course of action, and commonly also display ________________ (conflicting feelings) about most things.

d. Social Withdrawal, 462

5. Schizophrenic people withdraw from the "real" external world and become preoccupied with their own ________________ and ________________, leading to deterioration in social skills.

3. Psychomotor Symptoms, 462

1. The extreme forms of the *psychomotor symptoms* of schizophrenia are collectively known as **catatonia.** Complete this table by providing the names of the types of catatonia being described.

Type of Catatonia	Description
	assuming awkward, bizarre positions for long periods of time
	indefinitely maintaining postures into which they have been placed by someone else
	being totally unaware of and unresponsive to the external world, remaining motionless and silent for long stretches of time
	moving excitedly, sometimes with wild waving of arms and legs
	remaining in an unmoving, upright posture for hours and resisting efforts to be moved

B. What Is the Course of Schizophrenia?, 463

Schizophrenia usually emerges between the late teens and mid-30s. The most typical course the disorder follows is to go through three distinct phases. Study this diagram, which shows these phases and their characteristics.

The Prodromal Phase

- Schizophrenic symptoms are not yet prominent
- The person has begun to deteriorate from previous levels of functioning

The Active Phase

- Schizophrenic symptoms become prominent
- In some instances, the active phase is triggered by stress in the person's life

The Residual Phase

- A return to the prodromal level of functioning
- The florid symptoms of the active phase recede
- Many individuals remain in a general state of decline

1. While approximately _____ percent of schizophrenic patients recover completely, the majority shows signs of residual _______________ .

2. The several characteristics that are predictive of recovery in schizophrenic patients include good premorbid functioning. List two other characteristics.

____

C. Diagnosing Schizophrenia, 463

1. Complete these two general DSM-IV-TR diagnostic criteria for schizophrenia.

   a. Signs of schizophrenia present for at least _____ months.

   b. Deterioration from previous levels of functioning in _______________ , _______________ relations, and self-care.

2. Like Kraepelin, the DSM-IV-TR categorizes types of schizophrenia based on descriptions of patients' behaviors. In this table, write key words that will help you remember the central features of each type of disorder. Then, match each type with the example that best illustrates it.

Category	Key Words for Central Factors	Example
Disorganized		
Catatonic		
Paranoid		
Undifferentiated		
Residual		

Examples:

a. Daniel lost his job as a corporate attorney about a year ago, which seemed to trigger an intense phase of schizophrenic symptoms. Most of them have passed, but Daniel no longer seems to show much emotion about anything.

b. Jenny excitedly waves her arms about wildly in an attempt to fight off the "evil spirits" who tell her they are going to hurt her.

c. Albert lives in a large city where he is homeless. He spends most days sitting in a small park, speaking to no one, and quietly laughing and grimacing as thousands of people walk past him.

d. Bob is convinced that government agents are trying to kill him because President Kennedy has "spoken" to him, telling Bob the truth about his assassination.

e. Ellen is a 45-year-old ex-teacher, who had to quit her job when her schizophrenic symptoms took over her life. She can usually be found sitting in her kitchen, where she often will barely move a muscle for hours at a time.

3. List the major characteristics for each of the two types of schizophrenia many researchers believe exist.

   a. Type I schizophrenia: ______________________________

   b. Type II schizophrenia: ______________________________

4. What are the major differences that have been observed between the course of Type I schizophrenia and the course of Type II schizophrenia?

   ____

   ____

II. How Do Theorists Explain Schizophrenia?, 464–477

A. Biological Views, 464

Coverage of this subsection is broken down into its three parts—genetic factors, biochemical abnormalities, and abnormal brain structure.

1. Genetic Factors, 464

1. Although it seems clear that the risk of developing schizophrenia is significantly greater in people who are closely related to schizophrenic probands, the trend does not (in itself) establish a genetic basis for the disorder. Why?

   ____

   ____

2. If genetic factors were at work in schizophrenia, ______________ twins would have a higher concordance rate for the disorder than ______________ twins.

3. What have studies shown with regard to the fact stated above in item 2?

   ____

   ____

4. Other than genetic factors, what is one biological explanation for the concordance patterns found by researchers studying schizophrenia among identical and fraternal twins?

   ____

   ____

   ____

5. In adoption studies, the prevalence of schizophrenic symptoms in both the biological and the adoptive relatives of people with schizophrenia (who were adopted away from their biological parents in infancy) is compared. Complete the following statements related to adoption studies.

   a. ______________ influences would be indicated when *adoptive* relatives have symptoms of schizophrenia, whereas ______________ influences would be suggested when *biological* relatives have symptoms of schizophrenia.

   b. In adoption studies, ______________ relatives of people with schizophrenia are more likely to display symptoms than ______________ relatives.

6. Complete the following information relating to the adoption studies by Seymour Kety et al., which provided support for the genetic view of schizophrenia.

   a. *Subjects:* 33 people with schizophrenia who had been adopted and:

____

____

b. *Method:* Researchers identified 365 biological and adoptive relatives of both the schizophrenic and the "normal" subjects. Relatives were divided into four groups (see below). Each relative was interviewed and evaluated by psychiatrists who did not know from which groups subjects came.

c. *Results:* Based on the evaluations, 37 of the relatives received a diagnosis of either "definite schizophrenia " or "uncertain schizophrenia." The table below shows the percentage of relatives from each group who received one of these diagnoses. (Finish labeling the diagnoses according to the four groups).

	"Schizophrenic" Diagnosis	**"Normal"**
____________ relative	14%	3.4%
____________ relative	2.7%	5.5%

7. Researchers using *genetic linkage* and *molecular biology* strategies have identified possible gene defects on a number of chromosomes that could predispose people to develop schizophrenia. In fact, various studies have identified 9 different chromosomes that show these defects. What are three possible reasons for these varied findings?

a. ____

____

b. ____

____

c. ____

____

A Closer Look: Postpartum Psychosis: The Case of Andrea Yates, 468

1. Like Andrea Yates, 1 to 2 in _________ mothers who have recently given birth experience postpartum psychosis, although only a small fraction of those who suffer this disorder actually harm their children.
2. Name some symptoms of postpartum psychosis.

____

____

3. *Reflect on the case of Andrea Yates. In addition to the blame assigned to Yates, her husband, her doctors, and her insurers have all come in for criticism by some for their handling of her postpartum psychosis before she drowned her five children. Who or what do you think most deserves the criticism and for what reasons?*

2. Biochemical Abnormalities, 466

The first of the two distinct biological views of the development of schizophrenia centers on the ***dopamine hypothesis.*** *It states that in schizophrenia, neurons that use the neurotransmitter dopamine fire too often and thus transmit too many messages, leading to symptoms of the disorder. Researchers formulated this hypothesis after observing some interesting effects of antipsychotic medications known as* ***phenothiazines.***

Researchers identified the phenothiazines in the 1950s and used them to treat schizophrenia—Why they were effective was not known

↓

Clinicians noticed that patients with schizophrenia using phenothiazines had the same kind of muscle tremors as patients with Parkinson's disease

↓

Clues that Linked Schizophrenia to Dopamine Activity

Researchers knew that Parkinson's patients have low levels of dopamine, which causes their tremors	It was also known that L-dopa, a precursor of dopamine, was helpful in treating Parkinson's because it raised dopamine levels
↓	↓

As a Result, Two Hypotheses Were Formed

If antipsychotic drugs generate symptoms of Parkinson's while alleviating schizophrenia, then the drugs must reduce dopamine activity	If increasing dopamine activity too much creates symptoms of schizophrenia in Parkinson's patients, then schizophrenia must be related to excessive dopamine activity.

1. Amphetamines induce or exacerbate psychotic symptoms (called "amphetamine psychosis") because they ________________ dopamine activity in the brain.
2. Antipsychotic drugs are dopamine ________________ , which means that they bind to dopamine receptors (especially *D-2 receptors*), prevent dopamine from binding to those receptor sites, and thus prevent dopaminergic neurons from ________________ .
3. People with schizophrenia might have a ________________ than usual number of dopamine (especially D-2) receptors, which would lead to dopamine overactivity in the brains of those individuals.
4. The dopamine hypothesis has been challenged by the discovery that a new group of drugs, called ________________ antipsychotics, are even more effective than the traditional drugs. These drugs, however, bind to D-2 receptors *and* to receptor sites for ________________ and other neurotransmitters.
5. A second challenge to the dopamine hypothesis is that it appears to contribute to the ________________ symptoms of schizophrenia, but not to the ________________ symptoms of schizophrenia.

3. Abnormal Brain Structure, 469

The second distinct biological view of the cause of schizophrenia relates to abnormal brain structure. It has been strengthened by research in the last decade that has linked schizophrenia, particularly cases dominated by negative symptoms, with specific structural abnormalities in the brain.

1. Researchers have found that many people with schizophrenia have enlarged ________________ .
2. List characteristics of people with schizophrenia who have this brain abnormality.

   ____

   ____

3. Other significant abnormalities found in people with schizophrenia are reduced or heightened ________________ ________________ in their brains, smaller ________________ and ________________ lobes, and smaller amounts of cortical gray matter.

4. Viral Problems, 470

1. Complete the list of factors that have been linked to the brain abnormalities found in people with schizophrenia.
   a. Genetic factors
   b. Poor ______________
   c. ______________ development
   d. ______________ complications
   e. ______________ reactions
   f. toxins
2. According to the viral theory of schizophrenia, symptoms come about as a result of a virus entering the brain during the ______________ period and remain latent until puberty or young adulthood, when it is activated by ______________ changes or another viral infection.
3. Summarize the evidence for the viral theory of schizophrenia related to:
   a. season of birth

   ____

   ____

   b. fingerprints

   ____

   ____

   c. viral exposure and antibodies

   ____

   ____

B. Psychological Views, 471

In this subsection, each of the leading psychological theories of schizophrenia is addressed in its own part.

1. The Psychodynamic Explanation, 471

1. Complete these statements regarding Freud's theory of the development of schizophrenia.
   a. Regression, the first part of the two-part process, is when a person regresses to a pre-ego state of primary ______________, resulting in symptoms such as neologisms, loose associations, and delusions of grandeur.
   b. During the second part of the process, the person attempts to regain ego control and establish contact with ______________; symptoms representing an unconscious attempt to substitute for a lost sense of reality arise, such as ______________ ______________.
2. Although unsupported by empirical evidence, Fromm-Reichmann's theory suggests that so-called ______________ (schizophrenia-causing) mothers have certain personality characteristics that "set the stage" for the development of schizophrenia in their children.
3. Below, list some of the characteristics of these mothers.

   ____

   ____

2. The Behavioral View, 472

1. Fill in the missing information in this diagram depicting the behavioral view of schizophrenia that emphasizes the key role of operant conditioning.

Unusual circumstances, or socially inadequate individuals, prevent a person from being reinforced for paying attention to social cues in his or her environment.	→	As a result, the person stops attending to normal social cues and instead focuses on other, often irrelevant cues, such as _______________ _______________	→	As the person attends more and more to the irrelevant cues, his or her responses become increasingly more bizarre Such responses in turn elicit: _______________ _______________ _______________

3. The Cognitive View, 472

Study the diagram below, which depicts the cognitive explanations of schizophrenia.

Biological abnormalities result in schizophrenic symptoms, such as visual and auditory hallucinations

↓

The schizophrenic person turns to others in an attempt to understand his or her new sensory experiences

↓

When others deny the existence of the experiences, the schizophrenic person soon believes that the truth is being hidden and rejects all feedback from others

↓

Resulting in Delusional Thinking

The schizophrenic person then develops delusional beliefs that he or she is being manipulated or persecuted

1. Although people with schizophrenia do experience sensory and perceptual problems, research has failed to support the idea that the misinterpretation of these problems _______________ the syndrome of schizophrenia.

C. Sociocultural Views, 473

1. Multicultural Factors, 473

1. Prevalence rates of schizophrenia seem to differ among different racial and ethnic groups. For example, the rate of schizophrenia among African Americans is significantly __________ than the rate of schizophrenia among white Americans.

2. Identify three possible reasons for the difference in prevalence noted in question 1.

   a. ____

   ____

   b. ____

____

c. ____

____

3. According to a major study conducted by the World Health Organization, patients with schizophrenia living in developing countries have ________________ recovery rates than patients with schizophrenia living in Western and developed countries.
4. Identify two explanations that have been put forward for the disparity in recovery rates noted in question 3.

   a. ____

   b. ____

2. Social Labeling, 474

1. Sociocultural theorists believe that the ________________ itself causes many of the features of schizophrenia.
2. Once the label is assigned, it becomes a "________________ ________________ prophecy," that leads to schizophrenic symptoms.

You may find it useful to go back and study the coverage related to the Rosenhan (1973) study in Chapter 3, which is discussed again in this subsection.

3. Family Dysfunctioning, 475

Bateson's ***double-bind hypothesis*** *suggests that children respond to their parents' mutually contradictory messages by developing schizophrenic symptoms. Read this case study relating to this hypothesis, then complete the exercise following it.*

Case Study

Pamela is the 10-year-old daughter of divorced parents who are constantly in conflict with each other, particularly concerning visitation issues. Here is an example of a typical interaction between Pamela and her parents:

Mother: (sarcastically) Pamela, you know it is very important that you go to your father's this weekend, because it was part of our agreement.

Pamela: Do you want me to stay with you this weekend? I could call him . . .

Mother: No, I want you to go. I'll be fine here by myself. (crosses arms, facial expression of anger)

Pamela: Well . . . okay. Are you sure?

Mother: Yes, of course I'm sure. (Mother hugs Pamela and begins to cry)

Pamela then goes to her room and sits on her bed. She feels confused and paralyzed. Should she go to her father's house and risk hurting her mother? However, her mother said she wanted her to go. Pamela knows that if she doesn't go, her father will be angry with her.

1. Restate (a) the mother's primary communication and (b) her metacommunication.

   a. ____

   b. ____

2. What does research indicate about the validity of the double-bind hypothesis?

____

3. The study of families of schizophrenic people have yielded three trends that support some aspects of the family systems view. One is that parents of schizophrenic people display more conflict. List the other two.

   a. _______________

   b. _______________

4. Researchers have found that people with schizophrenia are four times more likely to relapse if they live in a family characterized by *high expressed emotion* compared to those who live in families with low expressed emotion. Describe features of the former types of family below.

____

____

____

4. R. D. Laing's View, 476

1. R. D. Laing's theory asserts that we find meaning in our lives by finding our true selves, which is difficult because society requires us to develop "false selves" to meet the demands and expectations of others. Complete the following questions regarding Laing's conceptualization of schizophrenia.

   a. Because they cannot meet the needs of their families and society, some people withdraw into an inner search for strength and purpose.

   b. According to Laing, what would happen if these people were left to themselves?

   ____

   c. However, society responds by telling these people they are _______________ .

   d. Ultimately, these individuals assume the role of patient and submit to treatments that actually produce more symptoms.

III. Putting It Together: Psychological and Sociocultural Models Lag Behind, 477–478

1. In what way has the last 30 years of research answered the question, Is schizophrenia a single disorder with many "faces"?

____

____

MULTIPLE CHOICE

1. The term *dementia preaecox*, what we now call schizophrenia, was coined by
   a. Eugen Bleuler.
   b. Emil Kraepelin.
   c. Benedict Morel.
   d. Sigmund Freud.

2. Approximately _____ percent of people worldwide suffer from schizophrenia.
   a. 1
   b. 5
   c. 10
   d. 25

3. Harry believes that Martians have infiltrated the CIA. This is an example of a(n):
   a. loose association.
   b. delusion.
   c. hallucination.
   d. neologism.

4. The area of the brain that is most involved in language production is
   a. Broca's area.
   b. Wernicke's area.
   c. the left temporal lobe.
   d. inactive during auditory hallucinations.

5. Premorbid functioning refers to a schizophrenic person's functioning
   a. just prior to death.
   b. during early childhood.
   c. prior to recovery from the disorder.
   d. prior to the appearance of the disorder.

6. The most common form of hallucination experienced by people with schizophrenia is:
   a. visual
   b. somatic
   c. olfactory
   d. auditory

7. Donald is plagued by delusions and hallucinations. His schizophrenia is most likely related to
   a. serotonin.
   b. dopamine.
   c. acetylcholine.
   d. norepinephrine.

8. According to the _______________ perspective, schizophrenia is a result of extreme regression and attempts by the ego to reassert control.
   a. cognitive
   b. existential
   c. behavioral
   d. psychodynamic

9. According to the double-bind hypothesis, a person who is repeatedly exposed to internally contradicting messages may develop schizophrenia if he or she adopts a strategy of
   a. ignoring the primary communication.
   b. responding only to congruent communications.
   c. asking for clarification about the communication.
   d. alternating attention to the primary communication and to the metacommunication.

CHAPTER

15 Treatments for Schizophrenia and Other Severe Mental Disorders

CHAPTER OUTLINE

REVIEW EXERCISES

I. Institutional Care in the Past, 482–483

1. Philippe Pinel's practice of ______________ treatment spread to the United States, resulting in the creation of large ______________ ______________ rather than asylums to care for mentally disturbed individuals.
2. Required by U.S. law, ______________ hospitals were established so that institutional care would be available to both poor and rich people.
3. The state hospital system developed numerous problems; list three.
   a. State ______________ was too low.
   b. There was a decline in the ______________ of care.
   c. ____
4. Complete these statements about the 100-year decline in mental health care that began in the mid-nineteenth century.
   a. Priorities of public mental health institutions changed dramatically from ______________ care to custodial care or order-keeping.
   b. During this time, hospitals increasingly relied upon ______________, isolation, and ______________ to treat disruptive patients.
   c. "Advanced" forms of intervention included medical approaches such as ______________.
5. Describe characteristics of *social breakdown syndrome*, a result of institutionalization.

____

____

____

II. Institutional Care Takes a Turn for the Better, 484–486

During the 1950s, milieu therapy (based on humanistic principles) and token economy programs (based on behavioral principles) gained prominence as methods of treatment in institutions for mentally ill people. Exercises in this subsection cover the two approaches separately.

A. Milieu Therapy, 484

1. In the **milieu therapy** approach, a climate that builds self-respect, responsibility, and activity is provided to patients within the psychiatric setting. Below, list two specific aspects of the lives of patients who are treated with milieu therapy.
   a. ____
   ____
   b. ____
   ____
2. Research indicates that patients with chronic schizophrenia in milieu programs improve at higher rates than do such patients in ______________ care programs, and the approach has proven to be an effective adjunct to other hospital treatments.

B. The Token Economy, 485

1. **Token economy programs** apply the systematic application of ________________ conditioning techniques.

2. In this exercise you will put yourself in the place of the therapist assigned to design a token economy program for Claude L., a 42-year-old man with schizophrenia. Use your knowledge of the deficits and excesses of behavior that people with the disorder exhibit to complete a list of target behaviors that could be rewarded, set the daily reward in numbers of "TEs" (token exchanges), and complete the list of reinforcements that Claude could purchase with his tokens.

City Hospital Department of Psychiatry

Treatment plan for: Claude L.
Therapist:
Treatment program: Token economy

Self-Care/Hygiene Tasks

1. showering daily (TE = 1 per day)
2.
3.

Social/Behavioral Skills

1. showing physical self-control with others/not fighting (TE = 2 per day)
2.
3.

Ward Responsibilities

1. setting table in dining room (TE = 5)
2.
3.

Reinforcements

1. candy bars and soda (TE = 2)
2. going on an escorted trip to the zoo or the museum (TE = 100)
3.
4.

3. By the end of the structured token economy implemented by Paul and Lentz (1977), _____ percent of the patients had been released to sheltered-care facilities. In comparison, only 71 percent of the patients treated in ________________ therapy and 45 percent of patients receiving ________________ care had been released.

4. Lack of an appropriate ________________ group in many studies of token economies limits the validity of these studies, and renders their results questionable.

5. Again putting yourself in the place of a therapist at City Hospital, suppose that one of your colleagues proposes a token economy that requires patients to earn tokens to buy pillows, meals, and

any "outdoor" time. Write a statement on the ethical and legal problems this program would give the hospital.

____

____

____

6. Another therapist at City Hospital has been treating a woman with schizophrenia who insisted on talking to her "evil twin" every day in the mirror. After six months in your colleague's token economy program, the woman stops this behavior.

   a. Critique your colleague's subsequent claim that the program had "worked."

   ____

   ____

   b. How might your colleague rebut your critique?

   ____

   ____

III. Antipsychotic Drugs, 486–491

1. Complete these statements that delineate the history of **antipsychotic medications.**

   a. The group of antihistamine drugs called ________________ were administered by the surgeon Henri Laborit to calm patients undergoing surgery.

   b. Because of their calming effects, researchers speculated that this group of drugs could be used to treat ________________ disorders.

   c. After being tested in laboratory and clinical settings, chlorpromazine was marketed as the first antipsychotic drug under the trade name ________________ .

   d. Since the discovery of this drug, other "conventional" antipsychotics have been developed and are known collectively as ________________ drugs.

Go back to Chapter 14 and review how the antipsychotic drugs are believed to relieve symptoms of schizophrenia.

A. How Effective Are Antipsychotic Drugs?, 487

1. Antipsychotic drugs seem to relieve symptoms of schizophrenia in at least ________ percent of patients using these medications, and represent the most effective form of intervention for the disorder.

2. In a study demonstrating the risk of relapse among patients with schizophrenia who discontinued antipsychotic drug therapy too soon, researchers found that ______ percent of patients whose medications were changed to a placebo after five years relapsed, whereas only ______ percent of those who continued receiving medications relapsed.

3. List symptoms that (a) are reduced and (b) are less affected by the phenothiazines and related antipsychotic drugs.

   a. ____

   b. ____

B. The Unwanted Effects of Conventional Antipsychotic Drugs, 488

1. ______________ effects are movement abnormalities produced by antipsychotic medications.
2. Complete the following table that summarizes important features of some unwanted effects of antipsychotic medications described in the textbook.

Parkinsonian and Related Symptoms	
Prevalence	
Symptoms	
Treatment	prescribe anti-Parkinsonian drugs along with antipsychotic drugs
Neuroleptic Malignant Syndrome	
Prevalence	
Symptoms	
Treatment	
Tardive Dyskinesia	
Prevalence	at least 10 percent of patients will eventually develop to some degree
Symptoms	
Treatment	

3. Tardive dyskinesia is called a late-appearing movement disorder because symptoms do not appear until the patient has been on the medication for at least _______ _______ .
4. Imagine that you are training a group of psychiatric residents on appropriate antipsychotic prescription procedures. What three points will you emphasize?
   a. If the patient does not respond to neuroleptic drugs, you should:
   ____
   b. When you begin a neuroleptic drug regimen for a patient, you should prescribe the ______________ dosage possible.
   c. After the patient reestablishes nonpsychotic functioning you should:
   ____

C. New Antipsychotic Drugs, 490

Because some patients with schizophrenia do not respond to, or cannot tolerate the effects of, traditional neuroleptic drugs, new antipsychotic drugs have been developed to treat them. These drugs, which include clozapine (Clozaril) and risperidone (Risperdal), have been found to be effective in 85 percent of cases.

1. In addition to being more effective drugs, atypical antipsychotic medications have several other advantages over traditional neuroleptic drugs. Complete the list of advantages.

   a. The atypical antipsychotics are much more effective in treating those who experience the _______________ symptoms of schizophrenia.

   b. These drugs cause few _______________ symptoms.

   c. They do not appear to cause _______________ _______________.

2. A major concern with clozapine is that it can lead to _______________, a potentially fatal drop in white blood cells in 1 percent of its users.

Eye on Culture: First Dibs on Atypical Antipsychotic Drugs, 491

1. Reread the box on page 491 of your textbook. Describe several prescription patterns that indicate that African Americans may be receiving less effective biological care than white Americans in many cases of schizophrenia. Suggest some reasons for this racial disparity.

   ____

   ____

   ____

   ____

   ____

IV. Psychotherapy, 491–497

Although some clinicians have treated schizophrenic people with psychotherapy alone (emphasizing a trusting and understanding relationship), the majority of practitioners today recognize that medication is a crucial component of the treatment process. Cognitive-behavioral therapy, family therapy, and social therapy can be very helpful to patients, especially after medication has relieved symptoms such as delusional thoughts and incoherence that are barriers to therapeutic interventions.

A. Cognitive-Behavioral Therapy, 492

1. What are the major goals of cognitive-behavioral therapy treatment for schizophrenia?

   ____

   ____

   ____

2. Identify the five main cognitive-behavioral techniques described in your textbook to achieve the goals discussed in question 1.

   a. ____

   b. ____

   c. ____

   d. ____

   e. ____

3. The new wave of cognitive-behavioral therapists, including those who are practitioners of acceptance and commitment therapy, seek to help clients become detached and comfortable _______________ of their hallucinations. They want the clients to be _______________ of and

_____________ their hallucinations, and thus learn to move forward with their lives.

4. What has research shown about the effectiveness of this form of cognitive-behavioral therapy?

____

The Media Speaks: Can You Live with the Voices in Your Head?, 494

1. Read the article about Angelo and the support group, Hearing Voices Network, he attends. Reflect on the ways in which the coping strategies espoused by H.V. N. and other groups like it are similar to the techniques and goals of the cognitive-behavioral treatment of schizophrenia. What do you think about the link between the two strategies? Are there ways in which the strategies are different?

____

____

B. Family Therapy, 496

1. Recovering patients with schizophrenia are greatly affected by the behavior and attitudes of _________________ at home, since over _____ percent of these individuals live with their parents, siblings, spouses, or children.
2. People with schizophrenia whose relatives have high levels of _________________ _________________ (i.e., high levels of criticism, emotional overinvolvement, and hostility) often have much higher relapse rates compared to those whose relatives do not.
3. Psychoeducation provides guidance, advice, support, and education about schizophrenia to families of people with the disorder.
   a. Psychoeducation also helps family members become _________________ in their expectations, more _________________ of deviant behavior, less guilt-ridden and confused, and more willing to try new patterns of interaction and communication.
   b. Psychoeducation also helps the person with schizophrenia:

   ____

   ____

C. Social Therapy, 497

1. Clinicians who use social therapy in the treatment of schizophrenia focus on the development of problem-solving, decision-making, and social skills in their patients. List two other "practical" interventions in this form of therapy.

____

V. The Community Approach, 497–504

1. Write a brief definition of each of the following terms.
   a. Community Mental Health Act of 1963

   ____

   ____

   b. Deinstitutionalization

   ____

   ____

c. "Revolving door" syndrome

____

____

A. What Are the Features of Effective Community Care?, 498

In order to address the needs of people with schizophrenia, the community care approach provides a range of services that are designed to maximize the potential of these individuals to live and function in the community.

1. Complete this summary table by describing the central characteristics of each component of the community care approach.

Component	Characteristics
Coordinated services	community mental health centers provide medication, therapy, and emergency care; they also coordinate services of other agencies, especially for MICAs
Short-term hospitalization	
Partial hospitalization	
Supervised residencies	
Occupational training	

B. How Has Community Treatment Failed?, 502

1. One inadequacy in community treatment for people with schizophrenia is poor coordination of services, including minimal ________________ between agencies and no overall strategy for the provision of services.
2. Describe the work of the **case manager.**

____

____

____

____

In addition to the shortage of needed community programs, there is an increasing trend in community mental health services away from their stated goals. Those goals are to (1) assist patients suffering from acute mental illness, (2) circumvent hospitalization before it becomes absolutely necessary, and (3) provide services to patients who have just been released from the hospital.

3. What is the "NIMBY" syndrome?

4. A large proportion of people with schizophrenia do not receive necessary services from the community and cannot afford private treatment. These individuals are forced to live in situations that can exacerbate their problems. Write a short paragraph describing the plight of these individuals who are forced to live in rooming houses or on the street. Be sure to consider the impact that the deinstitutionalization movement has had on these people.

5. As many as one of every ______________ homeless people has a severe mental disorder such as schizophrenia.

C. The Promise of Community Treatment, 504

1. Despite the serious problems of the community approach, there are several recently developed programs and groups that are committed to providing adequate services to people with schizophrenia. Describe the purpose and/or services offered by the national interest group the National Alliance on Mental Illness.

VI. Putting It Together: An Important Lesson, 505

1. Provide two pieces of evidence in support of the textbook author's statement that "no matter how compelling the evidence for biological causation [of schizophrenia] may be, a strictly biological approach to the treatment of psychological disorders is a mistake more often than not."

   a. ______________

   b. ______________

MULTIPLE CHOICE

1. What French physician is credited for beginning the movement toward more humane and moral treatment of mental patients?
   a. Henri Laborit
   b. Philippe Pinel
   c. Pierre Deniker
   d. Maxwell Jones

2. The creation of a therapeutic community was a feature of
   a. moral therapy.
   b. milieu therapy.
   c. a token economy.
   d. sociocultural therapy.

3. Which of the following are antipsychotic medications?
   a. tricyclics
   b. phenothiazines
   c. benzodiazepines
   d. MAO inhibitors

4. Which of the following is least likely to be relieved by an antipsychotic drug?
   a. delusions
   b. flat affect
   c. hallucinations
   d. bizarre behavior

5. The neuroleptic side effect characterized by involuntary muscular contractions and bizarre and uncontrollable movements is called
   a. dystonia.
   b. akathisia.
   c. mode rigidity.
   d. neuroleptic malignant syndrome.

6. All other things being equal, which of the following patients appears most likely to develop tardive dyskinesia from taking a neuroleptic?
   a. a male
   b. a female
   c. an older person
   d. a younger person

7. Which of the following is most likely to reduce the negative symptoms of schizophrenia?
   a. Haldol
   b. Clozapine
   c. psychotherapy
   d. the phenothiazines

8. Which of the following is not a symptom of schizophrenia?
   a. flat affect
   b. loss of volition
   c. tardive dyskinesia
   d. formal thought disorders

9. Tony spends his days at a center with other individuals with mental disorders. Staff at the center provide supervision as well as some therapy and occupational training. Tony goes home each night. This is an example of a(n):
   a. aftercare program.
   b. day hospital.
   c. semihospital.
   d. half-way house.

10. The trend in treatment for people with schizophrenia and other severe mental disorders since the 1960s has been toward
    a. more inpatient psychotherapy.
    b. short-term hospitalization and community-based services.
    c. a decrease in the hospital's use of medication to manage severe mental disorders.
    d. using only individual psychotherapy with patients prior to release from the hospital.

CHAPTER

16 Personality Disorders

CHAPTER OUTLINE

REVIEW EXERCISES

The following exercises cover chapter introductory material on pages 509–512.

1. Complete these exercises about the concepts that form the basis of this chapter.
   a. **Personality** refers to the ________________ and enduring patterns of inner experience and ________________ ________________ displayed by each individual.

b. Most of us maintain an adaptive flexibility in our changing environment by learning from experiences and experimenting with different responses in our efforts to cope.

c. Those with a **personality disorder** are frequently unable to do this. Give the definition of a personality disorder from the textbook.

____

____

____

2. Personality disorders are classified in DSM-IV-TR as Axis _____ disorders because they usually do not have periods of clear ________________ and do not vary greatly in intensity over time.

3. Personality disorders often coexist with Axis _____ disorders (a relationship that is called ________________).

I. "Odd" Personality Disorders, 512–518

Each of the 10 personality disorders identified by DSM-IV-TR is covered in its own part. Below is a partial representation of Figure 16–1 on page 511—a grid showing the various features of the 10 disorders. Read about the characteristics of each disorder (which comes at the beginning of the coverage of each), then go to this grid and check the features that you think fit it. Finally, compare your choices against the original grid on page 511 to see if you caught the central points.

"Odd" Personality Disorders

	Paranoid	**Schizoid**	**Schizotypal**
Relationship problems			
Suspicious/distrustful			
Hostile			
Blames others			
Deceitful			
Controlling/manipulative			
Jealous			
Sensitive			
Aloof/isolated			
Self-absorbed			
Self-critical			
Impulsive/reckless			
Grandiose/egocentric			
Emotionally unstable			
Overly emotional			

	Paranoid	Schizoid	Schizotypal
Depressed/helpless			
Anxious/tense			
Cognitive/perceptual eccentricities			
Attention deficiencies			
Psychotic-like episodes			

A. Paranoid Personality Disorder, 513

1. Complete this list of features of the **paranoid personality disorder.**
   a. distrustful and suspicious of others' _______________, and read "hidden" meaning and hostile intention into the actions of others
   b. quick to challenge the _______________ and trustworthiness of others
   c. critical of others' _______________ and faults, but unable to recognize their own _______________
   d. blame and regularly hold _______________ against others for things that go wrong
2. Between 0.5 and 3 percent of adults, and apparently more _______________ than the other gender, have paranoid personality disorder.

Psychodynamic theorists propose several ways a paranoid personality disorder can emerge from parental mistreatment, hostility, and absence of consistent nurturing. Study this diagram showing potential "outcomes" for people who experience this sort of parental environment, and who later develop a paranoid personality disorder.

Parental mistreatment, hostility, and absence of consistent nurturance leads to children who:

↓ come to view all environments as hostile and dangerous, resulting in a basic distrust of others ↘

↓ project feelings of hostility and rage onto others, leading to feelings of persecution ↙

Paranoid Personality Disorder

3. A possible _______________ factor in paranoid personality disorder was shown by one study of Australian twin pairs that found a high concordance of excessive suspiciousness.
4. One reason that clinicians find it difficult to treat people with paranoid personality disorder is that unless they are in crisis, few of these individuals think they need therapy. What is another reason?

____

____

5. Describe the goals of cognitive and behavioral therapies for paranoid personality disorder, which are often combined.

____

____

____

6. Generally, ______________ therapy has been relatively ineffective in the treatment of paranoid personality disorder.
7. The psychodynamic therapists, who are known as self-therapists, try to help clients suffering from paranoid personality disorder re-establish ______________-______________ (a unified personality), which the therapists believe has been lost.

B. Schizoid Personality Disorder, 515

1. People with paranoid personality disorder avoid social contact because they distrust others. Why do people with **schizoid personality disorder** avoid others?

   ____

2. In addition to having very little interest in relationships, a restricted range of ______________ expression is displayed by people with schizoid personality disorder.
3. Psychodynamic and object relations theorists hypothesize that, like other personality disorders, schizoid personality disorder develops as a result of inadequate parenting. Complete these questions about these explanations.
   a. According to these theorists, what characteristics do the parents of people with schizoid personality disorder tend to have?

      ____

   b. Unlike those with paranoid personality disorder, who react with distrust and hostility, those with schizoid personality disorder suffer an inability to ______________ or ______________ love.
4. Cognitive theorists believe that people with schizoid personality disorder suffer from certain deficits that account for their lack of responsiveness. List them.

   ____

   ____

5. Behavioral therapists, who often integrate their treatment with cognitive techniques, attempt to help their schizoid clients develop better ______________ skills.
6. Group therapy has helped some schizoid patients by providing a contained, safe setting for social contact. Describe one of its potential limitations.

   ____

C. Schizotypal Personality Disorder, 516

1. People with **schizotypal personality disorder** experience extreme discomfort in close ______________, cognitive or perceptual ______________, and behavioral eccentricities.
2. List two types of peculiar thought exhibited by some people with schizotypal personality disorder.

   ____

   ____

3. Describe some of the eccentric behaviors of people with schizotypal personality disorder.

   ____

   ____

4. Complete these questions relating to studies suggesting that schizophrenia and schizotypal personality disorders have similar roots.

   a. In a study of family relationships as a causal factor, schizotypal personality disorder—like schizophrenia—was linked to family ________________ and psychological disorders in parents.

   b. Studies utilizing backward masking tests indicate that defects in ________________ and memory processes might contribute to schizotypal personality disorder, just as these defects are related to schizophrenia.

   c. Research on biological factors found that schizotypal patients appear to have higher levels of dopamine activity, as do schizophrenic people. What other biological abnormality has been found in both groups of patients?

      ____

5. Regardless of the clinician's theoretical orientation, what are usually the central goals in the treatment of schizotypal personality disorder?

   ____

   ____

6. Complete the questions relating to the kinds of interventions offered by different types of treatment approaches to schizotypal personality disorder.

   a. On the cognitive end of cognitive-behavioral therapy, therapists teach clients to evaluate their unusual perceptions or thoughts according to objective evidence and to ignore ________________ thoughts.

   b. On the behavioral end of cognitive-behavioral therapy, therapists focuses on reeducative methods such as:

      ____

   c. ________________ doses of antipsychotic drugs seems to work best for some patients.

II. "Dramatic" Personality Disorders, 518–535

Here is a grid for testing your understanding of the features of "dramatic" disorders. Compare your selections with those in Figure 16–1 on textbook page 511.

"Dramatic" Personality Disorders

	Antisocial	Borderline	Histrionic	Narcissistic
Relationship problems				
Suspicious/distrustful				
Hostile				
Blames others				
Deceitful				
Controlling/manipulative				

	Antisocial	**Borderline**	**Histrionic**	**Narcissistic**
Jealous				
Sensitive				
Aloof/isolated				
Self-absorbed				
Self-critical				
Impulsive/reckless				
Grandiose/egocentric				
Emotionally unstable				
Overly emotional				
Depressed/helpless				
Anxious/tense				
Cognitive/perceptual eccentricities				
Attention deficiencies				
Psychotic-like episodes				

A. Antisocial Personality Disorder, 518

1. What are two other terms used for people with **antisocial personality disorder?**

   ____

2. The primary feature of antisocial personality disorder is a pervasive pattern of ______________ for and violation of the ______________ of others, which is reflected in the disorder's strong association with criminal behavior.

3. What are some of the antisocial behaviors typically seen before age 15 in people who will later be diagnosed with antisocial personality disorder?

   ____

   ____

4. Add to this list of adjectives that describe the characteristics of a person with antisocial personality disorder.

Deceitful	______________
Irresponsible	______________
______________	______________
______________	______________

5. Up to 3.5 percent of people in the United States meet the criteria for antisocial personality disorder; men are ________________ times more likely to be diagnosed than women.

6. Individuals with antisocial personality disorder have higher rates of alcoholism and substance-related disorders than the general population. Complete the following table related to three possible links between substance use and antisocial personality disorder described in your text.

Possibility #1	**Possibility #2**	**Possibility #3**
Early ________________ and substance abuse triggers the development of ________________ .	Antisocial personality disorder leaves a person more ________________ to develop ________________ ________________ problems.	Both antisocial personality disorder AND substance abuse are caused by a third factor such as the need to ________________ .

Study this diagram that depicts the psychodynamic explanation of antisocial personality disorder.

Absence of parental love leads to . . .

↓

Child lacks a basic trust of others

↓

Child becomes emotionally detached from all relationships

↓

Child attempts to bond
with others through use of
power and destructiveness

↓

and develops antisocial personality disorder

7. Complete the following statements relating to different explanations of antisocial personality disorder.

   a. Supporting the psychodynamic view, studies indicate that people with the disorder are more likely to have experienced stressful childhood events, such as poverty and family violence, parental conflicts, or divorce.

   b. Behavioral views hold that people with the disorder might acquire their symptoms through ________________ the behaviors of parents and others, and/or that parents may unwittingly reinforce antisocial behaviors.

   c. Cognitive theorists believe that people with the disorder trivialize the ________________ of others and have difficulty seeing other ________________ .

8. Researchers have found that people with antisocial personality disorder feel less ________________ than others, which could explain why they fail to learn from ________________ experiences and seem to "tune out" the emotional ________________ of others.

9. Laboratory studies have shown that people with antisocial personality disorder respond to expectations of a stressful event with low levels of physiological ________________ , indicating that these individuals may be more able to ignore ________________ or emotional situations.

10. Laboratory studies have also shown that antisocial people display both lower than usual

__________ activity, which is associated with impulsivity and aggression, and defiant functioning in their brains' __________ __________, which are involved in planning, strategizing, and personal relations.

11. Complete the following statements regarding treatment of people with antisocial personality disorder.
    a. No treatment intervention for antisocial personality disorder seems to be __________.
    b. Most people with the disorder do not voluntarily seek treatment, and most of those who do receive it (either voluntarily or not) terminate treatment prematurely. What is the major difficulty in treating these individuals? __________
    ____
    c. Cognitive-behavioral therapists attempt to get people with antisocial personality disorder to consider __________ issues and the __________ of others.
    d. Structured environment approaches emphasize __________ toward others.

B. Borderline Personality Disorder, 523

DSM-IV-TR defines borderline personality disorder is a pervasive pattern of instability in interpersonal relationships, self-image, and mood, as well as marked impulsivity. Read the following case study related to borderline personality disorder which will be followed by an exercise.

Case Study

Belinda T. is a 27-year-old woman who decided to seek therapy from Dr. Platt, an established and highly regarded clinician. During the initial interview, Belinda told Dr. Platt the following: "Things have been getting worse and worse for me. Even when it seems like I'm having a good day, suddenly something goes wrong and I get depressed, or so mad that I see red. [1] A few nights ago I smashed every glass plate in the house and kicked my dog so hard that I had to take him to the vet. [2] The next day I felt so horrible that I drank until I passed out. I get to feeling really awful and alone, like I'm a big nothing inside. Sometimes I cut my arms and stomach with a razor. [3] When I feel the pain and see the blood, I get a rush . . . almost like I feel more "real." [4] This therapy is my last chance; if it doesn't work, I may as well just give up and die."

Dr. Platt agreed to work with Belinda in therapy and made a provisional diagnosis of borderline personality disorder. After her first therapy session, Belinda told her friends that Dr. Platt was "the most wonderful person in the world," and that she had never met anyone with such understanding and compassion. She said that she was certain Dr. Platt could help her. But just five sessions later, Belinda confronted Dr. Platt by saying, "You are an unfeeling, incompetent bitch! You are the one who needs a shrink." [5] Dr. Platt responded by asking, "I wonder if some of your anger is about my being on vacation last week?" Belinda confirmed Dr. Platt's hypothesis by angrily claiming that Dr. Platt had deserted her and no longer cared about her. [6] Sobbing, Belinda rolled up her sleeve and revealed several new cuts on her arm. "Look at what you made me do! Please don't leave me alone again; I can't stand it. The next time you cancel a session, I might kill myself." [7]

1. Each of the numbered statements in this sample case relate to a particular characteristic of people who suffer from **borderline personality disorder.** Match each statement with the characteristics (a–g) that follow.

   [1]____ [2]____ [3]____ [4]____ [5]____ [6]____ [7]____

Characteristics:

a. Anger is expressed in aggressive, violent behavior outward.

b. Fearing desertion, manipulative behavior such as suicidal threats is used to maintain relationships.

c. Anger is expressed and directed inward through self-destructive and self-mutilating behaviors.

d. Vacillation occurs between overidealizing and devaluing others in relationships.

e. Dramatic, often sudden shifts in mood are common.

f. Rage and extreme disappointment are felt when expectations, particularly about others "being there" at all times in a relationship, are not met.

g. Self-destructive and self-mutilating behavior can serve to relieve chronic feelings of boredom and emptiness and to validate "personhood."

2. Complete the following statements regarding the prevalence and course of borderline personality disorder.

   a. About 75 percent of the estimated 1–2.5 percent of the general population with borderline personality disorder are ________________ .

   b. The symptoms of the disorder most commonly seem to peak during ________________ adulthood and decrease with age.

3. Psychodynamic research has focused on the excessive fear of ________________ in people with borderline personality disorder, which has led to a hypothesis that parents' lack of acceptance causes a loss in self-esteem, dependency, and difficulty in coping with ________________ .

4. In addition to family instability, conflict, and parental loss, early trauma such as physical, ________________, and ________________ abuse is prevalent in the backgrounds of people diagnosed with borderline personality disorder.

5. Biological factors that have been implicated in borderline personality disorder include low ________________ activity (linked to aggression against self and others), abnormalities in the ________________ gene (associated with depression), and other genetic factors.

6. According to the *biosocial theory* of borderline personality disorder, the disorder results from a combination of ________________ forces, such as abnormal neurotransmitter reactions and difficulty controlling emotions, and ________________ forces, such as environments in which a child's emotions are misinterpreted by parents, or punished, ignored, and trivialized.

7. Sociocultural theorists hypothesize that the increasing prevalence of borderline personality disorder is related to a rapidly changing culture and breakdown of the ________________ unit.

8. What are some reasons why some therapists refuse to see clients with borderline personality disorder?

   ____

   ____

   ____

   ____

   ____

9. Complete these statements about treatment for borderline personality disorder.

   a. Contemporary psychodynamic therapy focuses on ________________ disturbance, poor sense of ________________, and pervasive ________________ and emptiness.

b. Describe the features of dialectical behavior therapy (DBT), the integrative treatment approach that is now considered in many circles to be the treatment of choice for borderline personality disorder.

____

____

____

c. The use of drugs (such as antidepressants or antipsychotics) in therapy is controversial in part because of the elevated risk of ______________ ______________ by patients with borderline personality disorder.

The Media Speaks: Self-Cutting: The Wound That Will Not Heal, 526

Read the first-hand account of a self-cutter. Reflect on how the experience of cutting, as described in the article, is similar or different to the beliefs of various theorists who attempt to explain the self-injurious behavior of people with borderline personality disorder. NOTE: The author of this first-hand account has not, so far as we know, been diagnosed with a personality disorder.

C. Histrionic Personality Disorder, 529

1. Complete the following list of features of persons diagnosed with **histrionic personality disorder.**

   a. They are described as "______________ charged" and have exaggerated, rapid mood swings.

   b. Always "______________," these people are grandiose and theatrical in their language and gestures.

   c. They are ______________, self-centered, and ______________ in their extreme need for attention.

   d. They exaggerate physical ______________ and weaknesses, as well as the intensity of their relationships with others.

   e. They may behave in a sexually ______________ manner as a way to get attention from and seduce others.

2. What have recent studies indicated about the prevalence rates of histrionic personality disorder among men versus women?

   ____

3. Psychodynamic theorists believe that histrionic people defend against deep fears of ______________ by being overly emotional and inventing crises so that other people will act ______________ toward them.

4. Many cognitive explanations focus on the deficient functionings of those with histrionic personality disorder, such as their "lack of substance," extreme ______________, and assumption that they are helpless.

5. Sociocultural theorists point to society's ______________ and expectations that encouraged childishness in women, resulting in histrionic behaviors that may be viewed as a caricature of ______________ as our culture once defined it.

6. List two challenges faced by therapists who treat patients with histrionic personality disorder.

   a. ____

   ____

b. ______________________________

____

7. What is a central goal in the treatment of histrionic personality disorder?

____

D. Narcissistic Personality Disorder, 531

1. **Narcissistic personality disorder** is characterized by excessive grandiosity, need for admiration, and lack of empathy. Read the lettered statements below made by a man with this disorder, then describe the characteristic of the disorder that is being displayed in the spaces for letters a–c following the statements.

   Statements:

   a. I think it's quite obvious that I saved the company's ass with my work on that project. I set a standard for the industry. The work could be described as nothing less than brilliant.

   b. Almost nobody is savvy enough to understand how my mind works. Maybe Bill Gates and Ted Turner . . . no, I doubt if even they could understand me.

   c. All the time my co-worker Lance spent lying around the hospital really added to the amount of work I was given, and it wasn't fair! I know he had a heart attack, but I have my own problems.

   a. grandiose sense of self-importance, exaggeration of achievements, arrogance

   b. ______________________________

   c. ______________________________

2. Of the roughly 1 percent of the adult population with narcissistic personality disorder, up to 75 percent are ________________ .

3. Psychodynamic theorists propose that cold and rejecting parents cause children to feel rejected and unworthy, and that some of these children grow up to defend against these feelings by telling themselves they are ________________ and desirable.

4. Behavioral and cognitive theorists give a very different explanation of narcissistic personality disorder, suggesting that people diagnosed with this disorder were treated too ________________ early in life.

5. Sociocultural theorists propose that individual cases of narcissistic personality disorder result from societal breakdowns during "________________ of narcissism."

6. Narcissistic people might enter therapy with a sense of entitlement that may be manifest in manipulating the therapist to support their sense of ________________ .

Psych Watch: Lying: "Oh, What a Tangled Web...", 532

1. Briefly describe how each of the following theorists and researchers believe why people lie.

   a. Psychodynamic theorists ______________________________

   ____

   b. Behavioral theorists ______________________________

   ____

   c. Sociocultural theorists ______________________________

   ____

d. Biological researchers ____

____

III. "Anxious" Personality Disorders, 535–541

Here is a grid for testing your understanding of the features of "anxious" personality disorders—the last of the three groups. Remember to check the features that you think apply to each disorder, then compare your selections with those in Figure 16–1 on textbook page 511.

"Anxious" Personality Disorders

	Avoidant	**Dependent**	**Obsessive-Compulsive**
Relationship problems			
Suspicious/distrustful			
Hostile			
Blames others			
Deceitful			
Controlling/manipulative			
Jealous			
Sensitive			
Aloof/isolated			
Self-absorbed			
Self-critical			
Impulsive/reckless			
Grandiose/egocentric			
Emotionally unstable			
Overly emotional			
Depressed/helpless			
Anxious/tense			
Cognitive/perceptual eccentricities			
Attention deficiencies			
Psychotic-like episodes			

A. Avoidant Personality Disorder, 535

1. **Avoidant personality disorder** is characterized by social avoidance, persistent feelings of ________________, and hypersensitivity to ________________ evaluations and rejection.

2. Complete the following questions relating to the relationship between avoidant personality disorder and social phobias.

   a. Symptoms that are common to both disorders include fear of ________________ and low ________________.

b. Some theorists believe that important differences between the two disorders include the fact that people with social phobias primarily fear social ________________, whereas people with avoidant personality disorder mostly fear social ________________.

3. Psychodynamic theorists suggest that after being repeatedly ________________ or punished by parents during toilet training, children develop a negative self-image, a distrust of others, and a belief that "I am unlovable"—all of which contribute to avoidant personality disorder.

4. The ________________ view of avoidant personality disorder suggests that because of past criticisms, those affected expect and fear ________________, misinterpret people's reactions, and discount positive feedback.

5. Describe why therapists often find it difficult to keep individuals with avoidant personality disorder in treatment.

____

____

6. Treatment for avoidant personality disorder is very similar to treatment for people with ________________ disorders such as social phobias.

7. Complete this table by giving an example of an intervention for people with avoidant personality disorder from each of the perspectives given.

Perspective	Example of Intervention
Psychodynamic	
Cognitive	
Behavioral	provide social skills training and exposure treatment requiring clients to gradually increase their social contacts
Biological	

B. Dependent Personality Disorder, 537

1. In each of the following areas, give *two* examples of behaviors that might be characteristic of Wilma, a woman with **dependent personality disorder.**

Relationships:

a. *Wilma's extreme fear of separation and need to be "taken care of" results in submissive, clinging, and obedient behavior.*

b. ____

____

Decision making:

a. ____

____

b. ____

____

Emotions/Mood:

a. ____

____

b. ____

____

2. Complete the following statements regarding the various explanations of dependent personality disorder.

   a. In the past, psychodynamic theorists believed that, like depression, dependent personality disorders were a result of a fixation at the ______________ stage of psychosexual development.

   b. Other psychodynamic theorists hold that the parents of people with the disorder were overprotective, thus fostering dependent behaviors and heightening the child's feelings of insecurity and anxiety about ______________ .

   c. ______________ theorists believed that parents unintentionally rewarded their child's clinging behavior and punished ______________ behavior.

   d. According to cognitive theorists, one maladaptive assumption underlying this disorder held by those who have it is that they are inadequate and helpless to deal with the world. What is the other underlying maladaptive assumption?

   ____

3. Key concerns for clinicians in the treatment of patients with dependent personality disorder include how to get them to accept ______________ for themselves and what to do about the patient's ______________ or parent—who is probably playing a role in the maintenance of dependent behaviors.

4. Psychodynamic therapists must inevitably work through the dependent patient's ______________ of dependency needs onto the therapist.

C. Obsessive-Compulsive Personality Disorder, 539

1. People with **obsessive-compulsive personality disorder** are preoccupied with order, ______________ and ______________ .

2. Complete this list by providing the usual result or outcome of each characteristic of obsessive-compulsive personality disorder.

   a. Fixation on organization and details: ______________________________

   ____

   b. High standards for self and others: ______________________________

   ____

   c. Fear of making mistakes: ______________________________

   d. Inflexible morals, ethics, and values: ______________________________

   e. Miserly behavior: ______________________________

3. While many people diagnosed with obsessive-compulsive (anxiety) disorder also have an obsessive-compulsive personality disorder, no specific link has found empirical support.

4. According to Freudian theorists, people with obsessive-compulsive personality disorder are described as ______________ ______________ (characterized by orderly, stubborn, and re-

strained behavior) as a result of their parents being very harsh and punitive toward them during the toilet-training stage.

5. Cognitive theorists believe that illogical thinking processes, such as ________________ thinking, maintain the symptoms of people with obsessive-compulsive personality disorder.
6. One difference between obsessive-compulsive *anxiety* disorder and obsessive-compulsive *personality* disorder is how they are treated. Rather than drug or behavioral therapy, which treatments are most effective for the obsessive-compulsive personality disorder?

   ____

IV. Multicultural Factors: Research Neglect, 541–542

1. Although there has not been systematic research on the issue, identify two possible explanations that theorists have put forth for the fact that 75 percent of people diagnosed with borderline personality disorder are female.

   ____

   ____

   ____

2. Some multicultural theorists believe that borderline personality disorder may be attributable more to social ____________ than to ____________ factors.
3. A research study has shown a disproportionately high prevalence of borderline personality disorder among Hispanic Americans, as compared to white Americans and African Americans. What are the explanations for this result that some multicultural theorists are suggesting?

   ____

   ____

   ____

V. What Problems Are Posed by the DSM-IV-TR Categories?, 542–543

1. Of all the categories in the DSM-IV-TR, personality disorders are among the most difficult to accurately diagnose. Complete the following statements related to three central problems that can lead to misdiagnosis of these disorders.
   a. Many diagnostic criteria cannot be directly ________________, so they must rely on the impression of ________________ clinicians.
   b. There is considerable ________________, or overlap, of symptoms *within* clusters of personality disorders and even *between* the clusters themselves.
   c. People with very ________________ personalities are often given the same diagnosis.

VI. Are There Better Ways to Classify Personality Disorders?, 543-544

1. Today's leading criticism of DSM-IV-TR's approach to personality disorders is that the classification system uses categories rather than ________________ of personality, assuming a personality disorder is either entirely present or absent.
2. Briefly describe a dimensional approach to classifying personality pathology.

____

____

____

3. List the five "supertraits," or personality factors identified by proponents of the "Big Five" theory of personality and personality disorders.

   a. ____

   b. ____

   c. ____

   d. ____

   e. ____

4. How many broad personality factors are identified in Jonathan Shedler and Drew Westen's dimensional model of personality, put forth as an alternative to the "Big Five" model?

VII. Putting It Together: Disorders of Personality Are Rediscovered, 545–546

1. Complete this list of questions about personality disorders that researchers and clinicians continue to ask.

   a. How common are the various personality disorders?

   b. ____

   c. ____

   d. ____

   e. ____

MULTIPLE CHOICE

1. An inflexible pattern of inner experience and outward behavior that deviates markedly from the expectations of one's culture is called a
   a. neurosis.
   b. fugue state.
   c. personality trait.
   d. personality disorder.

2. In a study of role playing, subjects with paranoid personality disorder generally responded to ambiguous behavior with
   a. anger.
   b. confusion.
   c. withdrawal.
   d. confrontation.

3. A lack of interest in sexual behavior is likely to be a feature of the
   a. schizoid personality disorder.
   b. paranoid personality disorder.
   c. antisocial personality disorder.
   d. dependent personality disorder.

4. The symptom of bodily illusions displayed by many schizotypal patients involves
   a. loose associations.
   b. sensing an external force or presence.
   c. the belief that unrelated events pertain to them.
   d. conversing in a vague manner and making inappropriately elaborate statements.

5. What childhood patterns place a person at risk for developing antisocial personality disorder as an adult?
   a. autism
   b. serious misbehavior (conduct disorder)
   c. childhood depression
   d. generalized anxiety disorder

6. Which characteristic is not typical of borderline personality disorder?
   a. major mood changes
   b. unstable self-image
   c. constant depression
   d. impulsivity

7. People who are diagnosable with histrionic personality disorder are somewhat unusual compared to those with other personality disorders in that they
   a. are unhappy.
   b. tend to seek treatment.
   c. display strange behavior.
   d. behave in a maladaptive way.

8. The avoidant personality disorder is one of the
   a. odd personality disorders.
   b. Axis I personality disorders.
   c. anxious personality disorders.
   d. dramatic personality disorders.

9. Decision making is a particular problem for the person who suffers from
   a. borderline personality disorder.
   b. dependent personality disorder.
   c. narcissistic personality disorder.
   d. obsessive-compulsive personality disorder.

10. Max spends so much time organizing his attack on the problem that he never gets to work on the problem. This is a habitual pattern with him. His behavior is a symptom of
    a. avoidant personality disorder.
    b. antisocial personality disorder.
    c. dependent personality disorder.
    d. obsessive-compulsive personality disorder.

CHAPTER

17 Disorders of Childhood and Adolescence

CHAPTER OUTLINE

REVIEW EXERCISES

I. Childhood and Adolescence, 550

1. Even youth who do not have a diagnosable disorder experience difficulties from time to time.
   a. About _____ of all children worry about things such as school, health, and their safety.
   b. Other common problems among children include ________________, nightmares, ________________, and restlessness.
   c. Teenagers often feel anxious or confused over ________________ and ________________ changes, or social and academic ________________.
   d. As compared to their parents, today's teenagers feel less ________________, more ________________, and more isolated from their families.
2. About one-________________ of children and adolescents in the United States experience a diagnosable psychological disorder.
3. ________________ with psychological disorders outnumber ________________, which is interesting because the prevalence of disorders by gender is generally the opposite in adulthood.

II. Childhood Anxiety Problems, 551–553

1. Identify three major factors that contribute to childhood and adolescent anxiety.
   a. ____
   b. ____
   c. ____

A. Childhood Anxiety Disorders, 551

1. Like adults, children can suffer from specific phobias, __________ phobias, and ____________ anxiety disorder.
2. Although childhood anxiety disorders can be explained in the same way as adult anxiety disorders, anxiety disorders in children can also develop as a result of some unique features of childhood. To each unique feature listed, give an example of something that might contribute to the development of an anxiety disorder.
   a. *Compared to adults, children have few experiences with the world.*
   ____
   ____
   b. *Today's society exposes children to many frightening images and messages.*
   ____
   ____
   c. *Children are highly dependent on their parents for emotional support and guidance.*
   ____
   ____

3. Why do generalized anxiety disorder and social phobia rarely appear in earnest until children are at least 7 years old?

____

____

4. Children who suffer from **separation anxiety disorder** experience ______________ anxiety whenever they are separated from ____________ or a parent.

5. In some cases, a childhood separation anxiety disorder can further take the form of a school ______________, or a school refusal.

B. Treatments for Childhood Anxiety Disorders, 552

1. In addition to treatment techniques that mirror adult therapies for anxiety disorders but are tailored to a child's unique life experience, some therapists use play therapy and hypnotherapy when treating children who are suffering anxiety disorders. Briefly describe the two techniques and why they are effective for children.

   a. Play therapy

   ____

   ____

   b. Hypnotherapy

   ____

   ____

III. Childhood Mood Problems, 553–557

A. Major Depressive Disorder, 553

1. Around _____ percent of children currently experience major depressive disorder. What is a major reason for the disparity between this rate and the rate of depression among adults?

____

____

2. Depression in younger children can be caused by negative _________ _________, major changes, ___________, or ongoing _______________.

3. Identify two ways in which the features of childhood depression differ from the features of adult depression.

   a. ____

   b. ____

4. Before the age of 13, there is no significant difference in rates of depression between boys and girls. However, by age 16, ___________ are twice as likely as the other gender to experience depression.

5. What are some possible reasons for the major shift in depression prevalence by gender in the early teenage years?

____

____

6. Most research has indicated that cognitive-behavioral therapy, interpersonal approaches, and antidepressant drugs have all proven effective in the treatment of childhood and adolescent depression. Identify two recent developments that have called this into question, and briefly summarize the controversy that attends both developments.

   a. ____________________

   b. ____________________

B. Bipolar Disorder, 556

1. Bipolar disorder had previously been considered an adult-only disorder, but in the past fifteen years a sharply increasing number of children and adolescents have been diagnosed with bipolar disorders. How do most theorists explain this new trend?

   ____

   ____

2. Why do some theorists disagree with the increased diagnoses of bipolar disorder among children?

   ____

   ____

3. Around one-__________ of children in treatment for bipolar disorder receive an antipsychotic drug; one-__________ of them receive an antibipolar (mood stabilizing) drug, and many others receive __________ or __________ drugs. Relatively few of these drugs have been tested on and specifically approved for children.

IV. Oppositional Defiant Disorder and Conduct Disorder, 557–563

1. In this table, summarize the characteristics and prevalence rates of the two types of disruptive behavior disorders listed.

Disorder	Characteristics	Prevalence
Oppositional defiant disorder		10 percent of children
Conduct disorder		

2. List the most common behaviors leading to the arrest of juvenile (a) boys and (b) girls.

   a. ____________________

   b. ____________________

A. What Are the Causes of Conduct Disorder?, 561

1. Along with drug use and biological, genetic, and socioeconomic factors, family ________________ is often a cause in the development of conduct disorders.
2. Give three examples of parental behaviors that have been associated with the emergence of conduct disorders.

____

____

B. How Do Clinicians Treat Conduct Disorder?, 562

1. Treatment for conduct disorders is generally more effective with children under the age of _____, because disruptive behavior patterns become more resistant to change as a child grows older.
2. Family interventions are often effective in the treatment of conduct disorder. List two aspects of family intervention below.
   a. ____
   b. ____
3. Institutionalization in ________________ ________________ centers appears to exacerbate behavior problems among young offenders.
4. ________________ programs that begin in early childhood are also very promising because they focus on increasing training opportunities, ________________ facilities, alleviating poverty, ________________ care, and improving ________________ skills.

V. Attention-Deficit/Hyperactivity Disorder, 564–569

1. After reading through the case of "Steven" in the text, list five behaviors that exemplify his overactivity and impulsivity.

____

____

____

2. ADHD often coexists with ________________, or communication problems, poor school performance, and social skills deficits.
3. Complete these statements about the prevalence of ADHD.
   a. Of the 5 percent of children with ADHD, as many as _____ percent are boys.
   b. The disorder persists into adulthood in between _____ and _____ percent of affected people.

A. What Are the Causes of ADHD?, 565

1. Biological factors, high levels of ________________, and ________________ dysfunction are all possible causal factors in ADHD, although none has received consistent empirical support.
2. The symptoms of ADHD, as well as the diagnostic label itself, can exacerbate ________________ problems of children with the disorder and can even produce additional ________________.
3. While receiving considerable press attention, ________________, food additives, and environmental ________________ do not appear to cause ADHD.

B. How Do Clinicians Assess ADHD?, 566

1. ADHD is a difficult disorder to assess. List five important assessment tools and techniques that clinicians use to assess ADHD.

   a. ______________________________

   b. ______________________________

   c. ______________________________

   d. ______________________________

   e. ______________________________

2. Many children are diagnosed with ADHD by pediatricians or family physicians. Studies suggest that only _____ to _____ of these diagnoses are based on psychological or educational testing.

C. How Is ADHD Treated?, 566

1. Complete these statements relating to drug treatment for children with ADHD.

   a. The stimulant drug **methylphenidate (Ritalin)** has a ______________ effect on many children with ADHD.

   b. Methylphenidate increases the ability of children to solve ______________ and to control ______________ at home and school.

2. Many children with ADHD are taken off Ritalin, often in reaction to the negative publicity the drug has received regarding its safety, over-prescription, and potential for abuse. What do studies show is the outcome for many of these children after they are taken off the drug?

   ____

3. Given that Ritalin can affect the growth of some children, how do doctors prevent such an effect in their patients who take it?

   ____

4. Behaviorists use operant conditioning treatments that involve teaching parents to systematically ______________ appropriate behavior—a method that seems most effective when it is combined with ______________ therapy.

D. Multicultural Factors and ADHD, 568

1. Identify three possible reasons why American children from racial minority groups are less likely than white American children to receive an ADHD diagnosis and undergo treatment.

   ____

   ____

VI. Elimination Disorders, 569–571

1. Elimination disorders are characterized by the repeated urination or defecation in clothes, beds, or on the floor, after an age at which the child should be able to ______________ these bodily functions.

2. Complete these statements regarding **enuresis,** the usually involuntary bed-wetting or wetting of one's clothes.

   a. Children must be at least _____ years old to receive this diagnosis.

   b. Prevalence of enuresis ______________ with age for both sexes, and no more than _____ percent of 15 year olds experience it.

c. A ________________ event such as hospitalization, the birth of a sibling, or entrance into ________________ can precipitate the resumption of bed-wetting even after the child has been dry prior to these events.

3. Describe the explanations for enuresis by theorists of the (a) psychodynamic, (b) family systems, (c) behavioral, and (d) biological perspectives.

   a. it is a symptom of other conflicts and anxieties.

   b. ________________________________

   c. ________________________________

   d. ________________________________

4. Study the top part of this diagram describing a classical conditioning approach to the treatment of enuresis, then provide the appropriate components that are missing from the bottom part of the diagram.

---

1 A bell and a battery are wired to a pad consisting of two metallic foil sheets, and the entire apparatus is placed under the child at bedtime.

2 A single drop of urine sets off the bell.

3 The child is awakened immediately after he or she starts to wet.

________________ + ________________ = ________________

Unconditioned Stimulus | *Conditioned Stimulus* | *Conditioned Response*

---

5. A less common elimination disorder is **encopresis,** which is repeatedly and involuntarily ________________ into one's clothing, usually beginning after the age of ______ .

VII. Long-Term Disorders That Begin in Childhood, 572–589

A. Pervasive Devlopmental Disorders, 572

1. Pervasive developmental disorders are often marked by impaired ________________ ________________, unusual ________________, and inappropriate responses to ________________ in the environment.

2. Identify the four pervasive developmental disorders.

   a. ________________________________

   b. ________________________________

   c. ________________________________

   d. ________________________________

1. Autistic Disorder, 572

1. The symptoms of **autistic disorder** typically appear before the age of ______ and include extreme unresponsiveness to others, poor ________________ skills, and ________________ behavior.

2. Complete these statements that relate to the prevalence and course of autism.

   a. About 1 of every ________________ children are autistic.

   b. Approximately ______ percent of autistic children are boys.

c. ________________ out of ten autistic children remain severely impaired into adulthood.

3. Autistic children can display many behaviors that indicate a profound unresponsiveness to, and lack of interest in, other people (e.g., failure to make eye contact with parents). List three other examples of these behaviors.

____

____

____

____

4. About half of autistic children fail to speak or develop language skills. Those who do develop some level of verbal skills show many peculiarities in their communication patterns. Complete this description of these patterns.

a. In ________________, the child repeats exact words and phrases spoken by others without comprehension.

b. An example of ________________ ________________ would be an autistic child saying, "You want to watch TV now" when he or she wants to watch television.

Read this case study and complete the exercise that follows.

Case Study

Jodie is a 10-year-old autistic girl. Her parents are constructing a deck on the back of their house, and Jodie is having great difficulty dealing with this change, even though her parents are careful to keep everything in the house the same. Further, they are puzzled by the fact that Jodie does not seem to hear the extremely noisy electric saw but will turn her head if one of the workers drops a nail. Most distressing is the fact that when Jodie is agitated, she will bang her head on the wall repeatedly, a behavior that prompted her parents to keep a protective helmet in the closet. Jodie's parents have noticed other unusual, but less frightening behaviors in their child. For example, Jodie insists on picking up "dust bunnies" from underneath furniture and keeping them in her pocket at all times. She will take plates out of the kitchen cupboard, sit on the floor, and spin them around for hours on end. Jodie also seems fascinated by twirling her fingers near her face, an activity that seems to have a calming affect when she is upset.

5. As illustrated by this case, autistic children display very unusual responses to their environments. Describe each feature of autism listed in the table, then match the feature with the appropriate example in the sample case about Jodie.

Feature	Examples of Behavior Seen in the Case Study
Repetitive and rigid behavior	
Unusual motor movements	
Disturbed and paradoxical perceptual reactions	

2. Asperger's Disorder, 574

1. People with Asperger's disorder, or Asperger's syndrome, tend to experience many of the same impairments as people with autistic disorder. Identify four characteristics shared by most people with either Asperger's disorder or autism.

   a. ______________________________

   b. ______________________________

   c. ______________________________

   d. ______________________________

2. Unlike autistic individuals, people with Asperger's often have normal ______________, ______________, and ______________ skills.

3. Some researchers have distinguished three subtypes of Asperger's sufferers, and called them rule boys, logic boys, and emotion boys. Briefly describe each subtype.

   a. rule boys ______________________________

   ____

   b. logic boys ______________________________

   ____

   c. emotion boys ______________________________

   ____

3. What Are the Causes of Pervasive Developmental Disorders?, 575

Currently many clinicians and researchers believe that other pervasive developmental disorders are caused by many of the same factors as autism. However, as these disorders are further researched, more differences in their causes and treatments may be identified.

Although the idea that family and environment play a causal role in autism has lost most of its popularity (because of lack of empirical support, and because of the blame this view places on parents), these factors continue to influence the clinical field.

1. Complete these statements related to sociocultural views of autism.

   a. Leo Kanner argued that certain personality characteristics of "refrigerator parents," such as being very ______________, yet obsessive and ______________, contributed to autism.

   b. Some theorists believe that ______________ and ______________ stress contribute to autism; this view has not been supported by research.

One psychological theory of autism holds that, compared to normal children, autistic children have not developed a ***theory of mind*** *that would allow them to engage in make-believe play, develop relationships, and use language in ways that appreciate others' perspectives.*

2. Apply this theory to explain the following behavior of a child with autism: Eight-year-old Timothy asks for ice cream, then has a tantrum when his mother brings him some. He wanted strawberry ice cream, not the chocolate ice cream his mother gave him.

   ____

   ____

3. For the first two of the listed biological factors implicated in autistic disorder, a research finding that supports it is given. Provide another.

   a. *Genetic factors:*

   The prevalence of autism among siblings of autistic children is much higher than in the general population.

   ____

   b. *Prenatal difficulties or birth complications:*

   The rate of rubella among mothers giving birth to autistic children is much higher than expected.

   ____

   c. *Name some specific biological abnormalities found in many individuals with autism:*

   ____

4. How Do Clinicians and Educators Treat Pervasive Developmental Disorders?, 577

1. What are the goals of behavioral interventions for autistic children?

____

____

____

____

2. ____________ techniques attempt to get autistic children to imitate appropriate behaviors of others, and ____________ conditioning strategies reinforce adaptive behaviors in the autistic child.

3. A recent long-term controlled study examined the effectiveness of a behavioral intervention program with autistic children. Nineteen autistic children received intensive behavioral interventions from ages 3 to 7, whereas a control group of autistic children did not receive these interventions. How did these groups compare at the end of the study?

____

____

____

4. The *Learning Experiences . . . An Alternative Program (LEAP)* for preschoolers with autism integrates autistic children and normal children in a classroom setting to teach social and communication skills to the autistic children. Briefly describe how the autistic children have fared under this program, and how the normal children have fared.

____

____

____

5. Under the Individuals with Disabilities Education Act, a federal law, autism is one of 10 disorders for which school districts must provide a free education from birth to age ____________ .

6. In ____________ ____________ integration therapy programs, children with Asperger's disorder are taught to be more flexible with regard to rules, problem solving, and behavioral choices.

7. _______________ training helps the 50 percent of children with autism who do not speak to develop other forms of language; these interventions include teaching sign language, _______________ communication, and **augmentative communication systems.**

8. Some treatment programs for autistic children use _______________ - _______________ interactions to improve their communication skills. In these programs, _______________ reinforcers, rather than trivial ones, are identified and used to inspire better communication.

9. Thinking back to the case study of Jodie, how might Jodie's parent be included in a treatment program?

____

____

10. Programs such as _______________ homes and sheltered _______________ help people with autism live and work in the community.

B. Mental Retardation, 579

1. A DSM-IV-TR diagnosis of **mental retardation** is warranted if a person develops the following symptoms before the age of 18.

   a. A person manifests subaverage general _______________ functioning (an IQ of _______ or below), and

   b. displays concurrent deficits or impairments in present adaptive behavior—that is to say, he or she cannot meet set standards in at least two of these skill areas:

   ____

   ____

1. Assessing Intelligence, 580

1. Complete this list of statements that relate to concerns about the validity of intelligence tests.

   a. Correlations between IQ scores and _______________ performance is around .50, which is a less-than-perfect relationship.

   b. IQ tests seem to be socioculturally _______________, as evidenced by the fact that middle- to upper-socioeconomic-level households have an advantage because they are regularly exposed to the same kinds of tasks that the tests measure.

   c. IQ tests do not measure "street sense," which requires intellectual ability.

2. Assessing Adaptive Functioning, 581

1. Various scales have been developed to measure adaptive behavior. Because these scales are not always accurate, clinicians must _______________ and judge the functioning level of each individual, and take into account the person's _______________ and community standards.

3. What Are the Features of Mental Retardation?, 581

1. The most important, consistent difference between retarded and nonretarded people is that retarded people _______________ more slowly; the other differences relate to attention, _______________ memory, _______________ and language.

2. In the following table, give the DSM-IV-TR and the American Association of Mental Retardation (AAMR) terms for levels of mental retardation based on IQ range. The AAMR identifications are based on the level of support needed.

IQ	DSM-IV-TR	AAMR (Level of Support Required)
50–70	mild	intermittent
35–49		
20–34		
below 20		

3. As many as _____ percent of all people with mental retardation are **mildly retarded,** or "_________________ retarded."
4. Mild mental retardation is usually first detected when the child enters _________________; intellectual performance seems to _________________ as the child ages and progresses through school.
5. Give two examples of (a) sociocultural/psychological factors and (b) biological factors that are linked to mild mental retardation. *(Note that sociocultural/psychological factors seem to play the primary causal role in mild mental retardation.)*

   a. _________________

   b. _________________
6. Complete this summary table by giving the percentages and characteristics of each listed group of individuals with mental retardation (MR).

Disorder	Prevalence	Characteristics
Moderate retardation (IQ 35–49)	10 percent of the population of persons with MR	
Severe retardation (IQ 20–34)		
Profound retardation (IQ under 20)		

4. What Are the Causes of Mental Retardation?, 584

1. The primary causes of moderate to profound retardation are _________________.
2. Complete the statements about **Down syndrome,** the most common chromosomal disorder that leads to mental retardation.

   a. Fewer than one in every _________________ children are born with Down syndrome.

   b. Among children born to women over the age of _____, the incidence rises considerably.

3. The physical characteristics of people with Down syndrome include a small head, ________________ face, slanted eyes, high cheekbones, and, in some cases, a protruding ________________ .

4. One of the three types of chromosomal abnormalities that may cause Down syndrome is named *trisomy 21.* (a) Describe trisomy 21, then (b) list and describe another type of chromosomal abnormality linked to Down syndrome.

   a. ____

   b. ____

5. The IQ of most people with Down syndrome ranges from _____ to _____ .

6. The ________________ process seems to occur more rapidly in people with Down syndrome; many show signs of ________________ as they approach age 40.

7. Metabolic disorders that result in retardation are caused by the pairing of two defective ________________ genes, one from each parent.

8. Infants screened for *phenylketonuria (PKU)* can develop normal ________________ , as long as they are started on a low-phenylalanine diet before 3 months of age.

9. *Tay-Sachs disease* is a metabolic disorder found primarily in people of Eastern ________________ ________________ ancestry that is characterized by progressive ________________ deterioration, loss of visual and ________________ function, and finally death.

10. Complete this table, by describing prenatal and birth-related causes of retardation.

Problem	**Cause**
Cretinism	
	mother abuses alcohol during pregnancy
Birth-related causes	a. b.

11. Serious head injuries, as a result of an accident or abuse, can result in mental retardation. List other accident- or injury-related causes of mental retardation in children.

____

____

5. Interventions for People with Mental Retardation, 586

1. People with mental retardation were usually cared for in their homes until the mid-nineteenth century when ________________ schools, which tended to be overcrowded and neglectful, were established.

2. Denmark and Sweden initiated ______________ programs that provided people with mental retardation flexible routines, opportunities to make their own decisions, social and ______________ opportunities, and economic freedom.

3. Define each type of educational program and strategies for children with mental retardation.

   Special education:

   ____

   ____

   Mainstreaming, or *Inclusion:*

   ____

   ____

   Operant conditioning:

   ____

   ____

4. Because about _____ percent of people with mental retardation also experience psychological disorders, individual, group, and drug therapies may be provided to them.

   On pages 588 and 589 of the textbook, read about ***dating skills programs*** *and* ***sheltered workshops*** *that provide individuals with mental retardation opportunities to enhance their personal, social, and occupational skills.*

VIII. Putting It Together: Clinicians Discover Childhood and Adolescence, 589

1. Mental health professionals acknowledge that the **family perspective** is particularly useful in terms of explaining and treating psychological problems among youth. Explain why this is the case.

   ____

   ____

   ____

   ____

   ____

2. However, there are some dangers in relying exclusively on the family perspective. List two of these risks or dangers.

   ____

   ____

   ____

MULTIPLE CHOICE

1. Nadia frequently becomes nauseous when she is faced with being away from her mother. Consequently, Nadia often stays home from school and refuses to go to other children's houses to play. Nadia's mother describes her as needy and clingy. Nadia might be diagnosed with
   a. separation anxiety disorder.
   b. depression.
   c. oppositional defiant disorder.
   d. autism.

2. The development of juvenile delinquency appears to be closely tied to problems in
   a. socioeconomic class.
   b. attention deficit disorder.
   c. parent-child relationships.
   d. parental monitoring of child behaviors.

3. The drugs that are sometimes helpful for children with attention-deficit/hyperactivity disorder are
   a. stimulant drugs.
   b. antianxiety drugs.
   c. antipsychotic drugs.
   d. antidepressant drugs.

4. Tara often says "me" when she apparently means "you." She just cannot seem to get this part of speech correct. This error is called
   a. echolalia.
   b. neologism.
   c. nominal aphasia.
   d. pronominal reversal.

5. The diagnosis of profound mental retardation is given when the IQ score is
   a. 50–70.
   b. 35–49.
   c. 20–34.
   d. below 20.

6. Down syndrome is caused by
   a. the presence of a third, free floating twenty-first chromosome.
   b. the presence of a third twenty-first chromosome attached to another chromosome.
   c. a mixture of cells with 2 or 3 twenty-first chromosomes.
   d. all of the above may cause Down syndrome.

7. Melissa's baby was born looking a bit dwarflike. Early testing revealed a thyroid gland deficiency. The diagnosis of the baby's condition is likely to be
   a. cretinism.
   b. Tay-Sachs disease.
   c. fragile X syndrome.
   d. phenylketonuria (PKU).

8. Which of the following focuses on helping people who are mentally retarded learn job skills?
   a. special education
   b. mainstreaming
   c. state schools
   d. sheltered workshops

9. Troy is a nine year old who is in therapy because he is terrified of going to school. His therapist has encouraged him to draw pictures and to write a fun story. This is an example of
   a. group therapy.
   b. play therapy.
   c. hypnotherapy.
   d. family therapy.

10. The *Treatments for Adolescents with Depression Study (TADS)* found which treatment method, typically believed to be effective in treating depression in adolescents, to be barely more helpful than placebo therapy?
    a. antidepressant prescription
    b. electroconvulsive therapy
    c. cognitive-behavioral therapy
    d. group therapy

CHAPTER

18 Disorders of Aging and Cognition

CHAPTER OUTLINE

REVIEW EXERCISES

I. Old Age and Stress, 594–595

1. "Old age" is arbitrarily defined as life after the age of _____ .
2. List three stressful changes that are more likely to occur as people age.

____

____

____

3. Studies have shown that although as many as ____ percent of older individuals could benefit from psychological services, fewer than ____ percent actually receive these services.

4. About ____ percent of clinicians specialize in ____________, psychology dedicated to the mental health of the elderly.

II. Depression in Later Life, 595–597

1. Complete these statements regarding the prevalence of depression in older adults.
   a. Older people who have suffered the loss of a ____________ (or some similar trauma) and who have serious ____________ illnesses have the highest rate of depression.
   b. As many as ____ percent of older adults experience depression.

2. List three medical problems that appear to be exacerbated by depression in older adults.

   ____

   ____

3. Risk of suicide increases steadily as people age. White American men over the age of 85 have the highest rate of ____________ per 100,000 persons.

4. More than ____ percent of elderly patients are helped with combinations of cognitive-behavioral therapy, interpersonal therapy, and antidepressant medications. Why must special precautions be used with prescribing medications to the elderly? ____________

   ____

III. Anxiety Disorders in Later Life, 598

1. ____________ anxiety disorder is especially common in older individuals, but might be under-reported because physical symptoms of anxiety such as ____________ ____________ and sweating could be attributed to a medical condition.

2. Elizabeth is 82 years old and has been diagnosed with generalized anxiety disorder. What may have caused her disorder? How might she be treated?
   a. possible causes: ____________
   b. possible treatment: ____________

IV. Substance Abuse in Later Life, 598–600

1. The prevalence of substance abuse problems seems to decline among those who are age ____ and over; however, rates are significantly higher among older patients who are ____________.

2. Early-onset problem drinkers are aging abusers who typically have had alcohol-related problems since their 20s or 30s. When do late-onset alcohol abusers typically start drinking? Why do they typically start drinking?

   ____

   ____

3. The often unintentional misuse of ____________ drugs is a leading substance problem among the elderly.

4. Research suggests that ____________ drugs are being given to 30 percent of the nursing home population in the United States in order to sedate patients, despite the fact that many of the people receiving the drugs do not display symptoms that would indicate a need for them.

V. Psychotic Disorders in Later Life, 600–601

1. Symptoms of schizophrenia often ______________ in later life, and new cases are extremely rare.
2. Delusional disorder is characterized by ____

____.

VI. Disorders of Cognition, 601–614

A. Delirium, 601

1. Delirium is a clouding of ______________ that is characterized by confusion, as well as attention and concentration difficulties.
2. List some of the causes of delirium.

____

____

B. Dementia, 602

1. List the symptoms of dementia.

____

____

____

2. The prevalence of dementia increases with age, affecting only about 1 to 2 percent of those age 65, but as much as _____ percent of those over age 85.
3. Although some causes of dementia, such as ______________ disorders, are reversible, most cases of dementia are caused by irreversible problems such as ______________ disease.

1. Alzheimer's Disease, 602

1. As many as _____ percent of all cases of dementia are a result of **Alzheimer's disease** (making this the most common form of dementia).
2. This exercise asks you to describe key features associated with the early and later stages of Alzheimer's disease. Features of the middle stages are provided for you.

	Features of Alzheimer's Disease
Early stages	
Middle stages	Difficulty completing complicated tasks, memory difficulties worsen, decreasing awareness of limitations, general physical health remains intact
Later stages	

3. Structural changes in the brain occur in all people as they grow older. Some of these changes seem to be excessive in people with Alzheimer's disease, however. Complete the statements below related to these structural changes. *People with Alzheimer's disease have . . .*

a. an unusually high number of ________________ ________________, which are twisted strands of protein found ________________ cells of the hippocampus and other brain areas.

b. excessive formation of ________________ ________________, which are deposits of beta-amyloid proteins that form in the spaces ________________ cells and which can lead to the breakdown and death of these cells.

4. In some individuals, Alzheimer's disease could be caused by genetic factors. Specifically, some people may have inherited a mutated (or abnormal) gene, which is responsible for the production of several ________________.

5. Complete this diagram that depicts the two memory systems described in the text.

Short-term (or Working) Memory

Collects new information, that is then transferred or consolidated into:

↓

Long-term Memory (LTM)

The repository of all information stored over the years.
Information in LTM is classified as memory of two types:

↓	↓
________________ ***Memory***	________________ ***Memory***
Information, such as names, dates, and phone numbers, that is accessible to consciousness	Learned skills, such as how to ride a bike or use a phone, that we can perform without really thinking

6. The most important brain areas associated with short-term memory are the ________________ ________________, whereas the ________________ lobes and the diencephalon are very important to long-term memory.

7. Biological researchers have discovered that certain chemicals (such as acetylcholine, ________________, RNA, and ________________) "tell" key brain cells to produce ________________, which are crucial to the formation of memories.

8. What could happen if the activity of these chemicals is disrupted in some way?

____

____

____

9. Complete the following statements describing four possible geological causes of Alzheimer's disease.

a. Abnormal activity of ________________ protein and ________________ protein may cause plaques and tangles in the hippocampus.

b. Abnormal activity of the neurotransmitters ________________ and ________________ may be involved.

c. Environmental toxins such as ________________ or ________________ may be involved.

d. An ________________ ________________ might trigger the immune system to react against the body's own tissues.

2. Other Forms of Dementia, 608

1. The symptoms of **vascular dementia** (also known as ________________ dementia) may be caused by a stroke that results in loss of ________________ flow and subsequent damage to specific areas of the brain.

2. Below, write in the name of the particular disease that can result in dementia next to the descriptions provided.

   ________________ a progressive, neurological disorder characterized by motor symptoms (e.g., tremors, rigidity), as well as dementia in some cases

   ________________ a disorder very similar to Alzheimer's disease (but more rare) that impairs functioning of the frontal and temporal lobes

   ________________ a disorder marked by memory, mood, personality, and movement problems that is caused by genetic factors

   ________________ a disorder that leads to dementia and is caused by a slow-acting virus

3. Dementia may be caused by other physical disorders. List four of these below.

   ____

   ____

3. The Assessment and Treatment of Dementia, 609

1. Brain researcher Lisa Mosconi's long-term PET scan studies found that those who develop mild dementia and Alzheimer's displayed lower ________________ activity on initial PET scans, before developing symptoms, than those who did not later develop symptoms. Overall, the PET scans predicted mild dementia with an accuracy rate of _____ percent, and Alzheimer's disease with an accuracy rate of _____ percent.

2. Researcher Neill Graff-Radford found in 2005 that subjects whose blood contained an unusually high proportion of ________________ were three times more likely to develop mild dementia or Alzheimer's disease.

3. Describe the action and effects of *tacrine* (trade name, Cognex), *donepezil* (Aricept), rivastigmine (Exelon), and *galantamine* (Reminyl), which are used to *treat* (not cure) Alzheimer's disease.

   Action:

   ____

   ____

   Effects:

   ____

   ____

4. Other medications that seem to reduce the risk of Alzheimer's disease include the hormone ________________ and the nonsteroid anti-inflammatory drugs ________________ and ________________ .

5. Behavioral therapists teach family members how and when to apply ________________ in order to change problematic patient behaviors such as ________________ at night or incontinence.

6. Research suggests that cognitive activity can help ________________ or ______________ mild cognitive impairment or Alzheimer's disease.

7. Clinicians are becoming increasingly aware of the need to provide services to caregivers of individuals with amnestic disorders and dementia, who frequently report feeling angry, depressed, and overwhelmed by their responsibilities. Complete the list below of services provided to caregivers.

   a. Programs that educate families about their loved one's disease

   b. ____________________

   c. ____________________

8. Explain how assisted living facilities might be designed to meet needs of patients with dementia.

   ____

VII. Issues Affecting the Mental Health of the Elderly, 614–615

1. In recent years, clinicians have focused on several central concerns regarding the provision of mental health care to elderly individuals. Give specific examples of why each of the two issues listed below can be problematic or distressing.

   a. *Elderly individuals representing ethnic minority groups may be discriminated against or face unique barriers in mental health settings.*

   ____

   ____

   ____

   ____

   b. *Many older persons require long-term care.*

   ____

   ____

   ____

   ____

2. Increasingly, clinicians are advising young adults to take a health maintenance, or ____________ approach, to their aging process, because physical and psychological health promotes a more positive adaption to life changes and stressful events as people age.

VIII. Putting It Together: Clinicians Discover the Elderly, 616

1. How has clinicians' approach to treating the elderly changed in recent years? ____________

   ____

   ____

MULTIPLE CHOICE

1. One of the most common mental health problems of older adults is
   a. Pick's disease.
   b. depression.
   c. schizophrenia.
   d. substance abuse.

2. Who of the following is at the highest risk for abusing alcohol?
   a. Alex, male, age 25
   b. Brenda, female, age 25
   c. Charles, male, age 65
   d. Mildred, female, age 65

3. Mr. Mathews is 85 years old. He is in the emergency room because he is confused. He cannot seem to concentrate and is not apparently aware of his immediate surroundings. He cannot think straight. This happened over the last several hours. He is displaying
   a. delirium.
   b. dementia.
   c. depression.
   d. an anxiety attack.

4. Symptoms of the middle stage of Alzheimer's disease include
   a. denial of symptoms.
   b. anger about symptoms.
   c. indifference to symptoms.
   d. anxiety or depression about symptoms.

5. On autopsy a brain is seen to have an extraordinary number of neurofibrillary tangles and senile plaques. What did the person most likely have?
   a. presenile delirium
   b. Alzheimer's disease
   c. multiple-infarct dementia
   d. Creutzfeldt-Jakob

6. Adeline was diagnosed with Alzheimer's type dementia and no longer recognizes members of her family. This illustrates a failure in
   a. short-term memory.
   b. working memory.
   c. declarative memory.
   d. procedural memory.

7. Chronic alcoholism can lead to Korsakoff's syndrome which is characterized by the loss of
   a. memory for factual knowledge.
   b. memory for general knowledge.
   c. intelligence.
   d. procedural memories.

8. Ajay has experienced increasing memory problems, personality changes, and mood difficulties. Additionally, he experiences facial tics and spasms. Ajay might have
   a. Pick's disease.
   b. Creutzfeldt-Jakob disease.
   c. Huntington's disease.
   d. Parkinson's disease.

CHAPTER

19 Law, Society, and the Mental Health Profession

CHAPTER OUTLINE

REVIEW EXERCISES

The following questions refer to the introductory material on pages 619–620.

1. When clinicians and researchers act within the legal system, the relationship is termed ______________ ____ ______________ ; when legislative and judicial systems act upon the clinical field, the relationship is called ______________ ____ ______________ .
2. What are some activities of forensic psychologists? ____

   ____

I. Psychology in Law: How Do Clinicians Influence the Criminal Justice System?, 620–629

United States courts hand out punishment on the assumption that individuals are responsible for their crimes and are capable of defending themselves in court.

1. If either part of the assumption described in the statement above cannot be made, then our courts may not find these individuals ______________ for their actions, nor will they ______________ them in the usual manner.
2. There are two potential outcomes for people who are accused of a crime and who are deemed mentally unstable. Both involve **criminal commitment** in which the person is sent to a mental institution for treatment. Complete these statements regarding the two types of this kind of commitment.
   a. When individuals are deemed "mentally unstable at the time of their ______________ ," the court finds them **not guilty by reason of** ______________ .
   b. These individuals are committed for treatment until they improve enough to be ______________ .
   c. When a person is deemed "mentally unstable at the time of their ______________ ," it is because they are not capable of understanding court procedures or participating in their own defense.
   d. These individuals are committed for treatment until they are judged ______________ to stand trial.

A. Criminal Commitment and Insanity During Commission of a Crime, 621

1. Defendants with clinically diagnosed mental disorders do not necessarily meet the court's criteria for "insanity" because "insanity" is a ______________ term, not a clinical one, that is set by ______________ rather than clinicians.
2. In the John Hinckley case, the ______________ had to prove that the defendant was **sane** (which it failed to do). Currently, in federal and most state courts, it is the burden of the ______________ to prove that the defendant is **insane.**
3. Our tradition of a jury being able to acquit a defendant based on "insanity" goes back to nineteenth-century England. Several important changes in the definition of "insanity" have occurred since then. Complete the following table, which summarizes the tests of the insanity defense that have contributed to the current legal definition of "insanity."

Test	M'Naghten Test
Change in criteria	in addition to mental disorder, defendant must have been able to know right from wrong at the time of the crime
Test	**Irresistible Impulse Test**
Change in criteria	
Test	**Durham Test**
Change in criteria	
Criticisms or problems	definition was too broad; it could include virtually any problem listed in DSM-I and relied on contradictory opinions of clinicians
Test	**American Law Institute (ALI) Guidelines**
Change in criteria	
Criticisms or problems	in light of verdict in case of President Reagan's would-be assassin, guidelines were seen as too lenient

4. In 1983, the American Psychiatric Association recommended that legal definitions of insanity retain only the "right from wrong" criterion, essentially a return to the ________________ test; this test is used in federal courts and about 50 percent of state courts.

5. The other half of the state courts still use the broader ALI guidelines, except for Idaho, Kansas, Montana, Nevada, and Utah. What have those five states done?

   ____

6. About two-thirds of defendants who are acquitted by reason of insanity qualify for a diagnosis of schizophrenia. Describe some other characteristics of the typical person acquitted by reason of insanity.

   ____

   ____

One interesting criticism of the insanity defense lies in the seeming incompatibility between the assumptions, goals, and philosophy of the legal system and those of the behavioral sciences. Read the material in the section titled "What Concerns Are Raised by the Insanity Defense?, then think very carefully about this concern. Do you agree with it?

7. Other critics suggest that contradictory clinical testimony during trials points to a lack of professional consensus about mental health. What is one of the recent efforts to correct this impression that might be cited to counter this argument?

   ____

8. The widespread fear that the insanity defense systematically allows dangerous criminals to escape would seem to be belied by the fact that less than one in ________________ defendants in the United States is actually found not guilty by reason of insanity.

9. Complete these statements regarding criticisms of the insanity plea.

   a. Until recently, a defendant who successfully pled insanity received what amounted to a ________________ prison sentence because ________________ were reluctant to assert that the offender was unlikely to commit another crime.

   b. As a result of effective ________________ treatment in institutions, the bias against extended institutionalization, and the emphasis on patients' ________________, criminal defendants are being released sooner from mental hospitals of late.

   c. A 1992 Supreme Court ruling found the only basis for determining the release of offenders from mental hospitals is whether they are still ________________, not whether they might be ________________.

When defendants use the insanity plea, juries can find the defendant not guilty, acquit on the grounds of insanity, or find the defendant guilty. In 14 states, juries have another option—a verdict of ***guilty but mentally ill.*** *By rendering this verdict, juries are essentially saying, "We believe that you had a mental illness at the time of the crime, but we do not feel that this illness was sufficiently related to or responsible for the crime."*

10. Complete these statements relating to the "guilty but mentally ill" verdict.

    a. The verdict allows juries to ________________ a defendant, while trying to ensure that the person gets necessary mental health services.

    b. Research findings indicate that juries who are given the option of this verdict deliver insanity acquittals less often.

    c. Critics say that prisoners already have a right to mental health services, and that in truth, the verdict is no different than a ________________ verdict.

11. Another defense is sometimes called *guilty with diminished capacity.* Note that unlike "guilty but mentally ill," it is not a verdict that juries may render, but a defense plea. Complete these statements regarding this defense.

    a. A defense attorney using this plea argues that the defendant is guilty, but that his or her mental ________________ is an extenuating circumstance that should be considered to determine what crime the defendant was guilty of committing.

    b. Further, the defense attorney using this plea argues that the dysfunction prevented the defendant from ________________ to commit a particular crime, and that the defendant should therefore be convicted only of a lesser crime.

12. Complete these statements relating to "sex offender" statutes.

    a. Sex offender statutes traditionally presume that people who ________________ commit certain sex crimes are mentally ill, and are thus labeled *mentally disordered sex offenders.*

    b. Give an important *difference* between the way the legal system views mentally disordered sex offenders and those found not guilty by reason of insanity.

    ____

    ____

    c. Give an important *similarity* between the way the legal system views and deals with mentally disordered sex offenders and those found not guilty by reason of insanity.

    ____

    ____

B. Criminal Commitment and Incompetence to Stand Trial, 627

1. *Dusky v. United States* (1960) held that in order for a defendant to be found **mentally competent** to stand trial, he or she must demonstrate the following:

   a. an understanding of the ______________ he or she is facing

   b. sufficient ability to ______________ with his or her attorney in preparing and conducting an adequate ______________ .

2. To ensure due process, the judge may recommend a ______________ ______________ for any defendant whose competence is questioned.

3. If a court rules that a defendant is not competent to stand trial at the present time, what happens to the defendant?

   ____

When a defendant is criminally committed, it is usually because he or she was deemed mentally incompetent, rather than found "not guilty by reason of insanity."

4. What is the greatest inherent risk of competence provisions?

   ____

   ____

The risk described above was addressed by the U.S. Supreme Court in Jackson v. Indiana *(1972), when it ruled that an incompetent defendant cannot be committed as a "criminal" for an indefinite length of time. Specifically, what did the court rule? (Complete the following statement.)*

5. After a reasonable length of time, the defendant should be found ______________ and tried, set free, or transferred to a mental health facility under ______________ commitment procedures.

II. Law in Psychology: How Do the Legislative and Judicial Systems Influence Mental Health Care?, 629–636

1. **Civil commitment** is a legal procedure whereby certain people can be ______________ to undergo mental health treatment.

2. Psychologically disturbed people from racial minority groups are ______________ likely than disturbed white Americans to be sent to prison, as opposed to mental health facilities.

3. In the United States, when white and nonwhite defendants are evaluated for their competence to stand trial, nonwhite defendants are ______________ likely to be found incompetent to stand trial.

A. Civil Commitment, 629

1. Generally, individuals can be involuntarily committed if they are considered to be both in ______________ of treatment and ______________ to themselves or to others.

2. Complete the statements concerning the two principles upon which the state's authority to commit disturbed individuals rests.

   a. The principle of *parens patriae* allows the state to make decisions that promote the individual's best interest and protects him or her from ______________ .

b. *Police power* enables the state to protect ________________ from harm that may be inflicted by a person who is violent or otherwise dangerous.

3. Apply the Supreme Court's decisions related to civil commitment to the following situations. In each situation, describe the process the parents will have to follow in having their child committed.

   a. *A mother and father become increasingly concerned about the bizarre behavior of their daughter, who is a high school sophomore. Concerned that she might pose a danger to others, they seek to have her involuntarily committed.*

   ____

   ____

   b. *The situation is the same as in exercise a., except that the daughter is a 24-year-old woman, living on her own.*

   ____

   ____

4. In *Addington v. Texas* (1979), the Supreme Court stated that in order for a person to be committed, a ________________ standard of ________________ must be met; specifically, the court ruled that there must be "________________ and ________________" proof that the person is mentally ill and has met the state's criteria for involuntary commitment.

5. In what instance might an emergency commitment (without due process) occur?

   ____

   ____

6. What is a "2 PCs" certification?

   ____

   ____

7. Although about ______ percent of people with mental disorders are not violent, research findings indicate a ________________ relationship between severe mental disorders and violent behavior.

8. Research suggests that mental health professionals are not very good at accurately predicting dangerousness in their patients. Complete these statements regarding this research.

   a. These professionals tend to ________________ the likelihood that a patient will eventually engage in violent behavior (a long-term prediction).

   b. However, the short-term predictions of ________________ violence are more accurate than their long-term predictions.

9. One criticism of civil commitment is that the legal definitions of "mental illness" and "dangerousness" are so vague that they could be applied to people simply deemed undesirable in some way. What is another criticism?

   ____

   ____

   ____

Since the Robinson v. California *decision in 1962, civil commitment rates have declined. In part, this has been the result of the application of more specific criteria to commitment decisions. Read through the section on textbook pages 633 and 634 and consider the following question: Do you think that the narrowing of civil commitment criteria ultimately benefits society or not?*

B. Protecting Patients' Rights, 634

1. In *Wyatt v. Stickney* (1972) a federal court decision ordered Alabama to provide "adequate treatment" to all persons who had been involuntarily committed. In the ruling, specific services that Alabama was compelled to provide were spelled out. They included more therapists and better living conditions. List three more.

 ____

 ____

 ____

2. Complete the statements regarding two U.S. Supreme Court rulings on the right to treatment for those in mental health institutions.

 a. *O'Conner v. Donaldson* (1975) established that the institutions must engage in periodic reviews of patients' cases, and that the state cannot confine a non-________________ person who is capable of living successfully in the community.

 b. In *Youngberg v. Romeo* (1982), the court again broadened the rights of mental patients by ruling that the involuntarily committed have a right to "reasonably ________________ confinement conditions" and "reasonable care and safety."

3. In order to ensure that mental health patients maintained their rights, Congress passed the ________________ and ________________ for Mentally Ill Individuals Act in 1986, which gave patients' rights advocates the power to ________________ and legally pursue possible cases of patient abuse and neglect.

4. Briefly state why mental health advocates across the country are suing federal and state agencies to fulfill promises of the community mental health movement.

 ____

 ____

5. Most of the **right to refuse treatment** rulings have involved ________________ treatments such as psychosurgery that are viewed as more intrusive, aversive, and ________________ than psychotherapy.

6. Many states have recognized a patient's right to refuse ________________, although the extent to which states allow such refusals varies greatly.

7. Patients in some states have the right to refuse psychotropic drugs, but their refusal may be denied if it is deemed incompetent, ________________, or irrational.

8. In another court ruling regarding rights of patients, *Dixon v. Weinberger* (1975) found that individuals with psychological disorders have a right to treatment in the least ________________ facility available; the right to community treatment was later confirmed in *Olmstead v. L.C. et al.* (1999).

9. Consider what you have read in the first two sections of this chapter, then respond to the following statement:

 Mental health professionals—not the courts—are the only ones who should make decisions regarding the care and treatment of their patients.

 ____

 ____

 ____

III. In What Other Ways Do the Clinical and Legal Fields Interact?, 637–639

All four subsections of this brief section—malpractice suits, professional boundaries, jury selection, and psychological research of legal topics—will be covered in this part of the workbook.

1. What does the tongue-in-cheek term "litigaphobia" mean?

2. Lawsuits are filed against clinicians for many alleged acts of negligence or wrongdoing, including sexual activity with a client, improper termination of treatment, and negligence regarding a client who commits suicide. List three events that can precipitate claims against clinicians.

3. Briefly describe evidence reported by Brodsky and Poythress (1990), as well as a more recent study of psychiatrists in northern England, indicating that fear of litigation has affected clinicians' judgments about their patients:

4. In recent years, the legislative and judicial systems have given greater authority to psychologists—oftentimes authority that was once reserved for psychiatrists. Briefly describe an example of psychologists' increasing responsibilities in terms of patient care.

5. Clinicians known as "jury ____________" advise lawyers on jury selection and strategies on winning over jurors during trials.

6. Eyewitness testimony can be flawed due to a variety of factors. Describe the potential problems associated with each of the following.

   a. eyewitness memory: ____________

   b. suggestive questioning: ____________

   c. eyewitness confidence: ____________

7. Describe a potential problem of the process used for criminal profiling.

____

____

____

Psych Watch: Serial Murderers: Madness or Badness?, 640

Reread this box on pages 640 and 641 of your textbook. Identify some traits that are shared by the majority of serial killers, and suggest some factors that may partly explain what drives them to kill.

____

____

IV. What Ethical Principles Guide Mental Health Professionals?, 640–643

Mental health professionals regulate practices within their own profession by developing and enforcing ethical guidelines. The American Psychological Association (APA) has developed extensive guidelines that promote the ethical practice of psychologists and call for psychologists to guard against "factors that might lead to misuse of their influence."

1. Imagine that you are a member of an ethics board that fields questions posed by psychologists. Write responses based on APA ethical guidelines to the following questions.

> I have been ordered to testify in a legal case involving a client that I evaluated 1 year ago. What are the ethical guidelines I should attend to?

a. ____

____

> I completed treatment with a client 2 months ago, and now I would like to ask her out for a date. Is this okay?

b. ____

____

> I was asked to appear on a talk show to help couples negotiate areas of conflict. Am I allowed to do that?

c. ____

____

> I am interested in what the APA says about ethical guidelines for the publication of research. What can you tell me?

d. ____

____

2. **Confidentiality** in therapy means that clinicians are obligated to refrain from disclosing information about their clients to other people. However, there are certain circumstances under which confidentiality might be compromised. List two of them.

   ____

   ____

   ____

3. In *Tarasoff v. Regents of the University of California* (1976), the California Supreme Court declared that "the protective [client-therapist] privilege ends where the ____________ ____________ begins."

4. Psychologists' ethical guidelines mandate that therapists have a ____________ to ____________ their clients and others from harm, even if it means disclosing ____________ information that was obtained during a client's therapy sessions.

5. California courts have extended *Tarasoff* to include the duty to protect people who are close to a(n) ____________ victim.

V. Mental Health, Business, and Economics, 643–645

The two subsections of this section—"Bringing Mental Health Services to the Workplace" and "The Economics of Mental Health"—will be covered together in the workbook.

1. Psychological disorders are thought to be among the ____________ leading work-related disorders and injuries in the United States.

2. Businesses often pay for programs such as employee ____________ programs and stress-reduction and ____________ seminars conducted in occupational settings that are designed to help prevent and remedy psychological disorders in the workplace.

3. In particular, ____________ abuse and other ____________ problems significantly increase the rates of absenteeism, work-related accidents, and workers compensation claims.

4. Although government funding allocated to people with mental disorders has increased, the money seems to be spent on income support and housing subsidies for those individuals rather than on ____________ ____________ ____________, such as mental health medications.

5. The growing economic role of private insurance companies has had a significant effect on the way clinicians go about their work. Complete the following statements regarding ways in which that interaction has occurred.

   a. Many insurance companies have developed ____________ care systems in which the insurance company often determines which therapists clients may use, as well as the ____________ and the ____________ of sessions.

   b. **Peer review systems** have been instituted in which a panel of clinicians who work for the insurers may review a therapist's report of a client's treatment and recommend that ____________ ____________ either be continued or terminated.

   c. Many therapists and clients dislike managed care and peer reviews. List one of their criticisms.

      ____

      ____

VI. The Person Within the Profession, 645

The main purpose of this final section of the textbook is to get you to think about how society views mental health care professionals. Keep in mind that the work clinicians do is influenced by their own personal strengths and weaknesses. As you will read in the textbook, many of them have themselves sought treatment for the same problems they are treating in others. This is why it is important to consider the words of the textbook relating to the human context in which the study and practice of psychology exists: "Mental health researchers and clinicians are human beings, within a society of human beings, working to serve human beings."

VII. Putting It Together: Operating Within a Larger System, 645–647

1. This chapter makes clear the fact that when individuals seek help for psychological problems, they are entering a system that is influenced by many forces, only one of which is the actual treatment provider. Based on what you have read, discuss aspects or components of this system that you believe (a) contribute to and (b) detract from the quality of services provided to consumers.

   a. ____

   b. ____

MULTIPLE CHOICE

1. Mario has been accused of a killing. Just as the court date arrives, he starts displaying the symptoms of schizophrenia. In a couple of days he is essentially not functional anymore. What is likely to happen in court?
   a. He is likely to be tried for the crime.
   b. He is likely to be committed indefinitely.
   c. He is likely to get off because he is not competent.
   d. He is likely to be committed until he is competent to stand trial.

2. John Hinckley was found not guilty of shooting President Ronald Reagan in 1981. The basis for the finding was that:
   a. he had a mental disorder.
   b. no crime was committed.
   c. he was mentally unstable at the time of the crime.
   d. he was mentally unstable at the time of the trial and unable to defend himself.

3. According to the criteria of the American Law Institute, a person is judged not criminally responsible if he or she has functioned
   a. under a mental disease or mental defect.
   b. under a compulsion or an irresistible impulse to act.
   c. without the knowledge of the nature of the act he or she was doing or that what he or she was doing was wrong.
   d. without appreciation for the wrongfulness of his or her conduct, or lacking the ability to conform his or her conduct to the requirements of law, as a result of mental disease or defect.

4. What percent of defendants *who use the insanity plea* are actually found not guilty?
   a. 1%
   b. 10%
   c. 25%
   d. 30%

5. In *Jackson v. Indiana,* the U.S. Supreme Court ruled that when a person is judged not competent to stand trial
   a. prison confinement is an option.
   b. indefinite commitment is not legal.
   c. a person must be released from custody.
   d. a person may be committed indefinitely under criminal status.

6. One of the justifications for civil commitment is that a person
   a. needs treatment.
   b. has been found guilty but mentally ill.
   c. has been found not competent to stand trial.
   d. has been found not guilty by reason of insanity.

7. What is the function of the two-physician certificate ("2 PC") commitment procedure?
   a. It is used for the commitment of a child.
   b. It is only used in cases of criminal commitment.
   c. It allows family members to order civil commitment.
   d. It allows quick commitment in an emergency situation.

8. In the case of *Robinson v. California,* the U.S. Supreme Court ruled that
   a. involuntarily committed people had a right to treatment or release.
   b. committing drug addicts to treatment facilities may violate the Constitution.
   c. sending drug addicts to prison for being addicts may violate the Constitution.
   d. when a person is ruled legally not competent, he or she gives up all constitutional rights.

9. What form of therapy are patients most likely to be granted the right to refuse?
   a. ECT
   b. medications

c. psychosurgery
d. psychotherapy

10. New Mexico and Louisiana are currently the only states to give psychologists the privilege to
    a. prescribe drugs.
    b. do psychoanalysis.
    c. admit patients to hospitals.
    d. perform ECT and other forms of biological treatments of mental disorders.

ANSWER KEY

Answers to most short-answer questions are provided. For questions with longer answers, the textbook source for the question is noted. Where answers will vary, no answer is given.

CHAPTER 1 Abnormal Psychology: Past and Present

REVIEW EXERCISES

I. and II. What Is Psychological Abnormality? What Is Treatment?

1b. distress
1c. deviance
1d. dysfunction
2. pp. 4–5
3. abnormal; normal
4a. sufferer
4b. healer
4c. emotional; behavior
5. many possible answers

III. How Was Abnormality Viewed and Treated in the Past?

1. many possible answers

A Closer Look: Marching to a Different Drummer: Eccentrics

1. freely; pleasure
2. fewer

A. Ancient Views and Treatments

1. external
2a. trephination; p. 8
2b. exorcism; p. 8

B. Greek and Roman Views and Treatments

1. pp. 8 and 10
2a. brain
2b. humors

C. Europe in the Middle Ages: Demonology Returns

1. After the fall of Rome, the power of the clergy grew and with it a rejection of scientific beliefs.
2. mass madness
3a. tarantism; p. 10
3b. lycanthropy
4. p. 10
5. p. 10

Psych Watch: Modern Pressures: Modern Problems

1. ecopsychology
2. "terrorism terror"
3. information anxiety

D. The Renaissance and the Rise of Asylums

1. Weyer
2. p. 11
3. pp. 11–12

A Closer Look: The Moon and the Mind

1a. The moon affects bodily fluids like it affects the tides.
1b. Odd human behavior is affected by the moon's gravitational forces.

E. The Nineteenth Century: Reform and Moral Treatment

1. La Bicetre (Paris); Philippe Pinel
2. p. 13
3. Tuke
4. moral
5. p. 13
6. p. 13
7a. staff
7b. humanity/dignity
7c. prejudice

F. The Early Twentieth Century: The Somatogenic and Psychogenic Perspective

1a. and 1b. pp. 14–15
2. psychological

3. hysterical
4. physical symptoms, such as paralysis that do not have a physical cause
5. hypnosis; psychological
6. Josef Breuer
7. psychoanalysis; unconscious
8. insight; outpatient

IV. Current Trends

A. How Are People with Severe Disturbances Cared For?

1. deinstitutionalization
2. outpatient
3. pp. 17–18

B. How Are People with Less Severe Disturbances Treated?

1. p. 18
2. 5
3. anxiety; marital; school

C. A Growing Emphasis on Preventing Disorders and Promoting Health

1. prevention
2. p. 19

D. Multicultural Psychology

1. p. 20

E. The Growing Influence of Insurance Coverage

1. managed care
2. p. 20

F. What Are Today's Leading Theories and Professions?

1a. psychoanalytic; unconscious
1b. biological; psychotropic
2a. psychiatrists; 3 to 4
2b. internship
2c. psychiatric social workers

V. Putting It Together: A Work in Progress

1. p. 22

MULTIPLE CHOICE

1. b
2. c
3. d
4. b
5. d
6. b
7. b
8. b
9. c
10. d

CHAPTER 2 Research in Abnormal Psychology

REVIEW EXERCISES

I. What Do Clinical Researchers Do?

1. nomothetic understanding
2. p. 28
3. a change in one variable causes a change in another
4. pp. 28–29

II. The Case Study

1. pp. 29–31

A. How Are Case Studies Helpful?

1a. behavior; theory
1b. assumptions
1c. techniques
1d. p. 31

B. What Are the Limitations of Case Studies?

1.–6. pp. 31–32

III. The Correlational Method

1. p. 32
2. Is procrastination related to, or associated with, test anxiety?
   Do procrastinators also experience significant test anxiety?
3. p. 32

A. Describing a Correlation

1. see p. 34
2. strength
3. correlation coefficient
4. –.82; .61; –.58; .50; –.01

The Media Speaks: On Facebook, Scholars Link Up with Data

1. Facebook users do not represent the total population in terms of culture, education, or income. The membership of Facebook is self-selecting; there is controversy regarding whether Facebook users have given permission to be part of psychological research.

B. When Can Correlations Be Trusted?

1. chance
2. p. 36

C. What Are the Merits of the Correlational Method?

1. external; generalized
2. internal; relationship

3a. Being satisfied in the marriage leads couples to communicate better.

3b. People who communicate better have more satisfying marital relationships.

D. Special Forms of Correlational Research

1. *Incidence:* the number of *new* cases of a disorder that emerge during a given period of time (e.g., new diagnoses from 1995–2000)
   Prevalence: the *total* number of cases of a disorder in a population during a given period of time (e.g., all cases from 1995–2000)
2. p. 37
3. order; causes; causation

IV. The Experimental Method

1a. independent

1b. dependent

2. temperature of milk (warm or cold); type of shampoo; amount of hair loss; posttreatment depression level
3. p. 38
4. p. 38

A.–C. The Control Group, Random Assignment, and Blind Design

1. exposure to the independent variable
2. p. 40
3. help; subject bias
4. p. 40

5a.–5c. p. 40

6a.–6c. many possible answers

7. many possible answers (check the redesign of the study with your instructor)

V. Alternative Experimental Designs

A Closer Look: Humans Have Rights, Too

1a. new drug studies

1b. placebo studies

1c. symptom-exacerbation studies

1d. medication-withdrawal studies

2. symptom-exacerbation

A. Quasi-Experimental Designs

1. randomly; experimental; control
2. p. 42
3. p. 42

B. Natural Experiment

1. independent; observes

2a.–2c. p. 42

3. repeated; generalizations

C. Analogue Experiment

1. independent; ethical
2. p. 43
3. control

4a. and 4b. p. 43

5. p. 43

D. Single-Subject Experiment

1. p. 44
2. manipulations
3. p. 44
4. controls
5. p. 44
6. **B**-Expectation: head-banging should decrease in frequency.
   A-Step Taken: Nathan is no longer rewarded with fruit juice.
   B-Step Taken: fruit juice is re-introduced as a reward to Nathan for not banging his head.
   B-Expectation: head-banging should decrease in frequency.
7. the reinforcement program (the independent

variable) was the cause of the improvement in Nathan's behavior.

8a. reversals

8b. two; independent

9. variable; confounding

10. Single-subject experiments expose the participant to an independent variable.

VI. Putting It Together: The Use of Multiple Research Methods

1a.–1e. pp. 45–46

MULTIPLE CHOICE

1. b
2. c
3. d
4. b
5. a
6. d
7. b
8. d
9. c
10. d
11. b

CHAPTER 3 Models of Abnormality

REVIEW EXERCISES

I. The Biological Model

A. Biological Explanations

1. brain

2. neurons; glia

3a. nerve endings

3b. neurotransmitters

3c. dendrites

3d. receptors

3e. axon

3f. synapse

4a. anxiety

4b. dopamine

4c. depression

5. endocrine; hormones

6. cortisol

7. genes

8. p. 53

9. thrive; adapt

10. p. 53

11. viruses

12. viral; anxiety; psychotic

B. Biological Treatments

1. all answers on pp. 54–55

2a. depression

2b. 65 to 140; seizure

2c. 7 to 9

3. frontal lobes

4. not responded

C. Assessing the Biological Model

1a. interplay

1b. p. 56

1c. p. 56

II. The Psychodynamic Model

1a. conflicts

1b. relationships; traumatic

1c. deterministic

A. How Did Freud Explain Normal and Abnormal Functioning?

1. The Id

1. pleasure; gratification

2. sexual; libido

2. The Ego

1. p. 57

2. c; e; a; b; f; all definitions are in Table 3-1, p. 58

3. The Superego

1. introject; parents'

2. conscience

4. Developmental Stages

1. fixated

2. erogenous; 0–18 months; anal, 18 months–3 years; phallic, 3–5 years; latency, 5–12 years; genital, 12 years–adult

3. pp. 58–59

B. How Do Other Psychodynamic Explanations Differ from Freud's?

1. p. 59
2. p. 59
3. p. 59

C. Psychodynamic Therapies

1. p. 59
2. p. 59

3a. free association
3b. therapist

4. repression
5. manifest; latent
6. a reliving of past repressed feelings
7. "working through"
8. dynamic focus
9. relational psychoanalytic

D. Assessing the Psychodynamic Model

1. biological; systematically
2. unconscious

III. The Behavioral Model

1. pp. 63–64
2. laboratories; conditioning
3. p. 64

A. How Do Behaviorists Explain Abnormal Functioning?

1a. and 1b. p. 64

2. p. 64
3. US: car honking and tires screeching
   CS: Foo Fighters song
4. pp. 64–65

B. Behavioral Therapies

1. relaxation skills; fear hierarchy; relaxation; relax in the presence of all items on the fear hierarchy

C. Assessing the Behavioral Model

1b. and 1c. pp. 65–66

2. self-efficacy
3. cognitive–behavioral

IV. The Cognitive Model

A. How Do Cognitive Theorists Explain Abnormal Functioning?

1. pp. 67–68
2. pp. 67–68

B. Cognitive Therapies

1a. negative; interpretations
1b. challenge

C. Assessing the Cognitive Model

1. pp. 68–69
2. acceptance; commitment
3. mindfulness-based; acceptance

Psych Watch: Surfing for Help

1. opportunity to link geographically disparate people with similar issues; free exchange of advice and support
2. unknown people at other end; untested advice; potential for insult

3a. through 3d. p. 72

4. p. 72

V. The Humanistic–Existential Model

1. self-awareness, values, meaning, and choice
2. self-actualize
3. existential; p. 69
4. client-centered
5. actions

A. Rogers's Humanistic Theory and Therapy

1a. dysfunction
1b. regard
1c. positive regard; self-regard
2a., 2b., and 2c. p. 71

3. approaches; psychiatrists

B. Gestalt Theory and Therapy

1. Perls
2. acceptance; frustrating
3. pp. 71 and 73

C. Spiritual Views and Interventions

1. p. 73
2. lonely; depressed; anxious

D. Existential Theories and Therapy

1. freedom of choice; responsibility; frustration; alienation; depression; boredom
2. p. 74

E. Assessing the Humanistic-Existential Model

1a. and 1b. p. 75
2. p. 75

VI. The Sociocultural Model: The Family-Social and Multicultural Perspectives

1a. norms
1b. roles
1c. cultural; family
1d. view

A. How Do Sociocultural Theorists Explain Abnormal Functioning?

1. Social Labels and Roles

1. p. 76
2. p. 76; schizophrenia; 7 to 52; staff; powerless, invisible, and bored

2. Social Networks and Supports

1. p. 76

3. Family Structure and Communication

1. pp. 76–77
2. enmeshed; disengagement
3. p. 77

B. Family-Social Treatments

1. Group Therapy

1. p. 77
2. individual
3. clinician
4. 500,000; 3 million; 3; 4

2. Family Therapy

1. p. 80
2. power; relationships
3. conjoint

3. Couple Therapy

1a. and 1b. p. 80
2. half
3. younger; gender roles

4. Community Treatment

1. pp. 80–81
2a. primary
2b. identify; treat
2c. long-term
3. p. 81

C. How Do Multicultural Theorists Explain Abnormal Behavior?

1. values; beliefs; histories
2. pp. 81–82
3 multicultural
4 p. 82
5 p. 82
6a. special cultural instruction of therapists in graduate training programs
6b. awareness by therapist of client's cultural values
6c. awareness by therapist of stress, prejudice, and stereotypes client is exposed to due to minority status
6d. awareness by therapist of hardships faced by children of immigrants
6e. therapists help clients recognize the impact of both their own culture and the dominant culture
6f. therapists help clients identify and express suppressed anger and pain
6g. therapists help clients achieve a bicultural balance
6h. therapists help clients raise their self-esteem

D. Multicultural Treatments

1b. less often
1c. pp. 82–83
2. culture-sensitive; gender-sensitive

E. Assessing the Sociocultural Model

1a. and 1b. pp. 83–84

VII. Putting It Together: Integration of the Models

1. biopsychosocial
2. psychological; predisposition; stress
3. p. 85

MULTIPLE CHOICE

1. c

2. c
3. a
4. d
5. b
6. a
7. a
8. c
9. a
10. b
11. d
12. b
13. c
14. b

CHAPTER 4 Clinical Assessment, Diagnosis, and Treatment

REVIEW EXERCISES

I. Clinical Assessment

1b. to determine how a person might be helped
1c. to evaluate treatment progress
2. theoretical

A. Characteristics of Assessment Tools

1. p. 90
2a. consistency
2b. p. 90
2c. agree; scored and interpreted
3. accuracy
4a. face; trustworthy
4b. predictive validity
4c. measures (or scores) gathered from other assessment techniques

B. Clinical Interviews

1. pp. 91–92
2. cognitive; biological; behavioral; psychodynamic; humanistic; sociocultural
3a. and 3b. p. 92
4. structured; schedules
5. p. 92
6b. accurate
6c. interviewer biases—relying too much on first impressions; giving too much weight to unfavorable information; gender and race biases
6d. p. 93

C. Clinical Tests

1. Projective Tests

1. personality; task
2. p. 94
3. psychological
4a. and 4b. p. 94
5. What led up to it?; thinking and feeling; What is the outcome?
6. Sentence; Person
7a. and 7c. p. 96

Table 4-1: Multicultural Hot Spots in Assessment and Diagnosis
p. 97; many possible answers

2. Personality Inventories

1. Multiphasic Personality Inventory
2. c; g; i; f; e; b; a; h; j; d
3. 120; 70
4. p. 98
5b. objective scoring
5c. standardization
5d. greater test–retest reliability
6. cultural

3. Response Inventories

1. p. 98

4. Psychophysiological Tests

1. physical; psychological
2. p. 99
3a. and 3b. pp. 99–100

A Closer Look: The Truth, the Whole Truth, and Nothing but the Truth
1. 8

5. Neurological and Neuropsychological Tests

1. head injury, brain tumors, brain malfunctions, alcoholism, infections
2a., 2b., 2c., and 2d. pp. 100–101
3. perception; memory; coordination
4. pp. 101–102
5. battery

6. Intelligence Tests
1. p. 102
2. intelligence quotient; IQ
3. Wechsler Adult Intelligence Scale, Wechsler Intelligence Scale for Children, Stanford-Binet Intelligence Scale
4. p. 103

D. Clinical Observations

1a. and 1b. p. 103

2a., 2b., and 2c. p. 103

3. behavior is often specific to a particular situation, so observations in one situation cannot always be applied to other situations.
4. pp. 103–104

The Media Speaks: Tests, eBay, and the Public Good

1. p. 104

II. Diagnosis: Does the Client's Syndrome Match a Known Disorder?

A. Classification Systems

1. clinical picture; disorder

2a. International Classification of Diseases, the classification system used by the World Health Organization

2b. Diagnostic and Statistical Manual of Mental Disorders, the classification system developed by the American Psychiatric Association

Eye on Culture: Culture-Bound Abnormality

1. p. 107

B. DSM-IV-TR

1. 400
2. pp. 107–109
3. a, j, f;
   g, k; longstanding, frequently overlooked problems;
   e, l; general medical conditions (current);
   i, b; psychosocial and environmental problems;
   Global Assessment of Functioning (GAF) Scale, a general overall rating of the person's functioning

C. Is DSM-IV-TR an Effective Classification System?

1. p. 109
2. p. 109
3. predictive

4 a. qualitatively

4 b. discrete

D. Can Diagnosis and Labeling Cause Harm?

1. p. 111
2. p. 112

III. Treatment: How Might the Client Be Helped?

A. Treatment Decisions

1a. nature; causes

1b. diagnostic

1c. orientation

1d. research

B. The Effectiveness of Treatment

1. p. 114
2. 75
3. uniformity myth
4. p. 116
5. drug therapy; behavioral therapies

Psych Watch: Dark Sites

1. 500
2. p. 115

IV. Putting It Together: Renewed Respect for Assessment and Diagnosis

1. pp. 117–118

MULTIPLE CHOICE

1. d
2. a
3. c
4. c
5. a
6. c
7. b
8. a
9. b
10. a

CHAPTER 5 Anxiety Disorder

REVIEW EXERCISES

I. Generalized Anxiety Disorder

1. free-floating
2. 6 months

3a., 3b., 3c., and 3d. pp. 122–123

4. childhood; adolescence; two

A. The Sociocultural Perspective: Societal and Multicultural Factors

1. dangerous
2. p. 124
3. *nervios*

Table 5-2: Eye on Culture: Anxiety Disorders

1. higher
2. obsessive-compulsive disorder
3. specific phobias

B. The Psychodynamic Perspective

1a., 1b., and 1c. p. 124

2. p. 124

3a. normal subjects often forget/repress aspects of threatening events; people with GAD react defensively when asked to discuss upsetting experiences

3b. more anxiety in cultures that punish/threaten children; extreme parental overprotectiveness leads to anxiety in children

4. p. 125

5a. and 5b. p. 125

C. The Humanistic Perspective

1. they do not receive unconditional positive regard from others, develop conditions of worth, and experience great anxiety; p. 125
2. client-centered
3. p. 126

D. The Cognitive Perspective

1. maladaptive assumptions

2a. 4

2b. 2

2c. 1

2d. 5

2e. 3

3. unpredictable; negative
4. metacognitive theory; intolerance of uncertainty theory; avoidance theory

5b. and 5c. more appropriate assumptions are suggested; clients are helped with changing maladaptive assumptions

6. mindfulness-based

E. The Biological Perspective

1a. and 1b. p. 130

3a. brain supplies of GABA are too low

3b. too few GABA receptors

3c. GABA receptors do not capture GABA efficiently

4a. GABA

4b. human anxiety

4c. causal; GABA reception

5. barbiturate; drowsiness, physical dependence
6. GABA; stops; GABA's ability to bind to the receptor sites is enhanced, thereby reducing arousal

7b. physically dependent

7c. potentiate

8. p. 132
9. physical; psychological
10. electromyograph; muscles
11. reducing
12. physical

II. Phobias

1. unreasonable; object; activity; situation
2. p. 134

3a. persistent

3b. avoid

A. and B. Specific and Social Phobias

1. pp. 134–136
2. higher

C. What Causes Phobias?

1. How Are Fears Learned?

1. classical
2. car accident; cars; car travel; fear, panic
3. p. 137
4. stimulus generalization
5. pp. 137–138

2. How Have Behavioral Explanations Fared in Research?

1. p. 139

2a. and 2b. p. 139

3. even though phobias can be acquired through classical conditioning and modeling, they might not be ordinarily acquired this way

3. A Behavioral-Evolutionary Explanation

1. preparedness

2a. and 2b. pp. 139–140

3a. certain tendencies to fear have evolved over generations (transmitted genetically)

3b. we are taught early in life that certain objects/situations are legitimate sources of fear

D. How Are Phobias Treated?

1. Treatments for Specific Phobias

1. behavior
2. exposure; exposed

3a., 3b., 3c. pp. 140–141

4. exposed; harmless
5. relaxation; gradual
6. therapist; client
7. in vivo; covert

2. Treatments for Social Phobias

1. lack of social skills
2. antidepressant
3. exposure
4. p. 142
5. rational emotive
6. model; role-play; feedback

III. Panic Disorder

1. 10
2. p. 143
3. reason; unpredictably

4a. having another attack

4b. meaning of the attack

4c. behavior around a possible future attack

5. p. 144

Psych Watch: Panic: Everyone Is Vulnerable

1. Many possible answers

A. The Biological Perspective

1. benzodiazepine
2. locus ceruleus
3. amygdala; ventromedial nucleus of the hypothalamus; central gray matter; locus ceruleus
4. p. 146
5. p. 147
6. 80; 50
7. p. 147

B. The Cognitive Perspective

1. pp. 147–148
2. p. 148
3. p. 148
4. misinterpret

5a. and 5b. p. 148

6. 85
7. it is at least equally effective

IV. Obsessive-Compulsive Disorder

1a. unreasonable

1b. distress

1c. time-consuming

A. What Are the Features of Obsessions and Compulsions?

1. dystonic; foreign
2. anxiety increases and the obsessions come back more strongly than ever
3. d
4. e
5. a
6. c
7. b
8. pp. 150–151
9. both

10. The fear that they will act out their obsessions; it is usually not warranted.

B. The Psychodynamic Perspective

1. p. 152
2. control

C. The Behavioral Perspective

1. p. 152
2. obsessive; compulsive

3b.–3d. pp. 152 and 154

4. 55; 85
5. pp. 154–155

The Media Speaks: Dining Out: The Obsessive-Compulsive Experience

1. Many possible answers

D. The Cognitive Perspective

1. p. 155
2. they blame themselves for having them, and expect terrible things to happen
3. because neutralizing relieves anxiety, it is reinforcing and is likely to be used again and again

4a. depressed
4b. conduct; morality
4c. harm; responsibility
4d. control

5. p. 156
6. p. 156

E. The Biological Perspective

1a. antidepressant; serotonin; low serotonin
1b. sensory; actions
1c. sexual, violent
1d. actively
2. Anafranil, Prozac, or Luvox; serotonin

V. Putting It Together: Diathesis-Stress in Action

1. pp. 158–159

MULTIPLE CHOICE

1. a
2. b
3. a
4. a
5. a
6. d
7. c
8. b
9. d
10. d
11. a
12 d
13. a

CHAPTER 6 Stress Disorders

REVIEW EXERCISES

I. Chapter Introduction and Stress and Arousal: The Fight-or-Flight Response

1a. stressor; an event or situation that creates a demand to change
1b. stress response; an individual's particular reaction to those demands
2a. hypothalamus
2b. autonomic nervous system; central nervous system
2c. sympathetic; parasympathetic
2d. pituitary; adrenal; corticosteroids
3a. and 3b. p. 167

II. The Psychological Stress Disorders: Acute and Posttraumatic Stress Disorders

1. 4; months or years; 29; 30

2b. p. 168
2c. p. 168
2d. p. 168

A. What Triggers a Psychological Stress Disorder?

1. Combat and Stress Disorders

1b. shell shock
1c. combat fatigue
2. 29; 10
3. 20

2. Disasters and Stress Disorders

1. p. 169
2. pp. 169–170

3. Victimization and Stress Disorders

1. p. 170
2a. 29; 32; 29
2b. acquaintances; relatives
2c. acute stress disorder
2d. 30
3. pp. 171–72
4a. and 4b. many possible answers
5a. – 5d. pp. 172–173

B. Why Do People Develop a Psychological Stress Disorder?

1a., 1b., 1c., 1d., 1e, and 1f. pp. 173–178
2. Hispanic Americans may be more likely than other cultural groups to react to traumatic events with dissociative symptoms. Hispanic Americans may tend to view traumatic events as inevitable and unalterable. Hispanic-American cultural emphasis on social relationships and support may place them at a disadvantage when they are deprived of important support systems.

C. How Do Clinicians Treat the Psychological Stress Disorders?

1a., 1b., and 1c. p. 179

1. Treatment for Combat Veterans

1a.–1c. p. 179
2. p. 179
3. insight; impact
4. Rap
5. pp. 180–181

2. Psychological Debriefing: The Sociocultural Model in Action

1. psychological; critical incident
2. sessions are intended to prevent or reduce stress reactions
3. p. 181

3. Does Psychological Debriefing Work?

1. p. 182

III. The Physical Stress Disorders: Psychophysiological Disorders

A. Traditional Psychophysiological Disorders

1. pp. 185–186

1. Biological Factors

1b. the development of ulcers or asthma, respectively
1c. increased production of gastric acid, leading to ulcers

2. Psychological Factors

1. attitudes
2. repressive
3. A; coronary heart
4a. and 4b. p. 187
5a. and 5b. p. 187
6. hostility/anger/time urgency

3. Sociocultural Factors: The Multicultural Perspective

1b. and 1c. p. 188
2. racial; nonracial

B. New Psychophysiological Disorders

1. Are Physical Illnesses Related to Stress?

1. Holmes; Rahe; social adjustment
2. life change units
3. pp. 190–191

2. Psychoneuroimmunology

1. antigens
2. blood cells
3a. multiply
3b. seek out and destroy body cells infected by viruses
3c. antibodies; destruction
4. susceptibility
5. spouse; Alzheimer's
6a. norepinephrine
6b. increase; inhibitory
7. corticosteroids
8. cytokines; inflammation
9. p. 193
10. p. 193
11. helpless; anger
12. lonely

C. Psychological Treatments for Physical Disorders
   1. behavioral; prevent
   2. pp. 194–198

IV. Putting It Together: Expanding the Boundaries of Abnormal Psychology
   1. pp. 198–199; many possible answers

MULTIPLE CHOICE
1. b
2. c
3. d
4. b
5. b
6. b
7. c
8. c
9. b
10. c
11. a

CHAPTER 7 Somatoform and Dissociative Disorders

REVIEW EXERCISES

I. Somatoform Disorders
A. What Are Hysterical Somatoform Disorders?
   1. pp. 206–207
   2a. and 2b. p. 207
   3. malingering
   4. intentionally
   5a. and 5b. p. 208
   6. deny; leave
   7. Munchausen
   8. children; medical; social

B. What Are Preoccupation Somatoform Disorders?
   1. overreact; symptoms
   2. hypochondriasis
   3. p. 210
   4. dysmorphophobia; defects
   5. pp. 210–211
   6. pp. 210–211
   7. more
   8. body build; genitals

C. What Causes Somatoform Disorders?
   1. anxiety
   2. uterus; ungratified

   1. The Psychodynamic View
   1a. conversion; emotional
   1b. phallic
   1c. anxiety
   1d. p. 213
   2a. and 2b. p. 213

   2. The Behavioral View
   1. rewards
   2. many possible answers
   3. p. 214

   3. The Cognitive View
   1. communicate; fear
   2. p. 214

   4. The Multicultural View
   1. inappropriate; common
   2. highest; more
   3. p. 214

   5. A Possible Role for Biology
   1. placebos
   2. p. 215

D. How Are Somatoform Disorders Treated?
   1. anxiety; obsessive–compulsive; exposure; response
   2. reinforcement; confrontation; p. 218
   3. more—conversion and pain disorders; less—somatization disorders
   4. p. 216

II. Dissociative Disorders
   1. past; future
   2. dissociative identity disorder; depersonalization disorder; p. 219

A. Dissociative Amnesia
   1. traumatic; organic

2a.–2d. pp. 220–221
3. encyclopedic; personal or autobiographical; episodic
4. wartime; disasters
5. p. 221

B. Dissociative Fugue
1. identities; location
2. p. 221
3a. and 3b. p. 222
4a. suddenly
4b. recurrence
4c. changes

C. Dissociative Identity Disorder (Multiple Personality Disorder)
1. two; host
2. sudden; stressful
3a. adolescence; adulthood
3b. 5; abuse
3c. three
4. p. 225
5. 15; 8
6. *The Three Faces of Eve*
7. pp. 225–226
8a. suggest
8b. hypnosis
8c. reinforce
9. p. 226

D. How Do Theorists Explain Dissociative Disorders?

1. The Psychodynamic View
1. repression
2. single
3. traumatic
4. pretending; safely
5. case histories

2. The Behavioral View
1a. operant conditioning
1b. anxiety
1c. reinforces
2. p. 228
3. p. 228

3. State-Dependent Learning
1. p. 229
2. arousal
3. narrow; exclusively

4. Self-Hypnosis
1. suggestibility
2. p. 230
3a. p. 230
3b. p. 230
4. subjects; suggestible
5. pp. 230–231

E. How Are Dissociative Disorders Treated?

1. How Do Therapists Help People with Dissociative Amnesia and Fugue?
1. search
2. hypotherapy
3. barbiturate

2. How Do Therapists Help Individuals with Dissociative Identity Disorder?
1. pp. 232–235

The Media Speaks: Homeward Hound: A Case of Dog Fugue?
1. pp. 221–222; p. 233

F. Depersonalization Disorder
1. experience; mental functioning; unreal
2a. and 2b. p. 235
3. many possible answers
4. symptoms of depersonalization disorder are recurrent and persistent
5. panic disorder

III. Putting It Together: Disorders Rediscovered
1. p. 237

MULTIPLE CHOICE

1. c
2. c
3. d
4. a
5. b
6. b
7. a
8. c
9. b
10. d
11. d
12. b
13. a
14. d

CHAPTER 8 Mood Disorders

REVIEW EXERCISES

I. Unipolar Depression

A. How Common Is Unipolar Depression?

1b. 17
1c. increased
1d. women
1f. one-half; 90 percent
2. 34

B. What Are the Symptoms of Depression?

pp. 243–244

The Media Speaks: The Crying Game: Male vs. Female Tears

1. p. 245
2. Many possible answers

C. Diagnosing Unipolar Depression

1. 5; 2
2. seasonal; postpartum; recurrent; catatonic; melancholic

3a. disabling
3b. two years
3c. double depression

II. What Causes Unipolar Depression?

1. stressful

2a. and 2b. p. 247

A. The Biological View

1. Genetic Factors

1a. family pedigree
1b. 46; 20
1c. Biological; biological

Psych Watch: Sadness at the Happiest of Times

1. a year; 10; 30
2. p. 248
3. shame, fear of judgment, belief that new motherhood should be joyous

2. Biochemical Factors

1. lowered serotonin and/or norepinephrine activity; they increase either serotonin or norepinephrine activity
2. pp. 249–250

3a. cortisol; the stress hormone
3b. melatonin, the "dracula" hormone
4. p. 250

3. Brain Anatomy and Brain Circuits

1a. prefrontal cortex
1b. hippocampus
1c. amygdala
1d. Brodmann Area 25
2. prefrontal cortex
3. neurogenesis
4. amygdala
5. p. 251

B. Psychological Views

1. Psychodynamic View

1a. and 1b. those whose parents did not meet needs during the oral stage; those whose parents gratified oral stage needs excessively
2. symbolic or imagined loss
3. dependence; self-reliance
4a. anaclitic
4b. father
5. affectionless; protection
6a. research findings on the relationship between childhood loss and depression are inconsistent

2. The Behavioral View

1a. p. 255
1b. p. 255
2. social; depressive

3. Cognitive Views

a. Negative Thinking

1a. and 1b. p. 256
2. negative
3. experiences; future
4a. negative conclusions based on little evidence; p. 256
4b. minimizing importance of positive experiences/magnifying importance of negative experiences; p. 256
5. inadequacies; hopelessness
6. p. 257

b. Learned Helplessness

1a. and 1b. p. 258
2a. periodic
2c. p. 258
3. p. 258
4. p. 258
5a. and 5b. p. 258
6. f; c; b; e
7. internal; global; stable
8. hopelessness
9a. and 9b. p. 259

C. The Sociocultural View

1. pp. 259–263

1. The Family-Social Perspective

1. pp. 259-260
2. three; more
3. one-third

2. The Multicultural Perspective

1. twice
2a – 2g. pp. 261–262
3. physical; cognitive

III. Bipolar Disorders

A. What Are the Symptoms of Mania?

1. inappropriate
2. p. 264

B. Diagnosing Bipolar Disorders

1. high; irritable; three
2. hypomanic
3a. and 3b. p. 264
4a. ethnic
4b. 15; 44
5. cyclothymic

C. What Causes Bipolar Disorders?

1. p. 267
2. serotonin
3. serotonin; norepinephrine; norepinephrine
4a. sodium
4c. potassium
5. mania; depression
6. basal ganglia; cerebellum; dorsal raphe nucleus; striatum; amygdala; prefrontal cortex
7. genetic makeup
8a. generations
8c. color blindness, red hair, medical syndromes

IV. Putting it Together: Making Sense of All That Is Known

1. p. 271
2. biological

MULTIPLE CHOICE

1. c
2. b
3. b
4. c
5. d
6. b
7. d
8. a
9. a
10. d
11. c

CHAPTER 9 Treatment for Mood Disorders

REVIEW EXERCISES

I. Treatments for Unipolar Depression

A. Psychological Approaches

1. Psychodynamic Therapy

1. p. 278
2a. and 2b. pp. 278–279

2. Behavioral Therapy

1. p. 279
2. combine; mild

3. Cognitive Therapy

1. pp. 280–281
2. 50; 60
3. cognitive-behavioral
4. discard; acceptance and commitment therapy; accept

B. Sociocultural Approaches

1. cognitive-behavioral
2. less
3. p. 284

4. 50; 60
5. p. 260
6. half
7. p. 285

C. Biological Approaches

1. Electroconvulsive Therapy

1a. bilateral; unilateral
1b. seizure
1c. 6; 12; weeks
2a. metrazol
2b. Insulin coma
2c. Cerletti
3a. and 3b. p. 289
4. p. 289
5. severe depression with delusions

2. Antidepressant Drugs

a. MAO Inhibitors

1b. monoamine oxidase
1c. p. 290
1d. p. 290
2. p. 290

b. Tricyclics

1. imipramine
2. 60; 65; 10
3a. relapse
3b. 5 months; continuation
3c. 3; maintenance
4a.–4c. p. 291
5a. and 5b. pp. 291–292

c. Second-Generation Antidepressants

1. Serotonin reuptake inhibitors
2. p. 292

3. Brain Stimulation,

a. Vagus Nerve Stimulation

1. electroconvulsive therapy
2. pp. 293–294
3. p. 294

b. Transcranial Magnetic Stimulation

1. prefrontal cortex
2. p. 295

c. Deep Brain Stimulation

1. Area 25
2. p. 295

D. How Do the Treatments for Unipolar Depression Compare?

1. cognitive; cognitive-behavioral; biological
2a. elimination of symptoms in 50–60% of subjects
2b. 29% of subjects improved
2c. p. 296
2d. Cognitive; cognitive-behavioral; drug
3. 30; maintenance
4. couple
5. behavioral
6. psychodynamic
7. psychotherapy; drug
8a. quickly
8b. medications; ECT
8c. 50; 80

Eye on Culture: First Dibs on Antidepressant Drugs?

1. half
2. p. 293

II. Treatments for Bipolar Disorders

A. Lithium and Other Mood Stabilizers

1. blood; urine
2. p. 301
3. 60
4. 28; prophylactic
5a. phosphoinositides
6. substituting

B. Adjunctive Psychotherapy

1. psychotherapy; drug; individual; group; family
2. p. 303
3. p. 303
4. hospitalization; job retention

III. Putting It Together: With Success Come New Questions

1. p. 303

MULTIPLE CHOICE

1. c
2. d
3. d
4. c
5. b
6. a
7. c
8. b
9. a
10. c

CHAPTER 10 Suicide

REVIEW EXERCISES

1. 31,000; 600,000; parasuicides
2a. frowned on
2b. coroners cannot always separate suicides from unintentional or accidental deaths

I. What Is Suicide?

1. intentional; conscious
2. pp. 311–312; b; d; c; a
3. p. 312

A. How Is Suicide Studied?

1b. therapy
1c. suicide notes
1d. p. 312

B. Patterns and Statistics

1. p. 312
2. Religious
3. 1:3; 3:1
4. pp. 314–315
5a. divorced people
5b. single and widowed people
5c. married people (especially those with children)
6. twice; African
7. poverty, alcohol use, modeling, availability of guns

II. What Triggers a Suicide?

A. Stressful Events and Situations

1. pp. 315–316
2. p. 316

B. Mood and Thought Changes

1. anxiety, tension, frustration, anger, shame
2. p. 317

C. Alcohol and Other Drug Use

1. 70
2. fear; violence; judgments

Psych Watch: Abnormality and the Arts: Can Music Inspire Suicide?

1. many possible answers, p. 318

D. Mental Disorders

1. mood disorders, substance-related disorders, schizophrenia
2. pp. 319–320
3b. p. 320
4. demoralization

E. Modeling: The Contagion of Suicide

1. celebrities, highly publicized cases, co-workers/colleagues
2. many possible answers

III. What Are the Underlying Causes of Suicide?

A. The Psychodynamic View

1. depression; redirected
2. negative; anger; hatred
3. Thanatos; others; themselves
4. p. 323

B. The Sociocultural View

1. pp. 323–324

C. The Biological View

1. 4; 0
2. pp. 324–325
3. aggressive; impulsive
4. serotonin

IV. Is Suicide Linked to Age?

A. Children

1a. boys
1b. false
2. p. 327
3. p. 327

B. Adolescents

1. third
2. p. 330
3. impulsive
4a. and 4b. p. 328
5. p. 328
6. uncertain
7b. anomic; see p. 329
7c. and 7d. pp. 329–330
8a. p. 330
8b. p. 330
9. p. 330

A Closer Look: The Black Box Controversy: Do Antidepressants Cause Suicide?

1. p. 329

C. The Elderly

1. 19; 12
2. pp. 330–332
3a. and 3b. p. 332

V. Treatment and Suicide

A. What Treatments Are Used after Suicide Attempts?

1. psychotherapy
2a. help them achieve a nonsuicidal state of mind
2b. help them to develop better ways of handling stress
3. 16; 30
4a – 4d. p. 333

B. What Is Suicide Prevention?

1. suicide prevention programs, suicide hotlines
2. p. 333
3. understanding and clarifying the problem, b; assessing suicide potential, a; assessing and mobilizing the caller's resources, e; formulating a plan, c

C. Do Suicide Prevention Programs Work?

1. white men; African-American; female
2. 8,000
3. visible; available
4. p. 337
5. public education

VI. Putting It Together: Psychological and Biological Insights Lag Behind

1. and 2. pp. 337–338

MULTIPLE CHOICE

1. c
2. a
3. b
4. a
5. c
6. c
7. b
8. b
9. d

CHAPTER 11 Eating Disorders

REVIEW EXERCISES

I. Anorexia Nervosa

1a. 85
1b. overweight
1c. distorted
1d. menstruation
2. restricting
3a. 90; 95
3b. 14; 18
3c. 0.5–2
3d. stressful
3e. 2; 6; starvation

A. and B. The Clinical Picture and Medical Problems

1. pp. 344–345

II. Bulimia Nervosa

1. binge-purge
2. p. 345

3a. nonpurging type
3b. purging type
4. normal
5. binge-eating

A. Binges

1. pp. 347–348

B. Compensatory Behaviors

1a. and 1b. p. 348

C. Bulimia Nervosa vs. Anorexia Nervosa

1a.–1e. p. 350
2. bulimia nervosa; anorexia nervosa

III. What Causes Eating Disorders?

1. multidimensional risk

A. Psychodynamic Factors: Ego Deficiencies

1. psychodynamic
2. pp. 351–352

3a. people with eating disorders perceive internal cues inaccurately
3b. people with eating disorders rely excessively on the opinions and wishes of others

B. Cognitive Factors

1. core pathology

2a. and 2b. pp. 352–353

C. Mood Disorders

1. p. 353

D. Biological Factors

1a. 6
1b. 23; 9
2. serotonin
3. lateral; ventromedial
4. thermostat
5. LH; restore; producing; lowering
6. VMH; remove; reducing; increasing

E. Societal Pressures

1. p. 355
2. pp. 357–358

F. Family Environment

1. thinness; dieting
2. affectionate, loyal
3. case

G. Multicultural Factors: Racial and Ethnic Differences

1. p. 360

H. Multicultural Factors: Gender Differences

1. 5; 10

2a. and 2b. p. 361
3a. and 3b. pp. 361–362
4. reverse anorexia nervosa; muscle dysmorphobia

IV. How Are Eating Disorders Treated?

A. Treatments for Anorexia Nervosa

1. pp. 363–366

Posttreatment Positive Outcomes
2a. 25; 58
2b. menstruation
Posttreatment Negative Outcomes
2a. 20
2b. 50
3. lines drawn through; a lot of; short; He; older person; did

B. Treatments for Bulimia Nervosa

1. b, e;
a, d; effective in 75 percent of bulimia cases;
c, f;
g; 25–40 percent effectiveness in reducing binging and purging

2a. 40; 20
2b. 89
2c. stress
2d. 2

V. Putting It Together: A Standard for Integrating Perspectives

1. p. 369
2. pp. 369–370

MULTIPLE CHOICE

1. c
2. c
3. c

4. c
5. c
6. c
7. d
8. b
9. b
10. b
11. a

CHAPTER 12 Substance-Related Disorders

REVIEW EXERCISES

1. e
2. b
3. f
4. d
5. a
6. c
7. 26
8. Native; Asian

I. Depressants

A. Alcohol

1. 5; 5
2. two
3. blood
4. less; dehydrogenase
5. metabolized; sobering-up
6. time and metabolism

1. Alcohol Abuse and Dependence

1. seniors; elementary
2. two
3. pp. 378–379

4a. tolerance
4b. p. 379
4c. delirium tremens; hallucinations

2. What Is the Personal and Social Impact of Alcoholism?

1. p. 379
2. p. 380
3. thiamine; confusion, memory loss, confabulation
4. p. 380

B. Sedative-Hypnotic Drugs

1. calming; sleep

1. Barbiturates

1. receptors; GABA

2a. slow or inhibit
2b. respiration; lower
3. p. 381
4. lethal; tolerance

2. Benzodiazepines

1a. Xanax, Valium, Ativan
1b. drowsiness; overdose

C. Opioids

1a. heroin
1b. narcotics
1c. opium
1d. methadone
1e. morphine
2. mainlined; bloodstream
3a. rush, p. 382
3b. high, p. 382
4. endorphins; pain; reduce

1. Heroin Abuse and Dependence

1a. anxiety; sweating
1c. third; eighth

2. What Are the Dangers of Heroin Abuse?

1. respiratory
2. p. 383

II. Stimulants

A. Cocaine

1. natural; coca
2. smoked
3. p. 385
4. dopamine, norepinephrine, serotonin
5. p. 385
6. p. 386

7a. free-basing
7b. crack

B. Amphetamines

1. manufactured

2. p. 387
3. pill/capsule; crank
4b. letdown
4c. dopamine; norepinephrine; serotonin
5. pp. 387–388
6. 6
7. equally
8. neurotoxicity

C. Caffeine

1. p. 388
2. dopamine, serotonin, norepinephrine
3. (left column) I, I, I
   (right column) D, I, I
4. p. 388

III. Hallucinogens, Cannabis, and Combinations of Substances

A. Hallucinogens

1. trips
2. lysergic acid; ecstasy
3. ergot alkaloids
4. p. 390
5. synesthesia
6. 6
7a. powerful
7b. Recurrent; flashbacks

B. Cannabis

1. hemp; THC
2. hashish; marijuana
3b. time; sizes
3c. p. 391
4. 2; 6
5. today, marijuana is at least 4 times more powerful than what was available in the 1970s
6. pp. 392–394

C. Combinations of Substances

1. p. 395
2b. they all depress the central nervous system
2c. antagonist
2d. p. 396
3. polysubstance

IV. What Causes Substance-Related Disorders?

A. Sociocultural View

1a. alcoholism; unemployment
1b. socioeconomic
1d. limits

B. The Psychodynamic View

1. nurtured
2. dependent, antisocial, impulsive, novelty-seeking, depressive
3. pp. 397–398

C. The Cognitive-Behavioral Views

1a. pp. 398–399
1b. p. 399
1c. p. 399

D. The Biological View

1. Genetic Predisposition

1. p. 400

2. Biochemical Factors

1. GABA; endorphins; dopamine; possibly anandamide, a neurotransmitter that operates like THC
2. reward; pleasure; dopamine
3. reward deficiency

V. How Are Substance-Related Disorders Treated?

A. Psychodynamic Therapies

1. conflicts; effective

B. Behavioral Therapies

1. a
2. b
3. c
4. motivated

C. Cognitive-Behavioral Therapies

1a. p. 404
1b. p. 404
1c. limits; rate
1d. younger, not physically dependent
2. p. 404

D. Biological Treatments
1. systematic; withdrawal
2. pp. 404–405
3. psychotherapy
4. block; change
5a. Antabuse
5b. opiods; withdrawal
6. pp. 406–407

E. Sociocultural Therapies
1. pp. 408–409
2a. and 2b. p. 409
3. p. 410

The Media Speaks: In Real Time, Amy Winehouse's Deeper Descent
Many possible answers

VI. Putting It Together: New Wrinkles to a Familiar Story
1. pp. 410–411

MULTIPLE CHOICE
1. b
2. d
3. b
4. c
5. a
6. d
7. b
8. b
9. b
10. b

CHAPTER 13 Sexual Disorders and Gender Identity Disorder

REVIEW EXERCISES

I. Sexual Dysfunctions
1. p. 415
2. Desire phase: pp. 416–420; Excitement phase: pp. 420–422; Orgasm phase: pp. 422–426

A. Disorders of Desire
1a.–1c. p. 417; Psych Watch
2. high; low; either high or low
3. cocaine, marijuana, amphetamines, heroin
4. pp. 418 and 420

B. Disorders of Excitement
1. Female Sexual Arousal Disorder
1. orgasmic

2. Male Erectile Disorder
1. vascular
2. p. 421
3a. nocturnal penile tumescence
3b. REM sleep
3c. physical
4. job; financial
5b. p. 422

C. Disorders of Orgasm
1. Rapid, or Premature, Ejaculation
1. inexperienced; arousal
2. p. 423
3a. p. 423
3b. p. 423
3c. p. 423

2. Male Orgasmic Disorder
1a. p. 424
1b. p. 424

3. Female Orgasmic Disorder
1. assertive; masturbating
2. psychoanalytic; pathological; clitoris
3a. diabetes, multiple sclerosis
3b. in skin sensitivity and structure of the clitoris and vaginal walls
3c. women taking Prozac may have problems with arousal and orgasm
4. p. 425
5. sexuality
6. p. 426
7. p. 426
8. sexual molestation

D. Disorders of Sexual Pain

1a. muscles; contract
1b. learned; painful
2. p. 427
3. p. 427
4. p. 427
5a.–5d. pp. 427–428
6. hypoactive sexual desire

II. Treatments for Sexual Dysfunctions

A. What Are the General Features of Sex Therapy?

1a.–1h. pp. 429–431

B. What Techniques Are Applied to Particular Dysfunctions?

1. p. 431
2a. sensate; caresses
2b. Viagra; one
2c. vacuum erection; blood
2d. prosthesis
3. p. 433
4. pause; arousal
5. self-exploration; awareness
6b. during caressing by partners
6c. during intercourse
7. normal; education
8a. vaginal; voluntary
8b. dilators; penetration
9. p. 434

C. What Are the Current Trends in Sex Therapy?

1a. live together
1b. depression
1c. marital discord; handicapped
1d. homosexual; addictions

III. Paraphilias

1a. nonhuman; nonconsenting; humiliation
1b. 6
2. the large market for paraphillic pornography
3. pp. 436–443
4. p. 443

IV. Gender Identity Disorder

1. gender identity disorder
2. 2
3. pp. 443–445
4. transvestic fetishism
5. do not become adults with the disorder
6a. hypothalamus; half
6b. female
6c. sexual
7a. hormone
7b. amputation; vagina
7c. mastectomy; phalloplasty
8. many possible answers
9a. p. 446
9b. p. 446
9c. p. 446

The Media Speaks: Battling a Culture of Shame

Many possible answers

V. Putting It Together: A Private Topic Draws Public Attention

1. p. 499

MULTIPLE CHOICE

1. d
2. d
3. a
4. b
5. c
6. b
7. a
8. a
9. c
10. c

CHAPTER 14 Schizophrenia

REVIEW EXERCISES

1. Bleuler; split mind
2a. fragmentation
2b. thoughts; emotion
2c. reality
3. one
4a. poverty

4b. fall from a higher to a lower socioeconomic level
5. p. 454

I. The Clinical Picture of Schizophrenia

1. p. 454

A. What Are the Symptoms of Schizophrenia?

1. Positive Symptoms

1. fact
2. b; a; d; c; p. 458
3. thought; speech
4. d
5. a
6. c
7. b
8. sights; sounds
9. syllable; background
10. pursuit
11. p. 460
12. Auditory; commands
13. external; Broca's
14. c
15. e
16. d
17. a
18. f
19. b
20. p. 461

2. Negative Symptoms

1a. speech; content
1b. p. 462
2. p. 462
3. anhedonia
4. apathy; interest; ambivalence
5. ideas; fantasies

3. Psychomotor Symptoms

1. posturing; waxy flexibility; stupor; excitement; rigidity

B. What Is the Course of Schizophrenia?

1. 25; problems
2. p. 463

C. Diagnosing Schizophrenia

1a. six
1b. work; social
2. c; e; d; b; a; pp. 463–464
3a. and 3b. p. 464
4. p. 464

II. How Do Theorists Explain Schizophrenia?

A. Biological Views

1. Genetic factors

1. p. 465
2. identical; fraternal
3. p. 465
4. p. 465
5a. Environmental; genetic
5b. biological; adoptive
6a. 33 matching control (non-schizophrenic) subjects
6c. Biological; Adoptive
7. p. 466

A Closer Look: Postpartum Psychosis: The Case of Andrea Yates

1. 1,000
2. pp. 468–469
3. many possible answers

2. Biochemical Abnormalities

1. increase
2. antagonists; firing
3. larger
4. atypical; serotonin
5. positive; negative

3. Abnormal Brain Structure

1. ventricles
2. p. 470
3. blood flow; temporal; frontal

4. Viral Problems

1b. nutrition
1c. fetal
1d. birth
1e. immune
2. prenatal; hormonal
3a. pp. 471–472
3b. p. 471
3c. p. 471

B. Psychological Views

1. The Psychodynamic Explanation

1a. narcissism
1b. reality; auditory hallucinations
2. schizophrenogenic
3. p. 471

2. The Behavioral View

1. p. 472

3. The Cognitive View

1. produces

C. Sociocultural Views

1. Multicultural Factors

1. higher
2a. through 2c. p. 473
3. better
4a. and 4b. p. 474

2. Social Labeling

1. diagnosis
2. self-fulfilling

3. Family Dysfunctioning

1. p. 475
2. Its validity has not been supported.
3a. have more trouble communicating
3b. are more critical of and overinvolved with their children
4. p. 476

4. R. D. Laing's View

1b. p. 477
1c. sick

III. Putting It Together: Psychological and Sociocultural Models Lag Behind

1. pp. 477–478

MULTIPLE CHOICE

1. c
2. a
3. b
4. a
5. d
6. b
7. b
8. d
9. a

CHAPTER 15 Treatments for Schizophrenia and Other Severe Mental Disorders

REVIEW EXERCISES

I. Institutional Care in the Past

1. moral; mental hospital
2. state
3a. funding
3b. quality
3c. p. 482
4a. humanitarian
4b. restraints; punishment
4c. lobotomy
5. p. 482

II. Institutional Care Takes a Turn for the Better

A. Milieu Therapy

1a. and 1b. p. 484
2. custodial

B. The Token Economy

1. operant
2. pp. 485–486
3. 98; milieu; custodial
4. control
5. p. 485
6a. and 6b. pp. 485–486

III. Antipsychotic Drugs

1a. phenothiazines
1b. psychological
1c. Thorazine
1d. neuroleptic

A. How Effective Are Antipsychotic Drugs?

1. 65
2. 75; 33
3a. hallucinations; delusions

3b. flat affect, poverty of speech, loss of volition

B. The Unwanted Effects of Conventional Antipsychotic Drugs

1. Extrapyramidal
2. p. 489
3. one year
4a. stop the drugs
4b. lowest
4c. gradually reduce or stop the drug

C. New Antipsychotic Drugs

1a. negative
1b. extrapyramidal
1c. tardive dyskinesia
2. agranulocytosis

Eye On Culture: First Dibs on Atypical Antipsychotic Drugs

1. p. 491

IV. Psychotherapy

A. Cognitive-Behavioral Therapy

1. pp. 492–493
2a. –2e. p. 493
3. observers; mindful; accept
4. It is often very helpful to clients with schizophrenia.

The Media Speaks: Can You Live with the Voices in Your Head?

1. pp. 492–495; answers will vary

B. Family Therapy

1. relatives; 50
2. expressed emotion
3a. realistic; tolerant
3b. p. 496

C. Social Therapy

1. p. 497

V. The Community Approach

1a. p. 497
1b. pp. 497–498
1c. p. 498

A. What Are the Features of Effective Community Care?

1. pp. 498–501

B. How Has Community Treatment Failed?

1. communication
2. p. 502
3. p. 503
4. pp. 503–504
5. three

C. The Promise of Community Treatment

1. p. 504

VI. Putting It Together: An Important Lesson

1a. and 1b. many possible answers

MULTIPLE CHOICE

1. b
2. b
3. b
4. b
5. a
6. c
7. b
8. c
9. b
10. b

CHAPTER 16 Personality Disorders

REVIEW EXERCISES

1a. unique; outward behavior
1c. p. 509
2. II; improvement
3. I; comorbidity

I. "Odd" Personality Disorders

See grid on p. 511

A. Paranoid Personality Disorder

1a. motives
1b. loyalty

1c. weaknesses; mistakes
1d. grudges
2. men
3. genetic
4. p. 514
5. p. 514
6. drug
7. self-cohesion

B. Schizoid Personality Disorder
1. they truly prefer to be alone
2. emotional
3a. unaccepting, abusive
3b. give; receive
4. pp. 515–516
5. social
6. p. 516

C. Schizotypal Personality Disorder
1. relationships; oddities
2. pp. 516–517
3. p. 517
4a. conflicts
4b. attention
4c. enlarged brain ventricles, smaller temporal lobes, and loss of gray matter
5. p. 517
6a. inappropriate
6b. pp. 517–518
6c. low

II. "Dramatic" Personality Disorders
grid p. 511

A. Antisocial Personality Disorder
1. psychopath, sociopath
2. disregard; rights
3. p. 518
4. pp. 519–520
5. four
6. intoxication; antisocial PD; prone; substance abuse; take risks
7b. modeling
7c. needs; points of view
8. anxiety; negative; cues
9. arousal; threatening
10. serotonin; frontal lobes
11a. effective
11b. they lack a conscience and do not want to change, p. 523
11c. moral; needs
11d. responsibility

B. Borderline Personality Disorder
1. e; a; c; g; d; f; b
2a. women
2b. young
3. abandonment; separation
4. sexual; psychological
5. serotonin; 5-HTT
6. internal; external
7. family
8. pp. 528–529
9a. relationship; self; loneliness
9b. pp. 528–529
9c. attempted suicide

C. Histrionic Personality Disorder
1a. emotionally
1b. on-stage
1c. vain; demanding
1d. illnesses
1e. provocative
2. pp. 530–531
3. loss; protectively
4. suggestibility
5. norms; femininity
6. p. 531
7. p. 531

D. Narcissistic Personality Disorder
1b. pp. 531 and 534
1c. pp. 531 and 534
2. men
3. perfect
4. positively
5. eras
6. superiority

Psych Watch: Lying: "Oh, What a Tangled Web. . ."
1a. through 1d. pp. 532–533

III. "Anxious" Personality Disorders

See grid on p. 511

A. Avoidant Personality Disorder

1. inadequacy; negative
2a. humiliation; confidence
2b. circumstances; relationships
3. ridiculed
4. cognitive; rejection
5. p. 537
6. anxiety
7. p. 537

B. Dependent Personality Disorder

1. pp. 537–538
2a. oral
2b. separation
2c. behavioral; independent
2d. pp. 538–539
3. responsibility; spouse
4. transference

C. Obsessive-Compulsive Personality Disorder

1. perfection; control
2a.–2e. pp. 539–540
4. anal regressive
5. dichotomous
6. psychodynamic and cognitive

IV. Multicultural Factors: Research Neglect

1. pp. 541–542
2. inequalities; psychological
3. p. 542

V. What Problems Are Posed by the DSM-IV-TR Categories?

1a. observed; individual
1b. similarity
1c. different

VI. Are There Better Ways to Classify Personality Disorders?

1. dimensions
2. pp. 543–544
3. neuroticism; extroversion; openness to experiences; agreeableness; conscientiousness
4. 12

VII. Putting It Together: Disorders of Personality Are Rediscovered

1. pp. 545–546

MULTIPLE CHOICE

1. d
2. a
3. a
4. b
5. b
6. c
7. b
8. c
9. b
10. d

CHAPTER 17 Disorders of Childhood and Adolescence

REVIEW EXERCISES

I. Childhood and Adolescence

1a. half
1b. bed-wetting; temper tantrums
1c. physical; sexual; pressures
1d. trusting; sensitive
2. fifth
3. Boys; girls

II. Childhood Anxiety Problems

1a. p. 551
1b. p. 551
1c. p. 551

A. Childhood Anxiety Disorders

1. social; generalized
2a. p. 551
2b. p. 551

2c. p.551
3. p. 551
4. extreme; home
5. phobia

B. Treatments for Childhood Anxiety Disorders
1a. and 1b. p. 553

III. Childhood Mood Problems

A. Major Depressive Disorder
1. 2; children lack cognitive skills that help produce depression
2. life events; rejection; abuse
3a. children lack interest in toys and games, rather than loss of sex drive
3b. childhood depression often manifests itself as headache, stomach ache, or irritability
4. girls
5. p. 554
6a. and 6b. pp. 554–556

B. Bipolar Disorder
1. p. 556
2. p. 556
3. half; third; antidepressant; stimulant

IV. Opposition Defiant Disorder and Conduct Disorder

1. p. 557; 10 percent of children (more boys than girls)
2a. and 2b. p. 560

A. What Are the Causes of Conduct Disorder?
1. conflict
2. p. 561

B. How Do Clinicians Treat Conduct Disorder?
1. 13
2a. and 2b. p. 562
3. juvenile training
4. prevention; recreational; health; parenting

V. Attention-Deficit/Hyperactivity Disorder

1. p. 564
2. learning
3a. 90
3b. 35; 60

A. What Are the Causes of ADHD?
1. stress; family
2. interpersonal; symptoms
3. sugar; toxins

B. How Do Clinicians Assess ADHD?
1a.–1e. p. 566
2. one-third; one-half

C. How Is ADHD Treated?
1a. quieting
1b. problems; aggression
2. They fare poorly.
3. They have their patients take "drug holidays," where the patients periodically cease taking the drug.
4. reinforce; drug

D. Multicultural Factors and ADHD
1. pp. 568–569

VI. Elimination Disorders

1. control
2a. 5
2b. decreases; 1
2c. stressful; school
3b., 3c., and 3d. p. 570
4. bell; sensation of full bladder; waking up
5. defecating; 4

VII. Long-Term Disorders That Begin in Childhood

A. Pervasive Developmental Disorders
1. social interactions; communications; stimuli
2a.–2d. autistic disorder; Asperger's disorder; Rett's disorder; childhood disintegrative disorder

I. Autistic Disorder
1. 3; communication; repetitive
2a. 160–600
2b. 80
2c. Nine
3. p. 573
4a. echolalia
4b. pronominal reversal
5. p. 574

2. Asperger's Disorder
1. social deficits; impaired expressiveness; idiosyncratic interest; restricted and repetitive behaviors
2. intellectual; adaptive; language

3a.–3c. pp. 574–575

3. What Are the Causes of Pervasive Developmental Disorders?

1a. intelligent; cold
1b. social; environmental
2. pp. 575–576
3a.–3c. p. 577

4. How Do Clinicians and Educators Treat Pervasive Developmental Disorders?
1. p. 577
2. modeling; operant
3. p. 578
4. autistic children have significantly improved cognition, social engagement, peer interactions, play behaviors, and other behaviors; normal children experience no negative effects
5. 22
6. cognitive social
7. communication; simultaneous
8. child-initiated; intrinsic
9. p. 579
10. group; workshops

B. Mental Retardation

1a. intellectual; 70
1b. p. 580

1. Assessing Intelligence

1a. school
1b. biased

2. Assessing Adaptive Functioning
1. observe; background

3. What Are the Features of Mental Retardation?
1. learn; short-term; planning
2. moderate; limited; severe; extensive; profound; pervasive
3. 85; educably
4. school; improve

5a. and 5b. p. 583

6. 3–4 percent of retarded population; 1–2 percent of retarded population; pp. 583–584

4. What Are the Causes of Mental Retardation?
1. biological

2a. 1,000
2b. 35
3. flat; tongue
4a. person has 3 twenty-first chromosomes instead of 2
4b. translocation or mosaicism; p. 584
5. 35; 55
6. aging; dementia
7. recessive
8. intelligence
9. European Jewish; mental; motor
10. pp. 585–586
11. p. 586

5. Interventions for People with Mental Retardation
1. state
2. normalization; sexual
3. pp. 587–588
4. 25

VIII. Putting It Together: Clinicians Discover Childhood and Adolescence
1. p. 589
2. p. 589

MULTIPLE CHOICE
1. a
2. d
3. a
4. d
5. d
6. d
7. a
8. d
9. b
10. c

CHAPTER 18 Disorders of Aging and Cognition

REVIEW EXERCISES

I. Old Age and Stress

1. 65
2. p. 594
3. 50; 20
4. 4; geropsychology

II. Depression in Later Life

1a. spouse; physical
1b. 20
2. p. 596
3. 65
4. 50; p. 597

III. Anxiety Disorders in Later Life

1. Generalized; heart palpitations
2a. p. 598
2b. p. 598

IV. Substance Abuse in Later Life

1. 60; institutionalized
2. p. 599
3. prescription
4. antipsychotic

V. Psychotic Disorders in Later Life

1. lessen
2. p. 601

VI. Disorders of Cognition

A. Delirium

1. consciousness
2. p. 601

B. Dementia

1. p. 602
2. 50
3. nutritional; Alzheimer's

1. Alzheimer's Disease

1. 66
2. p. 603
3a. neurofibrillary tangles; within
3b. senile plaques; between
4. proteins
5. declarative; procedural
6. prefrontal lobles; temporal
7. glutamate; calcium; proteins
8. p. 606
9a. beta-amyloid; tau
9b. acetylcholine; glutamate
9c. zinc; lead
9d. autoimmune response

2. Other Forms of Dementia

1. multi-infarct; blood
2. Parkinson's disease; Pick's disease; Huntington's disease; Creutzfeldt-Jakob disease
3. p. 609

3. The Assessment and Treatment of Dementia

1. hippocampus; 71; 83
2. AB42 beta-amyloid proteins
3. p. 610
4. estrogen; ibuprofen; naprosyn
5. reinforcement; wandering
6. prevent; delay
7b. and 7c. p. 612
8. pp. 612–614

VII. Issues Affecting the Mental Health of the Elderly

1a. pp. 614–615
1b. p. 615
2. wellness

VIII. Putting It Together: Clinicians Discover the Elderly

1. p. 616

MULTIPLE CHOICE

1. b
2. a
3. a
4. d
5. b
6. c
7. a
8. c

CHAPTER 19 Law, Society, and the Mental Health Profession

REVIEW EXERCISES

1. psychology in law; law in psychology
2. p. 620

I. Psychology in Law: How Do Clinicians Influence the Criminal Justice System?

1. guilty; punish
2a. crimes; insanity
2b. released
2c. trial
2d. competent

A. Criminal Commitment and Insanity During Commission of a Crime

1. legal; legislators
2. prosecution; defense
3. p. 621
4. M'Naghten
5. more or less abolished the insanity plea
6. p. 622
7. p. 622
8. 400
9a. longer; clinicians
9b. drug; rights
9c. insane; dangerous
10a. convict
10c. guilty
11a. dysfunctioning
11b. intending
12a. repeatedly
12b. they are considered responsible for their crimes
12c. they are committed to a mental health facility

B. Criminal Commitment and Incompetence to Stand Trial

1a. charges
1b. work; defense
2. psychological examination
3. p. 627
4. p. 628
5. competent; civil

II. Law in Psychology: How Do the Legislative and Judicial Systems Influence Mental Health Care?

1. forced
2. more
3. more

A. Civil Commitment

1. need; dangerous
2a. self harm
2b. society
3a. pp. 629–630
3b. pp. 629–630
4. minimum; proof; clear; convincing
5. p. 630
6. p. 631
7. 90; small
8a. overestimate
8b. imminent
9. p. 632

B. Protecting Patients' Rights

1. p. 634
2a. dangerous
2b. nonrestrictive
3. Protection; Advocacy; investigate
4. p. 635
5. biological; dangerous
6. ECT
7. dangerous
8. restrictive
9. answers will vary

III. In What Other Ways Do the Clinical and Legal Fields Interact?

1. fear of being sued for malpractice
2. p. 637
3. p. 637
4. pp. 637–638
5. specialists
6a.–6c. pp. 638–639
7. p. 639

PsychWatch: Serial Murderers: Madness or Badness?
pp. 640–641

IV. What Ethical Principles Guide Mental Health Professionals?

1a.–1d. pp. 642–643
2. p. 643
3. public peril

4. duty; protect; confidential
5. intended

V. Mental Health, Business, and Economics

1. ten
2. assistance; problem-solving
3. alcohol; substance-related
4. mental health services

5a. managed; cost; number
5b. insurance benefits
5c. pp. 644–645

VII. Putting It Together: Operating Within a Larger System

1. many possible answers

MULTIPLE CHOICE

1. d
2. c
3. d
4. c
5. b
6. a
7. d
8. c
9. c
10. a